Howard Barker

PLAYS FIVE

THE LAST SUPPER
SEVEN LEARS
HATED NIGHTFALL
WOUNDS TO THE FACE

OBERON BOOKS
LONDON

First published in this collection in 2009
by Oberon Books Ltd
521 Caledonian Road, London N7 9RH
Tel: +44 (0) 20 7607 3637 / Fax: +44 (0) 20 7607 3629
e-mail: info@oberonbooks.com
www.oberonbooks.com

Reprinted 2010, 2014

The Last Supper first published in 1988 in the UK by John Calder
Ltd and in the US by Riverrun Press Inc

Seven Lears first published in 1990 in the UK by John Calder Ltd
and in the US by Riverrun Press Inc

Hated Nightfall and *Wounds to the Face* first published in 1994 in the
UK by John Calder Ltd and in the US by Riverrun Press Inc.

Cover photograph by Anna Stephens
www.annastephensphotography.co.uk

A catalogue record for this book is available from the British
Library.

ISBN: 978-1-84002-886-7

Printed and bound by Replika Press Pvt. Ltd., India.

Visit www.oberonbooks.com to read more about all our books
and to buy them. You will also find features, author interviews and
news of any author events, and you can sign up for e-newsletters
so that you're always first to hear about our new releases.

Contents

THE LAST SUPPER

Characters

LVOV A Thinker	DORA A Teacher
MARYA A Nurse	ANNA A Prostitute
ARNOLD A Salesman	FORJACKS A Scholar
IVORY An Aristocrat	APOLLO A Poet
SUSANNAH A Cook	ELLA A Student
SLOMAN A Carpenter	FIRST OFFICER
JUDITH A Widow	SECOND OFFICER
GISELA A Diaryist	FARMER

THE ACTORS OF THE PARABLES

MacATTLEE McSTAIN McNOY Soldiers	WOMAN LOOTER
	MALE DOCTOR
LITTLE MONK	A CHILD
ABBOTT	A WOMAN
A FEMALE CHILD	A GUNNER
A WIDOW	A SEAMSTRESS
VIOLINIST	THE CHORUS
NUN	

THE FIRST PROLOGUE

ELLA: We found God after all
   Thinking He had disappeared
DORA: He had not disappeared
   We found Him after all
   Like the vagrant under the wall
   He was only out of sight
ELLA: And He stood up in the light
   Of all our shame and said
   In the beam of our shame
   Rubbed His eyes and said
DORA: I am not dead
   I am the Public
ELLA: To me the heretics will
DORA: I am not dead
   I am the Public
ELLA: And the transgressors
DORA: Genuflect
ELLA: The incurably deviant
DORA: Adore
ELLA: The breakers of vows
DORA: Applaud
ELLA: The habitually glum
DORA/ELLA: LAUGH YOU BASTARD, THIS IS MY CREATION,
   LAUGH.
DORA: Did you think I'd died with religion?
   Did you think I would succumb?
   I have endured worse winters
   Under the arches entertained the louse
ELLA: Quitting the cathedral in the night
DORA: God the Public needs no house
ELLA: And the sexually active bishops
DORA: The theologians with radio technique
ELLA: The fathers of gifted children
DORA: The rock musicians with castles
ELLA: The summer school students in states of undress
DORA: The carnival organizers
ELLA: The sweet-natured pickpockets

DORA: Shop stewards red-eyed in the billiard hall
ELLA: Popes and Mercenaries all
DORA: Concurred
ELLA: The Public We
   The Public We
   The Public Had to be God
DORA: Since God had to be
DORA/ELLA: APPLAUD YOU BASTARDS!
   (*The terrible sound of laughter.*)

THE SECOND PROLOGUE

IVORY: I bring you an invitation
   Oh, no, she says, not an invitation
   Yes
   We are all so afraid
   Yes
   An invitation to hang up the
   SUFFOCATING OVERCOAT OF COMMUNICATION
   Hang it up
   And those with biros write upon your wrist
   THE PLAY CONTAINS NO INFORMATION
   Aren't you tired of journalists?
   Oh, aren't you tired of journalists?
   No one will hold your hand tonight
   Nor oil you with humour
   As the swimmer is greased to pass through
   Water quicker
   No
   When the poem became easy it also became poor
   When art became mechanized it became an addiction
   I lecture!
   Oh, I lecture you!
   (*A terrible storm of laughter.*)
   Forgive!
   Forgive!

THE PLAY

A FIGURE asleep in a hammock. An engine labouring. A WOMAN enters.

MARYA: I'm still insane.

Obviously insane as ever.

(*The train passes.*)

Goodbye you male scum! Goodbye you meat and gristle!

(*She bares her breasts. A MAN enters, watches her. The wheels fade.*)

ARNOLD: You shout at all the trains. You smear your breasts on all the windows. Goodbye you male scum! But how dedicated you are at the hospitals. Meeting the ambulances and wiping the broken bodies. Now, this is his influence. Isn't it? Your influence?

(*The FIGURE is still.*)

Pretend to be asleep. But I say it's your influence. YOU HAVE NO DESIRE TO CURE ANYBODY Sleeping, sleeping

(*IVORY enters.*)

Cunt!

IVORY: Let him sleep.

ARNOLD: Sleep? How can anyone sleep in the current state of things? We can only pretend, just as he is now pretending. He is fictive, aren't you? Fictive!

IVORY: We know he is fictive.

ARNOLD: We know it, but does he? Sleep is for times of stability. Even gardening has become impossible. Why do you say?

IVORY: No, I didn't say.

ARNOLD: Because it is absurd to plant what will never be allowed to nourish. I know you say plant anyway. Plant, and if it is trodden down, plant again. I have heard him say that.

MARYA: Plant, and even though armies trample fifty gardens one they will miss and there you may shelter.

ARNOLD: I have heard that –

IVORY: Often –

ARNOLD: Often I have heard that, but it is fictive, isn't it? Like all he says. WAKE UP YOU UTTER CUNT.

(*They look at ARNOLD.*)
It so happens I require your fictiveness. CUNT, WAKE UP.
(*He stares at the hammock and its occupant. The sound of desolation fills the stage.*)

THE FIRST PARABLE
The Irrepressible Optimism of the Demolition Squad

Three SOLDIERS enter.

ALL: We kill Nobody!

McSTAIN: They say civil wars are the worst but what's your evidence?

ALL: We kill Nobody!

MacATTLEE: They say it is terrible to lift your hand against your brother, but what's your evidence?

ALL: We kill Nobody!

McNOY: The Captain says the bell's our enemy. Seek out the churches, says our officer. He gave eight reasons for the unslinging of the bells.

McSTAIN: The sound of four ton bells crashing to the belfry floor is one nobody expects to hear repeated in his lifetime.

McNOY: We did however, hear it repeated.

MacATTLEE: In fact, the sound, for all its uniqueness, became routine.

ALL: We kill Nobody!

MacATTLEE: We suffer from the dim awareness that these acts are having no significant impact on the outcome of the war.

McSTAIN: Certainly there are fewer bells.

McNOY: But equally certainly the fighting has grown worse.

ALL: We kill Nobody!

McNOY: We suffer from the dim awareness that the future will be worse than the past we swore to extinguish.

MacATTLEE: We imagine what it is to be happy. But what once made us happy no longer does.

McSTAIN: We are forced to conclude that happiness, if it exists at all, is continuing to do what we are doing.

(*A MONK enters.*)

LITTLE MONK: Welcome to the monastery!

(*He bows.*)

There is food and drink in the refectory.

MacATTLEE: Food and drink?

McSTAIN: What food?

MacATTLEE: What drink?

McNOY: In the middle of a war?

MacATTLEE: If it is the middle.

LITTLE MONK: Hot water. Towels.

McSTAIN: Hot water?

LITTLE MONK: In the prebendary.

ALL: OLD TRICK.

McNOY: Ancient as the Greeks this insincere hospitality.

LITTLE MONK: (*Bowing.*) I admit it. I am thinking not of your hunger, or of your thirst, but of the bells.

McSTAIN: The bells...

MacATTLEE: The bells again...

LITTLE MONK: I owe it to my soul to be sincere. I could not care if you were fed or starved. Now I suppose you will beat me, and I deserve to be beaten for not succeeding in loving you.

(*He pulls up his habit, revealing his back.*)

Beat me, then. But leave the bells. Beat me to death for my sins!

ALL: We kill Nobody...

LITTLE MONK: You do not kill? But beat? Surely you beat?

McSTAIN: We have, we have beaten, haven't we?

McNOY: I dimly recollect a beating, but that was far from here.

MacATTLEE: Not far from here. We have merely marched in circles.

McSTAIN: It was near, rather.

McNOY: Dim, dim, that memory...

LITTLE MONK: (*Scrambling to his feet.*) GET AWAY FROM HERE, YOU SCUM!

MacATTLEE: You see, we must learn to keep our mouths shut.

LITTLE MONK: SCUM! I WILL THRASH YOU WITH A BRANCH!

(*He goes to kick MacATTLEE, who catches him by the foot.*)

McNOY: Tell us of the life of a monk.

LITTLE MONK: (*Shouting.*) Brothers! These soldiers do not kill!

McNOY: No, don't scream, tell us about the silent life.

LITTLE MONK: Monks! Monks!

(*The ABBOTT enters.*)

ABBOTT: Don't beat the little monk, I pray you.

McNOY: We leave the burning monasteries thinking, what kind of life was that?

ABBOTT: (*Kneeling.*) Beat me, if you must beat somebody.

LITTLE MONK: THEY DON'T BEAT!

ABBOTT: Soldiers who don't beat?

LITTLE MONK: Look!

McNOY: For example, the peace and quiet, does that stimulate the mind or deaden it?

ABBOTT: TAKE THEIR WEAPONS!

(*The LITTLE MONK frees himself with a kick and seizes the rifles. He runs off with them.*)

McSTAIN: You monks are all the same.

ABBOTT: Take yourselves to the crypt and lock the door!

McNOY: This could be paradise. Are you friendly with the nuns?

ABBOTT: If you return to your officers you will report the continued existence of the bells, and more soldiers will be sent, perhaps crueller than you. Obviously you must be locked away. Please co-operate. God loves the bells. We will free you when the war is over.

MacATTLEE: The war will not be over.

ABBOTT: We can pray.

MacATTLEE You can pray, but it will not be over.

(*The LITTLE MONK returns with a stick. He takes swipes at McNOY.*)

LITTLE MONK: Sinners! I will confess this, obviously.

ABBOTT: Restrain yourself.

LITTLE MONK: I can't help it!

ABBOTT: This is a foolish war. Everyone has forgotten why it started.

McSTAIN: That doesn't matter. It had a cause, that's the important thing. Now it exists for itself. It's the same with bells. The order to demolish has never been rescinded.

McNOY: Ow!

MacATTLEE: The officer who issued this order died in an air raid. We buried him in a town square near a fountain.

McSTAIN: Nish.

MacATTLEE: No, Pecs.

McSTAIN: Our memory fails us, but who wants a memory?

ABBOTT: Lie on the floor, or he will kick you.

(*They lie down.*)

Oh, God! I threatened them with violence and they acted!

LITTLE MONK: I want to beat them!

ABBOTT: No, no –

LITTLE MONK: I WANT TO BEAT THEM!

ABBOTT: (*Turning away.*) All right, beat them!

LITTLE MONK: Hey!

(*He whacks their backs.*)

ABBOTT: We are beating our enemies...

LITTLE MONK: Now I want to kill them!

ABBOTT: No!

LITTLE MONK: Yes! (*He goes to thrash them again. The ABBOTT grabs him.*) Why not! Why not!

ABBOTT: I don't know, I only – (*They grapple with each other.*)

LITTLE MONK: Let me go!

ABBOTT: In the name of God, I –

LITTLE MONK: I HATE YOU! I HATE YOU! (*He slaps the ABBOTT's face. He stops. They are breathless.*) You see how we...you see how...

(*A wind of desolation sweeps the stage.*)

ABBOTT: (*To the SOLDIERS.*) Go and take the bells down...go and...go and...

(*The SOLDIERS get up, begin to work.*)

END OF THE FIRST PARABLE

MARYA: Did you ever know anyone who slept so much?

IVORY: He stays up late.

MARYA: He stays up late, but did you ever know anyone who slept so much? I am offended by it. I regard it as an unfavourable comment on myself.

ARNOLD: On me, too.

MARYA: On all of us. As if what he dreamed were better than what we are.

IVORY: He dreams appalling truths.

MARYA: So what? I am a truth also. A MAD TRUTH OBVIOUSLY. I feel this need to kick him. Frequently I do.

ARNOLD: Kicks of love.

MARYA: Love kicks, yes.

ARNOLD: He knows this. He knows your kicks are compliments.

MARYA: That also is enraging. (*Sounds approaching.*) Another train!

(*She exposes her breasts to a passing train.*)

Goodbye you male scum! Goodbye you meat and gristle!

(*It passes, fades. A WOMAN enters with a sack.*)

IVORY: Susannah, you are the absolute in dedication –

SUSANNAH: Shut up –

IVORY: The absolute in concentration –

SUSANNAH: SHUT UP, WILL YOU!

IVORY: Consideration, solicitation –

SUSANNAH: (*Flinging down the sack, which spills loaves all over the floor.*) SHUT UP, I SAID!

MARYA: He means to compliment you.

SUSANNAH: He is ascribing tedious virtues to me. It's his way of belittling somebody.

ARNOLD: You can't say anything here…

SUSANNAH: If I don't do it, who will?

MARYA: Quite. Who will if you don't?

SUSANNAH: It is really so depressing, so enervating, that people like you who avoid every shred of responsibility or labour can demean the energy of others –

IVORY: I am not demeaning –

SUSANNAH: by applying sarcastic epithets to them such as –

IVORY: I abhor the charge –

SUSANNAH: Trust or honesty or –

IVORY: Abhor! Abhor!

SUSANNAH: Kindness in order to humiliate me! It is you who are humiliated! You! By idleness! By insolence! You! (*Pause.*)

ARNOLD: Extraordinary. Loaves! Extraordinary…
(*He stares at them.*)

SUSANNAH: The carthorse thanked. The donkey praised. (*She turns to go.*)
If you touch one crumb, I'll dislocate your spine.
(*She goes.*)

ARNOLD: Poor Susannah.

MARYA: What's poor about her? It's you who's poor.

ARNOLD: Where does she get loaves from? At a time like this? It's extraordinary.

IVORY: She has a gift…

MARYA: You call everything a gift in order to spare yourself the tedium of imitating it.

IVORY: I am an object of contempt, I see.

MARYA: Yes.

IVORY: I am a thing of filth and disapprobation.

MARYA: You know you are.

IVORY: (*Walking out.*) But there are worlds and worlds…

MARYA: You keep saying that. What does it mean?
(*IVORY goes out.*)
There are worlds and worlds, what does he mean?

ARNOLD: I think it's something he got from Lvov. (*He kneels. Begins to stack the loaves. Suddenly he stops.*) He gets furious if you wake him. (*Pause.*) Well, I say furious. I mean, there is a certain expression of – resentment – in his face. Probably he is dreaming of something of enormous significance. Probably he is in torment.
(*He peers at the SLEEPING MAN.*)
And his lips move, his lips go, and his brows are all, I say to him, you don't know the meaning of peace! To which he says –
(*A CHORUS of figures has appeared.*)

CHORUS: HE'S DREAMING US AGAIN.

ARNOLD: Peace?

CHORUS: US.

ARNOLD: Peace? (*He laughs.*)

CHORUS: US THE FATHER AND THE MOTHER.

ARNOLD: Peace!

CHORUS: UNANIMITY AND SOLIDARITY
COMMUNITY AND FAMILY
US
HE'S DREAMING US AGAIN
THE CROWD IS ALSO A DIVINITY
HE'S DREAMING OUR
REVENGE.
(*Pause.*)

LVOV: What are you afraid of?

ARNOLD: I don't know...

LVOV: You are always afraid of something. WHAT?

ARNOLD: I don't know, I don't know...
(*He starts stacking loaves.*)

LVOV: THEN WHY ARE YOU TREMBLING?
(*ARNOLD shakes his head.*)
It's no wonder I sleep so much, it is the only refuge from your misery. I ALSO AM FINITE.

ARNOLD: Of course...

LVOV: Pity is not bottomless. It is not a well, is it?

ARNOLD: No, indeed...

LVOV: Not a well at all. In my case, it is more like a saucer. Shallow. Simply spilled. Woops! Mine's spilled! No pity left! Where's everybody?

MARYA: Every day you say that. Every time you wake up. Where's everybody? Do you think we just sit about waiting for you to –

LVOV: Yes. (*Pause.*)

MARYA: Yes, it's true. (*She shrugs.*) It's true! When you are asleep we merely quarrel.

ARNOLD: There is no mutton to be had. No fowl. No fish. Nothing.

MARYA: How do you know?

ARNOLD: Sloman says.

MARYA: Sloman says? Why don't you look? Sloman says!

ARNOLD: YOU THRUST YOUR TITS AT TRAINS ALL DAY AND
THEN TELL ME TO LOOK FOR MUTTON I HATE YOUR
TITS YOU LOOK. (*Pause.*)

MARYA: You see? We quarrel even when you are awake. (*To
ARNOLD.*) There is food. There is always food. It conceals
itself, that's all.

(*An OFFICER enters.*)

OFFICER: Lvov? (*Pause.*) Which one of you's –

ARNOLD: He is Lvov.

(*The OFFICER goes towards LVOV.*)

Don't kill him.

(*The OFFICER looks at ARNOLD, confused.*)

So much – so much – killing…

(*He sits on a stool, shrunkenly. MARYA goes to him, nurses his
head.*)

OFFICER: (*To LVOV.*) My train leaves in an hour. Are you
Lvov? My train leaves in an hour. (*Pause.*) WELL, TELL ME
WHAT TO DO, THEN! (*He tears off his cap and sits earnestly
on a chair.*) It is so very easy to repeat the argument that
life should not be taken. I have read the argument and it
convinced me every time. And yet I never was convinced.
How could I have been because I – (*Pause.*) WELL, ARE
YOU LVOV OR NOT?

(*Pause. He snatches up his cap and leaves, as SLOMAN enters,
holding a sack.*)

SLOMAN: (*Holding out the sack.*) Mutton, no. But bitch! Not
a very healthy bitch, because the healthy dogs were
either nimble, and evaded capture, or if not nimble, then
already stewed and a figment in the alimentary memory.
Consequently, only she who looked fatal to digest could
be lured to my sack. Once in the sack I – (*Pause.*) It is
terribly hard to kill a dog. I suffered. Will against horror.
Will and more will. (*Pause.*) It is quite right that I who loved
dogs should have been sent. Quite right. Am I to skin it
also? (*LVOV ignores him.*) Silly question. (*He turns to go, then
abruptly flings the sack at LVOV, who catches it.*) You skin it.
(*Pause.*) If this is to be our final dinner I think you should
do some of the preparation. Seven years I have known you

and never once I SOUND LIKE A HOUSEWIFE ON THE
EDGE OF MUTINY not once have you. So you. (*Pause. LVOV
is still.*) He looks so –
He has his expression of –
ARE YOU CATCHING HIS EXPRESSION?

ARNOLD: Shut up, Sloman…

SLOMAN: His pained and injured – like a bruise burst open
expression – I have grown utterly to hate… (*Pause.*) Still,
we have, all of us, only a limited repertoire of expression. I
accept – barring the effect of gunfire on the physiognomy –
barring traumatic wounding – this is an expression we shall
have to live with. And there's the knife.
(*He chucks a blade at LVOV. It falls to the floor.*)
I never felt so strongly in my life – never more –
democratic. (*He looks to MARYA.*) Oh, say you know what I
mean!
(*He picks up the blade and takes the sack from LVOV.*)
I'll skin it obviously.
(*He goes out.*)

LVOV: You announce the last supper and they don't hurry
themselves, do they'?

MARYA: They are all over the continent and there is a
war on –

LVOV: They don't hurry themselves. They tidy their beds.
They nail soles on their boots. They linger in bookshops in
old cities. Don't they believe me any more?

ARNOLD: There is a war on, Lvov –

LVOV: I say this is the last supper and two, as usual, do all the
work.

ARNOLD: I would do more, but –

LVOV: The two who do the work perhaps do it because they
love me more. Or perhaps they do it because work is a
habit, and it comes easily to them. I don't praise them
for it.

MARYA: I would do more as well, but –

LVOV: I'm not asking for excuses –

MARYA: I'm not excusing myself, I want to explain –

LVOV: I am bored with explanations –

MARYA: I am a boring woman but bores must be indulged or fascination could not know itself –

LVOV: You quote me –

MARYA: All the time –

LVOV: With failing conviction –

MARYA: Possibly –

LVOV: Routinely –

MARYA: Possibly – no, not at all – you –

ARNOLD: I met him on a road between the coast and the silted harbour, and I said, even at twenty yards I said, there is no other man like this. From his features alone, I knew there was no other.

MARYA: That must be true of any face.

ARNOLD: Obviously.

MARYA: Since all faces are different.

ARNOLD: Obviously.

MARYA: We are an infinite variety.

ARNOLD: Any fool knows that. You are so trite for a lunatic. Any fool knows that. But his face. It was a face of extraordinary originality. Both coarse and refined. Even the passage of a cloud across the sun could bring out one, or other, aspect.

MARYA: It's true of any face –

ARNOLD: YOU ARE SO MERCILESSLY TRITE. Why be insane if you merely repeat slogans? What is the virtue in it?

MARYA: Why were you on the road?

ARNOLD: I was always on the road, wasn't I, Lvov? Always on the road?

(*SUSANNAH enters with a sack, she tips out a pile of potatoes.*)

My God, my God, Susannah…

SUSANNAH: Will. And more will!

(*She smiles triumphantly.*)

Do you hate me, Lvov? I do it for you, and your face is. Your frown is. A reproving ditch across your brow.

(*She looks at him, closely.*)

Never mind. I do it for you. I would have taken these from the groping hands of blinded babies. And still it would be for you. As it was I –

MARYA: SHE STOLE THEM FROM THE ORPHANAGE!

SUSANNAH: (*Not moving.*) Speak, then, Lvov…

MARYA: She stole them from the orphanage!

SUSANNAH: Speak then, you appalling man… (*Pause.*)

LVOV: They are very fine potatoes.

SUSANNAH: No, thank me.

MARYA: Anyone could steal them!

SUSANNAH: (*Turning on her.*) Could they? Can you imagine the will I found for that? My conscience I smothered with both hands. THANK ME YOU APPALLING MAN. (*Pause.*) He won't, will he?

LVOV: If you love me, should I be surprised you break with trivial conscience? That is the essence of love. But I kiss you anyway. Stealing from the rich is facile but – (*He dries, shudders.*)

ARNOLD: Train!

(*A fast train approaches. LVOV suddenly grabs SUSANNAH, shuddering. She looks at him, appalled. MARYA opens her gown to the train, then closes it again. The train goes.*)

MARYA: Guns…

ARNOLD: What's wrong with guns? Why not expose your tits to guns? A gun might blush, I daresay. A gun might suffer.

MARYA: You try to sound like Lvov, but all you do is make a fool of yourself. You think you are poetic but you are simply absurd.

ARNOLD: The absurd may be poetic.

MARYA: When I was in the hospital the doctors said, paint! Paint your feelings! Write! Write your feelings! I didn't want to. What do they think art is? Vomit?

ARNOLD: Art is sometimes vomit.

MARYA: How would you know! You are a travelling salesman.

ARNOLD: I know what it is to vomit –

LVOV: (*Freeing himself from SUSANNAH.*) Stop…do stop…this tide of wit and banter, stop…stop… When I'm gone you'll simply –

ARNOLD: Gone? Gone where?

LVOV: Simply degenerate into wit and banter.

ARNOLD: Gone where?

LVOV: Sitting at the road side gibbering…
(*An immaculately dressed WOMAN enters.*)
JUDITH: They have hanged some soldiers.
(*She takes off her gloves.*)
Quite rightly.
(*She looks around.*)
Am I early? The soldiers wanted to go home. No, said the
officers, the war's not over, how can you go home?
(*She looks around again.*)
No tables? No chairs? Still, we want to go home say the
soldiers in various illiterate tongues. This is supposed to be
some sort of occasion, isn't it and I've – well, I always dress
like this but – may I have a chair? (*ARNOLD brings her a
chair. She sits.*) What perfect potatoes! I never thought to see
potatoes so – inflexibly potato-like again – who –
(*She quickly kneels, picks one up.*)
May I keep this? To plant?
(*She sits again.*)
You see, I believe in the future.
(*She pops it in her bag.*)
But they are like heifers! They have a notion of home,
and wild with home sickness they charge the barrack
gates! Heads! Yes, heads against the solid planks, boom!
Boom! And blood! That is how mad they are! All this
is well enough, this is just the crazed instinct of males,
much applauded in battle and tolerated in the public bar
but then… (*Pause.*) One less, or more crazed than the
others, pulls from his pocket a handkerchief-sized, flimsy
and scarcely-recognizable emblem called – a flag. But
not the legal flag. This particular combination of colours
means – this pattern has – resonances and – hieroglyphic
significances which – its mere appearance is enough
to – AND UP GO THE GALLOWS! Tree trunks, one across
the other, most crude carpentry, the bark still on – and
they dangle two from either end, the homesick soldiers are
suspended like pheasants from a butcher's hook – do you
remember pheasants? And make an avenue down which –
(*Pause.*) They say of me, Judith will never be without

stockings if the war reduces the rest of us to nakedness. It appears I am a witch, but I merely read newspapers, and I thought ten years ago, stockings will cease, perhaps for all time, so I went from draper to draper, clearing them out. Admittedly, there is something absurd about them now... (*She strokes her knee.*) Lvov says, you are afraid of something, or you wouldn't dress so well, don't you, Lvov? Yes, I am afraid. I am afraid of Lvov. And he is vain, God knows, his simplicity is so orchestrated. At least I'm honest. HA! I HATE THAT PHRASE!
(*She takes the potato from her bag.*)
Can't wait.
(*She bites into it.*)
By the way I'm widowed.
(*They look at her. MARYA goes to comfort her.*)
No, don't touch!
(*She shuts her eyes.*)
Don't mutter or console...!

LVOV: How like you to announce this in such a calculated way. How insincere.

JUDITH: Yes.

LVOV: To make a work of art of it.

JUDITH: Yes. You taught me that. You taught me information is nothing and expression, all. You are the actor, and me, the scene shifter, learning from the wings...

ARNOLD: We are sorry. Notwithstanding you hate sentiment. I must tell you I am moved for you.

MARYA: WHY DOESN'T SHE JUST LET US GIVE!
(*SLOMAN enters with a server and lid.*)

SLOMAN: One joint of bitch.

MARYA: You must give. You will decay inside if you don't give.

SLOMAN: ONE JOINT OF BITCH!
(*He whisks off the lid, replaces it with a flourish.*)

MARYA: You will atrophy and stink. Your guts will rattle in your concave belly like string in a paper bag.

ARNOLD: Judith's husband is dead.

MARYA: IT'S TRUE WHAT I'M TELLING YOU! (*SLOMAN shrugs.*)

JUDITH: There are many advantages in this. For one thing, he is not maimed. I could not have borne the return of damaged goods. You have seen them, and so have I, and I always said to him, don't return like that, I have neither the pity nor the responsibility for it.

ARNOLD: You have the pity.

JUDITH: All right, yes, I have the pity, but the pity would destroy my life. (*She gets up.*) Perhaps he lay out in some wood somewhere, horribly hurt, and thinking of me, put a bullet in himself. Do you think that's possible?

MARYA: Very possible.

JUDITH: They do that. They do do that, don't they?

LVOV: He would have lain sick in a room, and you would have ignored him.

JUDITH: Yes.

LVOV: His eyes would follow you round the room.

JUDITH: If he had eyes.

LVOV: If he had eyes, you. And they would be a lake of misery, knowing you were coming here.

JUDITH: Yes. And you would not give me one hour more. Not yield one minute for his needs.

LVOV: Not one.

JUDITH: So, all this is good. All this is proper.

SLOMAN: It is not Lvov's way, is it, to let the weak distract the strong? Lvov surrenders nothing.

LVOV: Would you be here if I did? If I were naked, would you admire me? Because I have clothing, and there are many without. If I were filthy, would you admire me? For there are those without soap, and I keep soap. If I were all day carrying the crippled to the well, would you admire me? Because there are many without water, and I have strength. I am what I am and cannot be consumed in charity.

SLOMAN: No, nor in skinning dogs. Nor gathering potatoes. Or clearing drains when the drains are blocked.

IVORY: (*Entering.*) SHUT UP YOU WORTHLESS SHUT UP I HATE YOUR SHUT UP YOU DRAIN CLEANER.
(*He shudders, ceases. He goes to JUDITH and embraces her.*)

27

LVOV: (*To SLOMAN.*) You understand, while pretending not to. You make a rattle of democracy, while knowing how much better it is you cook than me. You see, and you deny. You have never ceased resenting, and when the truth stands out like a swollen vein, you resent that, too. Resent the stars if you wish. Or the fact that water runs downhill.

SLOMAN: No.

(*He shakes his head.*)

No.

No.

This is an odd time for an argument, but the best arguments break out at odd times. You are ascribing my democracy to a flaw in my character –

JUDITH: Your nature is flawed –

SLOMAN: My nature is neither here nor there –

IVORY: PUT THE DOG DOWN –

SLOMAN: You are obsessed with Lvov, all of you, and you interpret all he says in the light of truth, you will not see it when he trowels on spurious arguments, the more spurious he is the more you call it inspiration –

LVOV: THE DOG YOU BASTARD THE DOG –

SLOMAN: There is no flaw in my nature which is not also in his –

ARNOLD: You are spilling the dog –

SLOMAN: And what if I do ram my head against the trees? What if I do? Perhaps I hate the universe. Perhaps I wish water would run uphill. And if democracy is as hard as scooping the stars out of the sky, so what, the effort is good, the effort is admirable –

JUDITH: It is not admirable, it is futile and ridiculous –

SLOMAN: Seven years I have listened to his arguments and I feel like saying –

IVORY: DROP THE DOG AND I WILL BITE YOUR LUNGS OUT.

(*Pause. He laughs.*)

No, it's true, it's true, we are all incapable of discernment. It's perfectly true what he says we are infatuated. It's perfectly true we have allowed ourselves to be. It's perfectly true the power of Lvov resides solely in his refusal to apologize. Perfectly, perfectly true and I for one refuse to. I for one. (*Pause.*)

SLOMAN: (*To JUDITH.*) I'm sorry, I – I shouldn't have – when your husband is –

JUDITH: That is all absorbed. It lives only in the marrow now. Blind sediment.

SLOMAN: That may be so, but –

JUDITH: It is so.

(*SLOMAN goes out with the tray.*)

MARYA: Judith, you will live for such a long, long time.

JUDITH: Why do you say that?

MARYA: Because you are unloving. Unhating. But unloving too. I think you will live to be hundreds!

LVOV: She does love. It is knowledge she loves.

JUDITH: Yes! When the telegram arrived I was more interested in how I would react than I was in the information itself. For months I had prepared myself, and immediately I threw all his things in two large boxes, and sent the boxes to his mother.

LVOV: That was good. The things will help his mother to die, whereas they would only have prevented your living.

(*JUDITH absorbs this.*)

JUDITH: Lvov knows…! Lvov has never loved anyone, but he knows! When I was a girl I hunted men who knew things, who had done things. My husband, for example, had been a cowboy in Argentina! Yes, I never told you, but he had, and at fifteen had been a stowaway to the East Indies! What he didn't know! But Lvov, who lived all his life in one place Lvov knows more, don't you, Lvov? Will you teach us something new tonight? I must know something new…

(*The sound of desolation.*)

THE SECOND PARABLE
The Ashamed and the Unashamed

A CHILD enters. She looks around her. She lets out a cry.

CHILD: Help!
  Help!
  (*An OLD WOMAN appears.*)
WIDOW: Why should anyone help you?
CHILD: Because one day I'll be powerful and anyone who didn't help me will be made to suffer.
WIDOW: I'm suffering already and anyway you won't live to be adult. Someone will murder you and hide you in a ditch.
CHILD: How can you tell?
WIDOW: Your mouth.
CHILD: What about it?
WIDOW: Says murder me.
CHILD: Give us a room.
WIDOW: No rooms.
CHILD: GOT A BIG HOUSE.
WIDOW: Pigs in all the rooms.
CHILD: Pigs...?
WIDOW: Yes, you know pigs, they eat the dead.
CHILD: Turn a pig out.
WIDOW: For you? There's a war on.
CHILD: Always been a war on. As long as I can remember.
WIDOW: Me too.
CHILD: I'll die of cold.
WIDOW: No, you won't, you'll be murdered.
CHILD: I am one of a million homeless children, so I read.
WIDOW: I am one of a million miserable widows, so I heard.
CHILD: IT'S SNOWING.
WIDOW: (*Turning to go in.*) Thank God the pigs are dry.
CHILD: I'm not ashamed of being poor. I'm not ashamed of being homeless. I'm not ashamed of stealing. Nor of kicking old men when they're down.
WIDOW: No one is ashamed of anything any more. For example, I am not ashamed of having seven rooms. I am

30

not ashamed of eating pork. I am not ashamed of leaving children in the snow. This is the effect of unending war. Now clear off. I hate vagrants even more than they hate me.

(*She turns again.*)

CHILD: Just a minute!

(*THE WIDOW stops.*)

One of us could try to be ashamed. If you like, I will.

WIDOW: You don't look it. It's that mouth again.

CHILD: I don't know what ashamed looks like.

WIDOW: If I remember, it was sort of – I can't do it either –

CHILD: We can't do it because we don't feel it…

WIDOW: The snow's so deep I shan't get back to the house!

CHILD: Now you look ashamed! That's it!

WIDOW: It's not shame, I'm frightened –

(*She starts to go out, painfully.*)

CHILD: I'll get to the house before you! I'll shut the door and you can die to the sound of pig slaughtering!

WIDOW: Do you think that'll stop you being murdered? Delay it, that's all.

CHILD: That's all I ask. Delay and more delay. (*Pause.*) Now I can't see the house! Which way to the house?

WIDOW: Not telling.

CHILD: We'll drown in the snow!

WIDOW: I always thought I'd die alone, but no, it turns out differently…

CHILD: I can't move!

WIDOW: It was always like this in December…

(*Three figures appear, muffled, in the distance.*)

CHILD: Look! People!

WIDOW: Don't call them!

CHILD: I must!

WIDOW: If you call them, you'll only regret it.

CHILD: If I don't call them I'll regret it!

WIDOW: There are worse things than dying.

CHILD: HELP! HELP!

WIDOW: Idiot.

CHILD: They're waving!

WIDOW: Idiot. Idiot.

(*The THREE SOLDIERS appear.*)

McNOY: We're coming!

McSTAIN: We see you!

MacATTLEE: We kill nobody!

(*They pick their way over the stage.*)

WIDOW: You had to call help. Now look at us. If I had taken no notice how perfect everything would have been. I know I should never have left the house. One error! That's all it takes! One error and every error follows after! This comes of heeding the human voice.

ALL SOLDIERS: (*Looking.*) Women in holes...

WIDOW: Only pigs are worth replying to.

ALL SOLDIERS: PIGS! WHERE?

WIDOW: You see, everything's the result of everything else!

ALL SOLDIERS: WHAT PIGS?

CHILD: On the bed.

MacATTLEE: On the bed?

CHILD: In the bathroom.

McNOY: In the bathroom?

WIDOW: Kill everything. Kill the lot!

McSTAIN: To think we might have just passed by!

McNOY: We did pass by.

McSTAIN: When?

McNOY: Often. There is the house with the filthy shutters.

MacATTLEE: I dimly remember a house with shutters but that was far from here.

McNOY: Not far from here. We have merely marched in circles.

McSTAIN: My memory fails me, but who wants memory?

(*They make towards the house.*)

CHILD: Don't just go!

MacATTLEE: We thought you were hiding, but you fell in. It is always hard to tell why people are in holes.

(*He extends a hand to help her. She takes it.*)

What a wonderful mouth you have...

(*The CHILD looks to the WIDOW apprehensively.*)

CHILD: No, I think I will stay in the hole.

MacATTLEE: Please yourself.
(*He walks towards the house.*)
WIDOW: What about me!
McSTAIN: What about you?
WIDOW: Get me out!
McSTAIN: Get out yourself.
(*He walks away. Pause.*)
CHILD: My mouth could have got me out. My mouth was a rope. Whereas your mouth, pinched purse of a thing, keeps you in…
WIDOW: I tell you, when they have eaten the pigs, God help us.
CHILD: Why?
WIDOW: You know what happens when men have eaten.
CHILD: No, what happens?
WIDOW: They want love.
CHILD: LOVE?
WIDOW: Unfortunately, yes, I experienced a great deal of love when the war and I were still young…
(*Pig squeals offstage.*)
CHILD: Does it hurt?
WIDOW: Frequently, it's fatal.
CHILD: Smell that!
WIDOW: Pig fat. Our hour draws nearer. Our calvary.
CHILD: If the sun would shine, the snow would melt…
WIDOW: What do you call that? Wisdom?
(*Singing offstage.*)
CHILD: They should be ashamed…
WIDOW: I will suggest it to them. Because while we aren't ashamed, if they were, all would be well!
(*The SOLDIERS appear, smiling and lurching. They come to the rim of the holes. McNOY's hand reaches out to the CHILD.*)
You should be ashamed! Have you nothing better to do?
(*McNOY nudges MacATTLEE. MacATTLEE reaches out to the WIDOW.*)
Pinched purse or not. Now you see that loveliness has nothing to do with anything.

McSTAIN: They keep their haunches under the snow. So warm, the haunches...

ALL SOLDIERS: WE KILL NO – BODY

(*The hands are outstretched. At last the WOMEN concede, put out their hands. At the moment the hands touch, a distant sound seeps over the stage. The SOLDIERS listen, caught. It is the sound of bells. McSTAIN drifts under their spell, offstage. McNOY and MacATTLEE are unable to move.*)

END OF THE SECOND PARABLE

TWO WOMEN enter in coats.

GISELA: (*Putting down a bag.*) Things are getting worse. Or is that a superficial judgement?

DORA: They are not getting worse. They are merely becoming different.

GISELA: That's not a bit superficial!

(*She opens her arms, looking at LVOV. Then she goes to him and kisses him.*)

Mmmm!

JUDITH: Why do you always go mmmmm when you kiss someone? What is the mmmmm meant to imply?

DORA: We all have habits.

JUDITH: It is so false. It means, if it means anything at all, that you feel it should be a pleasure and it isn't. Is that what it means? If it is a pleasure go mmmmm and mean it, if it isn't, shut up.

DORA: We all have habits.

JUDITH: So you said.

DORA: And that is her habit.

JUDITH: Well, smash it. Do you desire Lvov? Of course you do. Then say so!

GISELA: (*Turning to JUDITH.*) You look more beautiful than you have ever looked.

(*LVOV bursts out laughing.*)

She does! That was not a tactic! She does!

JUDITH: Yes. I am impeccably got up.

IVORY: Underneath, a dog's dinner. But done up!

DORA: She is not a dog's dinner.

JUDITH: When did you last see me?

DORA: In the flesh? Never.

JUDITH: Well, allow me to judge. I am beautifully packed.

GISELA: We have only just arrived and already we are busily
flattering Judith. That is how quickly we slip into old
habits, wars or no wars. Lvov, if everyone arrives tonight,
it will be a miracle.

DORA: The roads are rivers, so to avoid the roads they drive
on the fields, and then the fields become rivers. The abuse!
The sullen style of abuse! Even the language is dying. We
are coming to the end.

MARYA: The end of what? What is coming to an end? The
war?

DORA: Complexity. We are witnessing the death of
complexity.

MARYA: Oh, that. Well, good.

DORA: You would say so. It bored you.

MARYA: It drove me mad.

DORA: It drove you mad, but for me, it was the whole point of
existence. I was teaching a class in the city, a class which
dwindled week by week, and today, no one appeared at
all. So I stood at the front and lectured, and I was more
articulate than at any other time of my life.

ARNOLD: It seemed so to you. But who was there to judge?

DORA: Everything I said was true. Everything, perfectly
expressed.

GISELA: (*Taking off her coat.*) It's true, I do desire Lvov. I
desire him, and he knows it. Why pretend I don't? But it's
complex. Sometimes I desire him, and sometimes I don't. I
think that is what I mean when I go mmm.

(*DORA laughs and hugs GISELA.*)

MARYA: Who cares what you mean? I don't.

(*LVOV moves to the front of the stage. The sound of a
murmuring crowd rises.*)

LVOV: I don't want to come! I don't want to come! (*The sound
is swamped by a mass of laughter.*) Of course they are absurd!

I see they are absurd, and the more absurd they are the less I want to leave them, why!
(*A mass of laughter.*)
CHORUS: THE MASSES
   THE MASSES
   THEY SING SO BEAUTIFULLY
   THE MASSES
   THEY TEAR THE FLAGS FROM GATES
   AND THE EAGLES FROM THE THRONES OF GOVERNORS
   AND PISS INTO THE MOUTHS OF DYING OFFICERS!
   (*The sound of a train.*)
ARNOLD: Ambulance train! Marya! They let one through!
MARYA: Oh, look at the length of it!
ARNOLD: Ambulance train!
   (*MARYA ties a scarf round her head and hurries out. At last the train passes. Fades.*)
   Normally they let them rot in sidings.
JUDITH: The army of the living must take precedence. I should have thought that was obvious.
ARNOLD: Dying in the sidings…
JUDITH: THEY DON'T DIE IN THE SIDINGS! THAT IS SO – THAT IS SO UTTERLY – (*Pause.*) What use are these emotional expressions –
IVORY: Their breath is like a wind which whistles down the corridors –
JUDITH: If they are not true? That surely is the rot of poetry?
LVOV: The posturing of pity obscures –
JUDITH: Yes, and nothing comes of it but sex. Sex and more sex!
DORA: You interrupted him. You interrupted Lvov.
JUDITH: Did I?
DORA: No one lets Lvov finish any more.
JUDITH: I'm sorry. I'm sorry, Lvov. (*Pause.*)
ARNOLD: She is tense. She is tense because –
JUDITH: I'm not. (*Pause.*) I apologise, but actually I think I could have finished it for him. He was going to say, obscures the secret pleasure in another's agony. Is that right?

LVOV: Yes. (*The mass of laughter passes.*) Yes, I was…
   (*Painful pause.*)

GISELA: It's obvious that anyone who has been taught as
   long as we have will know the method of the teacher. I
   see nothing very significant in our being able, after so
   long, to parody or imitate Lvov. It is perhaps, a sign of his
   greatness…

DORA: I think Gisela is aware, and possibly afraid, she could
   surpass Lvov…

GISELA: In Lvovness! In the elaboration of Lvov!

DORA: Yes…
   (*A further painful pause. The door opens with a flourish.*)

ANNA: Gin! Gin, bitches!
   (*She chucks the bottle at DORA, who catches it, laughing.
   LVOV goes to ANNA and embraces her again and again,
   silently, desperately.*)

ARNOLD: No one here drinks gin…

ANNA: Learn! It was a present from the last fat man in Dnieper!

JUDITH: Fresh from the brothel.

ANNA: Soldiers' stench in every pore and a slippery arse!

JUDITH: No time to wash –

ANNA: No time at all

JUDITH: Towel between the legs and –

ANNA: Money in the handbag!
   (*They both laugh. They embrace.*)

LVOV: Anna, you will bury us all.

ANNA: Not deep, Lvov…

LVOV: Not deep, no.

ANNA: No time for deep graves.

JUDITH: Prick in one hand, shovel in the other…

DORA: It isn't true that Anna will survive. Lvov wants to
   believe it. It is pure Lvov to want the whore to birth the
   future, but it isn't true, she will be strangled in a dirty
   room…

ANNA: Dora, you refuse all hope…!

DORA: Yes…

ANNA: I love you. How you refuse! Worthless hope!

DORA: I do. I do refuse. Kiss me!

(*They kiss, fondly.*)

GISELA: Lvov thinks corruption runs off Anna, like rain off an apple. We all have to believe in Anna's essential cleanliness. It is mandatory.

ANNA: Mandatory yes! What does that mean?

GISELA: You know perfectly well.

ANNA: I wish I was literate.

DORA: You are literate.

ANNA: I wish I was numerate.

DORA: You count money, don't you, at the door?

ANNA: I wish I was wicked!

JUDITH: You are wicked. What you mean is sinful, and sinful you will never be. A thousand men might lie on you, lathering, and you could skip up and your taste would all be honeyed. It's true isn't it? She is like that. She sweats purity. What do you say, Lvov? You are passionate about Anna.

LVOV: I think it is easy to love a prostitute. But because it is easy, it is not less worthy. I love Anna for her self. But I also love you, who is not yourself. It is only Dora I find hard to love. (*Pause.*)

DORA: I'm glad.

(*ANNA laughs loudly.*)

IT'S TRUE. I'M GLAD.

ANNA: I believe you!

JUDITH: Lvov did not answer my question, did you, Lvov?

ARNOLD: It's his method.

DORA: It's his method, yes.

GISELA: His method is to counter questions with a statement generally related to the theme but –

ANNA: Leave him alone, you cows…

DORA: That's true, gradually you discover what defines Lvov, and it's deflection. Skilful, I admit.

JUDITH: I asked if Anna could be sinful –

ANNA: I fucking can –

DORA: Fucking has nothing to do with it –

ANNA: You are such a bony cow.

GISELA: Shh –

ANNA: You stand there like a bony cow and –

LVOV: Shh –

ANNA: No, she is, she is, isn't she, Arnold, a bony cow?
(*He looks up from a chair.*)
Arnold!
(*She goes to him, puts her arms round his neck.*)
No, don't finger me! You say hello to Arnold and immediately he –

ARNOLD: That's not so! That's so unfair! That's not so!

IVORY: It is so.

ARNOLD: I resent that!

IVORY: It is so. It is in your nature.

LVOV: Let him finger you, if fingering is what he wants.

ARNOLD: Good God, if you can't put your – good God!
(*ANNA laughs.*)

SLOMAN: (*Who has entered and watched this.*) This is what I mean by equality.

ARNOLD: (*To LVOV.*) You give me permission – you condescend to – license me to –
(*He shakes his head with anger.*)

SLOMAN: This is what I mean when I talk of equality. There is none. This is what gets you in the end. The gnawing, humiliating absence of equality.

GISELA: What is humiliating about the absence of equality? Where is the humiliation in acknowledging another's qualities? His superiority even? Oh, God, what's humiliating in that?
(*SLOMAN looks at LVOV.*)

SLOMAN: It gnaws. (*Pause.*) It gnaws you even…

JUDITH: The ugly against the beautiful. The blind against the sighted.

SLOMAN: Yes.

JUDITH: The gnawing sense you lack blue eyes.

SLOMAN: I didn't say anything could be achieved. I said it gnaws. But Arnold cannot touch Anna, and Lvov can. It gnaws.

ARNOLD: No, I'm all right, I –

SLOMAN: Oh, Arnold, be gnawed! (*Pause.*) I also find Lvov –
    immaculate. I too, stoop to Lvov. And Susannah – (*She
    enters with a tray.*) – she carries EVERY FUCKING THING –
    (*ANNA goes to assist SUSANNAH.*) NO!
    (*ANNA stops.*)
    But Lvov would no more take her in his arms than he
    would – fornicate with a prolapsed mare…
GISELA: We come together and –
    We come together for –
    Lvov…!
    (*He is not observing them.*)
SLOMAN: I must – in the interests of clarity and truth – which
    was the first condition of our unity – speak what is to me
    at least – blindingly self-evident – but unperceived by
    you – which is that –
LVOV: You wish me to be inhuman.
    (*Pause.*)
SLOMAN: Yes. Obviously.
LVOV: I am perfectly human. And the perfectly human is as
    near to inhumanity as you should want. If I have power
    over Anna, you should be glad.
SLOMAN: Yes, but –
LVOV: You are angry that you are not me. Your body and
    your soul are raw, as if you were inverted and your red
    insides were smarting in the air.
SLOMAN: I can't reply to that –
LVOV: It is the terrible cry of the skinned wolf whose nostrils
    are brimming with its own blood…
SLOMAN: I can't reply. I would rather help Susannah –
LVOV: You are not helping Susannah, you are using her. You
    are using her against me.
    (*Pause.*)
SLOMAN: Yes…
    (*Pause. He gathers himself, goes to leave the room. As he does
    so, a FARMER enters, taking off his cap.*)
FARMER: Are you Lvov?
SLOMAN: I'm not Lvov.
    (*He goes out. The FARMER goes to ARNOLD.*)

FARMER: Are you Lvov?

(*ARNOLD shakes his head. The FARMER goes to IVORY.*)

I have a problem.

(*JUDITH laughs. The FARMER turns to leave.*)

GISELA: Don't go. It doesn't hurt to be laughed at. What you said was funny, whether you knew it or not.

FARMER: She sits there in her –

(*He shrugs.*)

She sits and – (*He shrugs.*)

GISELA: It doesn't hurt. The war is in its fourteenth year. The cattle are dead and so are the children. There's cholera in the water and pellagra in the bone. And you say you have a problem. She has a problem too. Her ribs are sticking through her skin.

FARMER: You talk too much. Which one's Lvov?

GISELA: You are bad-mannered, but that doesn't matter.

(*THE FARMER slaps GISELA in the face. She is silent. She takes out a handkerchief and dabs her mouth. LVOV goes towards him.*)

LVOV: If we embarrass you, perhaps it is because you are ashamed.

FARMER: I want advice.

LVOV: I don't give advice.

ANNA: There is a shed near the soup kitchen. It has a notice on it which says Advice. Or you could ask the gipsies. Or the comrades. They all give advice.

(*Pause. The FARMER turns to go.*)

LVOV: What have you done? Killed somebody? Unfortunately I am not free tonight. As you can see, I am giving supper here tonight. (*THE FARMER starts to go.*) You could have done a dozen murders, but I'm not free tonight.

FARMER: I'll wait.

LVOV: You are very patient, but tomorrow I shan't be –

FARMER: I said I'll wait.

(*He sits on the floor.*)

I've sat by cows all night and got a dead calf for it. So this is nothing. The soldiers made me stand for eighteen hours.

So this is nothing. And often, I'm drunk and lie in ditches days on end. So this is nothing.

(*Suddenly LVOV flies at the FARMER, seizing him and thrusting him out of the room. In a single, continuous movement he returns and leaps onto a chair. The FARMER shouts and hammers on the door.*)

LVOV: Losing the knack. The knack going. Losing the gift. The gift going. Finding it false and only forty-two. Come nearer those at the back! Those at the back file through! And the voice! The voice going! To hear me you must hardly breathe! Whoever coughs is not engaged, all coughers will be suffocated by their neighbours, you rob them of the right to hear, you rob them, shh! How rare this is, how rare to hear a teacher when the teachers are all dead, the teachers and the poets are all dead, instead we praise the actors, the geniuses posing for the cameras, how effortless they are and charming, this never-ageing charm will be the death of us, only catastrophe can keep us clean NO MORE GENIUSES IN WHITE SUITS, his garden, his summerhouse, his paddock and his rural bench, his PASSIONATE CONVIVIALITY, no, where are the teachers, you are so fortunate, you really are, so terribly fortunate, though the knack is going and I am only forty-two, the knack has gone, but I was never young, never, never young and at the brothel wept, I never laughed, I have no wit, the wit died in my jaw, how wonderful the absence of all wit, I sit so still and never tap my feet NEVER TRUST THE FOOT TAPPERS or touch a stranger intimately and at the dance-hall wept, yes, wept, I am so tired of rebels, I the rebel am so tired, are you not tired of being asked to rise, rise up, no stoop, you stoop, show me your stooping I will not rise for anyone who cannot stoop say to the hero in the funny hat, you will observe I have no hat, no aspect of what passes for my personality requires a hat and if the sun is hot I seek the shade, it is simplicity you lack and in exchange they give you comedy, I never made a joke, I never ever made a joke, THIS TERRIBLE DEFORMITY OF LAUGHTER makes

you ugly, no, do not heed the order rise, cease laughing
and pay your taxes –

(*A MAN has entered, scrupulously silent.*)

You're late.

(*The MAN smiles.*)

Not late. But certainly you cut it fine.

FORJACKS: I have excuses. But when were you ever interested
in excuses? You must make what you want of the fact that I
am very nearly late. Though not precisely so.

(*He removes his coat. The door is beaten violently.*)

You have so many enemies. Some of these enemies are
insane. But others are brilliant analysts, it must be said.

LVOV: (*Climbing off the chair.*) And the one outside? What is he?

FORJACKS: He believed in you, and you gave him nothing.

IVORY: WHO SAYS HE HAS TO GIVE SOMETHING! WHAT
IS HE, A SCAVENGER? WHAT IS HE, A JACKAL? STOP
BANGING, JACKAL OR I'LL BITE YOUR LIVER.

(*The FARMER ceases banging.*)

LVOV: (*To FORJACKS.*) All the same, I'm sorry you're late.

ANNA: He's not late!

LVOV: No, he isn't late, but I feel he is –

ANNA: That's ridiculous, he's –

LVOV: I SAID I FEEL HE IS LATE.

FORJACKS: If you wanted me to come earlier, I wish you'd
said –

GISELA: That would have ruined the point of it. He wanted
you to appear impatient.

FORJACKS: Yes. (*Pause.*) Yes. (*Pause.*) You once said – I wrote it
down –

ANNA: You write everything down!

FORJACKS: Yes – of course I do – be early for your enemies,
and late for your friends –

(*He looks at DORA.*)

Did you write that down?

DORA: I don't remember, I –

FORJACKS: I did write that down, and now –

GISELA: It's clearly redundant. Strike it out. In any case, Lvov
isn't a friend.

FORJACKS: No… No, he isn't, I'll strike it out.
(*He grins nervously.*)
The traffic is impossible! And the refugees! How easily
they die! But always in the most inconvenient positions, a
plane had strafed a column of –
(*He stops.*)
That's odd… I was about to describe in graphic detail
something that I thought appalled me, but actually – I
wanted to entertain you. We do love this war, don't we?
We do love suffering…
(*A train passes. They are still as its many wagons rattle past.
During this, a FIGURE enters, rotund in a mass of dirty coats.
He is still, and waits. The train fades.*)
LVOV: (*Looking at APOLLO.*) Oh, if there were a single life of
love…this man who carried girls from bedroom windows
and laid them in the clover half asleep, who serviced guns
bigger than houses and sent their shells to unknown targets
of innocence, and smashed himself, was sawn through
the skull by surgeons in a bloody tent, so his naked brain
pulsed in the ash-strewn air, and returning, with his clumsy
finger round a pencil stub, wrote poems small and shining
like impecunious stars…if there is a single life of love, it's
him… (*He bows to APOLLO.*)
APOLLO: I could have introduced myself better. And you have
nicked my style. But.
ANNA: Squeeze me!
(*He goes to ANNA, embraces her.*)
No, squeeze!
(*He crushes her.*)
You stink! Oh, God, you stink!
DORA: All men adore big men. And all women. Lvov adores
Apollo. Anna adores Apollo. And I must admit, I adore
him, too. Why?
GISELA: I don't adore him. I feel for Apollo – what, exactly – I
feel – gratified that he exists. That's all.
APOLLO: A poem for Gisela.
GISELA: Oh, no –
ANNA: Yes! A poem for Gisela!

APOLLO: Shh!

GISELA: I don't want a –

ALL: SHH.

(*Pause.*)

APOLLO: Her ribs will be a source of needles in the new stone
age... (*Pause.*) That's all.

(*He turns to LVOV.*)

Lvov, how quiet you have been, though I live near, I catch
no sounds of you...

ARNOLD: He has been ill.

APOLLO: So have we all! And now, this invitation!

LVOV: I have been sitting in the dark.

APOLLO: Excellent, but how quiet you have been...

(*He turns to them all.*)

It is wonderful to see us all again! Conventional sentiment,
but it is, it is! Sometimes we must give vent to common
sentiments, we must endow the truism with life, Lvov, are
you in pain?

(*He goes to LVOV, holds him.*)

Before you, I could not understand why I ached even as I
laughed, I could not understand the cruelty which flowed
over my lip even in the midst of my condolences, nor the
brevity of kindness...are you in pain?

(*SUSANNAH enters, bearing a table.*)

Let me carry a table! Brute to bear the tables! Brute!

(*SLOMAN follows her in, with a table.*)

SLOMAN: She isn't weak!

APOLLO: I merely demonstrate the absurdity of the
convention...

SUSANNAH: Table cloths!

(*ARNOLD goes out, for cloths.*)

FORJACKS: Lvov, every day I thought of you. Every day, I
think. I ran through my little book, the diary that I call
the Book of Lvov. Sometimes I read things which either I
had copied wrongly, or which entirely contradicted other
things. And I felt extremely angry, with myself, at first, and
then, with you.

SLOMAN: Table cloths!

(*He flings them out with a crack. Activity.*)

FORJACKS: For example, the concepts of gratification and abstinence.

SUSANNAH: Thirteen places!

SLOMAN: Thirteen chairs!

GISELA: Privilege expresses itself in different ways in different places. Given the shortage of firewood, to assemble thirteen chairs is reckless extravagance!

(*Chairs of odd kinds are carried in.*)

FORJACKS: In June you said –

(*He thumbs through a filthy book.*)

ANNA: Chair!

FORJACKS: Shh!

(*He thumbs.*)

In June you said – yes – Tolerance is impossible without gratification – though you later – not just later, often – questioned the value of tolerance – but then in September – PLEASE DON'T DELIBERATELY KNOCK INTO ME – sorry – in September – here it is – the 12th – and I may have got this wrong – you say – the knowledge of lack, when fulfilment is still possible – an orchard which a man chooses not to trespass in – produces a state of imaginative intensity which reality fails to satisfy, at least only in recollection, so that – what that suggests to me is the essential failure of all moments of consumption, but isn't that opposed to the first proposition, or am I –

(*LVOV doesn't respond.*)

Please don't bang me with that chair! I suppose I am trying to be consistent which in itself is – yes – that's the point, isn't it – as you said in April, the very attempt to inflict symmetrical systems is an oppression – ANNA!

(*She laughs.*)

I will collect a chair, I have every intention of –

APOLLO: The worst chair –

FORJACKS: The worst chair obviously, because I chose to think when grabbing was the order –

(*The CHORUS appears to LVOV.*)

IVORY: The chair of nails –

FORJACKS: The worst possible chair, of course –
   (*APOLLO holds one up.*)
   That's got no legs!
CHORUS: LVOV
   EVEN THE BLIND SEE
   AND DOUBT COMES TO THE INFATUATED
   LVOV
   (*A cloud of laughter.*)
LVOV: How can I hear myself!
CHORUS: LVOV
   WE ARE THE PEOPLE
   AND THE PEOPLE SEE YOUR SLIPPING SELF
   GIVE US A SLOGAN
   WE LOVE A SLOGAN
   WE WILL CARVE YOUR SLOGAN ON THE BRIDGE
   WHY DON'T YOU GIVE US A SLOGAN YOU SNOB
   (*A cloud of laughter.*)
   ARE YOU AFRAID?
   WE ALSO ARE AFRAID
   WE STAND BEHIND OUR DOORS WITH POKERS
   (*A cloud of laughter.*)
   YOU KNOCK THE WEAK ASIDE
   WE CAN'T HAVE THAT!
   YOU RIDICULE THE MASSES
   WE CAN'T HAVE THAT! (*A sound of desolation.*)
LVOV: I am not afraid of death. I am afraid of being
   revealed...

THE THIRD PARABLE
The Economy of the Itinerant Player

*A POOR FIGURE enters, blind, and with a violin. He stops, plays a
few bars. Pause. He plays a few more bars, stops.*

VIOLINIST: Nobody here, then?
   (*He moves around the stage, stops, plays, ceases.*)
   Nobody here, either?

I have got off the road.

Blind, and off the road.

I heard the guns. That's the way, I said, to the guns. Always to the guns. There is charity. And then they stopped. They stopped and started somewhere else. That is their way. But now it is days since I heard anything. Only a fool comes off the road. IS THAT SOMEONE?

(*He immediately begins playing, but stops, an ear cocked.*)

No, I am in trouble and no mistake. I broke the cardinal rule. OI! (*He waves the bow.*) Do you like Strauss? They laugh at Strauss. But Strauss knew. He knew their emptiness. He knew their hunger for oblivion. OI! (*A NUN appears, looks at him. The VIOLINIST plays some bars, and ceases. Pause.*) You do not applaud because you think applause will put you under an obligation. But frankly, I would be content with the applause.

(*The NUN begins to creep away.*)

OH, COME ON, CUNT!

(*She stops.*)

What are you, a deserter? I tell you this. A blind gipsy can hunt down a sighted man and cut his veins swifter than a kite plucks up a rabbit. I also carry a knife.

NUN: I can't help you.

VIOLINIST: What are you, a mother? If you're in milk, I'd suck and never mind the money...

NUN: I'm a youth, and in a terrible hurry.

VIOLINIST: Don't go, youth...

NUN: I must –

(*She turns. Suddenly the VIOLINIST snaps his bow across his knee. He holds it out in two pitiful sections. The NUN stares.*)

You have broken your...how will you... YOU ARE BLACKMAILING ME!

VIOLINIST: An expression of frustration, it occurs to all the great performers.

NUN: Liar, it's a blackmail. It's a blackmail and I won't submit.

(*She turns to go. He remains standing, arm outstretched. She stops.*)

It is so unjust! I protest!

VIOLINIST: What have you got in your purse?

NUN: Hardly a thing.

VIOLINIST: Half each.

NUN: I am on a mission of mercy and –

VIOLINIST: Me too. The perpetuation of the world.
(*He drops the instrument and holds out a dirty hand.*)
Anyway, you might have been waylaid, further up the field. This may be merciful.

NUN: (*Giving him a biscuit.*) You have all the answers.

VIOLINIST: (*Pocketing the biscuit.*) Let's get on, I will hold your shoulder.
(*He holds the NUN's shoulder.*)
You are frail. What are you, a brother? Give me your habit, brother. I am hanging out the holes of this lousy garment.

NUN: I can't do that.

VIOLINIST: Why not?

NUN: It is my identity. It is God's. And not mine to give.

VIOLINIST: Do you love Bartok? I would play Bartok, but he brings tears to my eyes. Take it off. He pleads for the unloved. Off with it, now.
(*Pause. Then the NUN disrobes.*)

NUN: Now let me go (*Suddenly the VIOLINIST bears her to the ground.*) Oh!

VIOLINIST: I MUST LIVE! I MUST LIVE!

NUN: Oh!

McSTAIN: (*A voice from offstage.*) Hey…!

VIOLINIST: Five days and never a soul! Five days and now – surplus!

McNOY: Hey! (*The VIOLINIST ceases to rape. The SOLDIERS enter, look at the sight.*)

MacATTLEE: A nun with no garments…
(*The VIOLINIST, sitting, begins to pluck a tune in pizzicato. The NUN sits up.*)

McNOY: Where there is a nun, there must be a convent.

MacATTLEE: (*To VIOLINIST.*) Have I seen you before?

VIOLINIST: I have heard you before.

MacATTLEE: I have. You play Bartok! You brought tears to my eyes!

VIOLINIST: I can. I can do that. But only with a bow.
  (*He shows the broken bow.*)
MacATTLEE: Who broke the bow?
VIOLINIST: Ask her.
  (*They look to the NUN, who is dressing.*)
MacATTLEE: You broke the bow? You broke the blind man's bow?
ALL SOLDIERS: We kill nobody –
MacATTLEE: Luckily for you. And I could have done with a little Bartok at this time of day. In the setting sun. When it is obvious the war will not end today after all. These are the hours you need to weep a little.
VIOLINIST: Open your knapsacks. Lend us a bite.
McNOY: There is nothing in our knapsacks. The fact we carry them at all is testimony to our unextinguishable optimism.
VIOLINIST: (*Standing.*) I'll march with you, then. Soldiers always find the roads. And what's a beggar without roads?
McSTAIN: This is the road.
VIOLINIST: This is the road? They are not what they used to be, then…
  (*They start to move.*)
NUN: Don't go without me!
VIOLINIST: Don't go? But you have a mission.
NUN: No. I never had a mission. I was running away.
VIOLINIST: Hold my shoulder, then, and if we meet peasants they will trust you, because of your habit. Then we can rob them better.
ALL SOLDIERS: THUS WE MIGHT ALL SURVIVE.

END OF THE THIRD PARABLE

They are arranging the tables. A GIRL enters. They stop.

ELLA: Not missed.
  Not mentioned.
  And not missed.
  THERE COMES A TIME THE SILENT WANT TO BURST!
LVOV: Yes…it's perfectly true, I had forgotten you.
  (*ELLA closes her eyes.*)

I could have eaten, and slept, and woke, and still would
not have said, she isn't here, Ella. It's testimony to our
contempt for you.

APOLLO: Oh, no, it –

LVOV: It's clear, for all of us, you have failed to make yourself
either loved or hated.

ELLA: Yes.

LVOV: It must be you who is to blame for it.

ELLA: Yes.

APOLLO: No, this is terrible, this is –

LVOV: No, don't apologize! She needs no, and asks for no, nor
credits any APOLOGY.

APOLLO: I am ashamed –

LVOV: No, it is her, let her be ashamed.

ELLA: I find it hard to speak. So terribly hard.

(*ANNA goes to embrace her.*)

LVOV: No, no! Let her endure it!

(*ELLA shakes her head, agonised.*)

SLOMAN: We had forgotten you, but that doesn't mean you
aren't welcome…

(*JUDITH laughs out loud.*)

What's funny? WHAT'S FUNNY!

JUDITH: You engineer the perfect compromise. You engineer.

SLOMAN: What's wrong with it?

JUDITH: Compromise?

SLOMAN: Yes!

JUDITH: It is a lovely thing in politics, and an ugly thing in art,
a miserable thing in marriage and in friendship – I don't
know. I have never had a friend. What does Ella think?

ELLA: I WANT TO BURST.

JUDITH: Yes, we know that.

ELLA: I want words, and sentences to splash all over you.
I want my self to come out and say THIS IS ELLA. IT IS
IMPOSSIBLE TO IGNORE ELLA.

ANNA: What words?

(*ELLA shakes her head.*)

ELLA: I am impossible to love.

SUSANNAH: For some, that might make you lovable.

ELLA: No. Lvov is right. Until I exist, I am contemptible.
 (*She sits on the floor, crossing one leg.*)
SLOMAN: We are being so – utterly and appallingly –
GISELA: Oh, do stop rasping out this useless and repetitive, unfocused and implacable SYMPATHY!
ELLA: Yes, please, it's no help to me …
 (*APOLLO throws her a cushion. They continue laying out the tables. MARYA enters, with a blood-stained dress.*)
MARYA: (*Lifting it to show.*) The amputees!
 (*She lets it fall, laughs.*)
 I carry their limbs to the hut. We pile them in the hut. The hut is bursting and the door has to be forced. I am simply not strong enough. I say to the sentry, come on, help me shut the hut! We put our backs to it. Lvov, this is a funny sight! This fat-backed soldier and this skinny girl, shutting the house of legs!
ARNOLD: There are eleven chairs, and Ella has a cushion.
MARYA: Ella?
ARNOLD: Has a cushion, yes.
MARYA: Who's Ella? Oh, Ella! I want to sit next to Lvov.
LVOV: I am not sitting.
SUSANNAH: Not sitting?
MARYA: All right, then I'll –
SUSANNAH: NOT SITTING?
LVOV: No, nor eating.
 (*SUSANNAH stares at him.*)
ARNOLD: It's a supper, you said, the final –
SUSANNAH: NOT EATING.
LVOV: (*Deliberately.*) No.
SUSANNAH: I could – why are you smiling – I could – YOU WOUND AND WOUND – why do you –
ARNOLD: You shouldn't do it, he only –
SUSANNAH: I FEED HIM.
 (*Pause.*)
 If you knew what I –
LVOV: Yes, I do know –
FORJACKS: We'll share out what he –
SUSANNAH: I FEED HIM.

DORA: (*To LVOV.*) Please, take a little of what she –

LVOV: No.

(*SUSANNAH stares at him. Suddenly, a fast train.*)

APOLLO: (*Looking at it.*) The officers!

(*He salutes. Lights flash on his face. It goes. SUSANNAH has not moved, or taken her eyes from LVOV.*)

They die,

They die,

So perfectly they die,

And I lend them the perfect velvet

Of my incredulity…

(*Pause.*)

Blue. The colour of my incredulity, I lay beneath immaculately coiffured heads. We shall never see such heads again. My own was opened. Out hopped Pity!

(*Pause.*)

I drove my car the night the war began, to hear Lvov. Dogs barked along the frontier and lights on mountain sides simmered behind blinds. The wind splashed me like a syphon. Soon we would be dead, or idiots. What a night! What a car! And Lvov, who then was very vain, was wearing blue, which clung to his body like a veil on the wet face of a widow, the beautiful Lvov, struggling to discard, but never able to…

FORJACKS: He never denied the power of materiality, did you Lvov? He was never less than human. Did he not say austerity was a flagellation, a mark of hatred of the world and of the body?

IVORY: I flagellate.

FORJACKS: You do –

IVORY: I flagellate, yes.

FORJACKS: Yes, yes, you do…

(*They are seated, but for LVOV, SUSANNAH, SLOMAN. SUSANNAH goes out.*)

DORA: Gisela, your hands are like cut flowers. You lay down your hands as if they were not joined to you. You place them. You arrange them like cut flowers.

APOLLO: How beautiful it is, this table cloth. No wonder you lay your hands like flowers. What does it matter if the menu stinks, we have a table cloth white as a glacier, stiff as a glacier... I used to sit in cafés with one glass...an oasis in a white landscape...all's well if the launderers are busy...!

ANNA: I brought the cloth. We fuck in table cloths.
(*JUDITH laughs.*)
We do! Obviously, there are no sheets, and since even the basest lout craves the false intimacy of sheets, we fuck in these...

IVORY: The lout wants his buttocks covered.

ANNA: He wants them covered, yes, and we found a hotel bombed. So much damask! So much stiff and monogrammed! But short. Our feet protrude...!

FORJACKS: It has all the logic of imperfect sex...

IVORY: WHAT'S IMPERFECT ABOUT IT! WHAT!

FORJACKS: The comic dimensions of imperfect sex...

IVORY: WHAT'S COMIC ABOUT IT? YOU KNOW NO SEX, COMIC OR OTHERWISE!

ARNOLD: All right, all right...

IVORY: He sits there –

ARNOLD: All right, all right...

IVORY: He sits there, he sits there...

MARYA: Shh... Shh...
(*A profound pause. They look, their looks are drawn toward LVOV.*)

LVOV: You came. All of you came. Even through contempt and dwindling fascination. I assembled you for a final act of love, but seeing you, it's obvious you haven't any more sufficient love for what's required –
(*The CHORUS asserts itself.*)

CHORUS: ARE YOU TRYING
YOU ARE TRYING TO ESCAPE
LVOV
LVOV
YOU AREN'T TRYING

LVOV: They look at me like –

CHORUS: WRONG WORDS
   TRY OTHER WORDS THEN
LVOV: You can see they think I'm –
CHORUS: ANY OLD EXCUSE WILL DO
LVOV: They are feeling sorry for me –
CHORUS: HOW RIGHT IT IS THAT YOU SHOULD DIE THEN
LVOV: I know that, I have established that –
CHORUS: NEW WORDS, THEN!
   (*LVOV sits on the floor.*)
   The Museum of the Masses will consist of ninety rooms,
   beginning with the wheel and ending with space travel.
   Our rise. Our painful ascent. The photographs show
   crowds attending rallies and carnivals at which. Our rise.
   Our painful ascent. In these photographs the faces of
   individuals are obscured by magnification. Our rise. Our.
   (*The cloud of laughter.*)
LVOV: I am turning their love into hate. It's difficult. I am so
   lovable. You can see, how difficult it is…
   (*The door opens. An OFFICER enters.*)
OFFICER: This is an illegal gathering. Are you Lvov?
LVOV: (*Springing into life.*) No, Lvov has gone.
OFFICER: Gone where?
LVOV: He left in a car.
OFFICER: (*Incredulous.*) A car? What car?
LVOV: A blue car, with one broken headlight.
OFFICER: You're lying.
LVOV: No! A red car with a roof rack.
OFFICER: A lie remains a lie, no matter how elaborate…
LVOV: You have been studying Lvov! His very tone!
OFFICER: I have read Lvov.
LVOV: Not easy, in this climate.
OFFICER: I found a copy in a waiting room.
LVOV: Oh, which? I should love to see it.
OFFICER: The up-line at Varna.
LVOV: Let's go, at once!
OFFICER: I know who you are. Do you think I am an idiot?
LVOV: Obviously it would assist me if you were.

OFFICER: Everything you say proves you are Lvov, and I am proceeding to dismiss this unlawful assembly under the regulations of December 19 –

LVOV: This comic formality becomes you very well –

OFFICER: (*Turning ferociously.*) I CAN ALSO BE A CUNT.
(*SLOMAN enters with a tray and the baked dog.*)

LVOV: Yes, and now I wonder, would you carve the meat for us?

OFFICER: Meat?
(*LVOV nods towards the table. The OFFICER drifts towards it.*)

JUDITH: (*To LVOV.*) How I love you. For a short time I believed I'd seen the last of you…

LVOV: (*Wearily.*) The last of me? In which form?

JUDITH: The form I loved.

OFFICER: It's a dog…

LVOV: Yes, it's a dog! A bitch mongrel, I understand, but the butcher would know better. There he is holding the carver, Barry, give him the knife…
(*SLOMAN holds out the carving knife. The OFFICER looks from face to face.*)

OFFICER: I CAN ALSO BE A CUNT!
(*They clap. He smiles, removes his cap and takes the knife.*)

ARNOLD: Everyone wishes to force everyone else to hear him. Even a madman banging a tin with a fork…

DORA: Everyone thinks his message is as good as anyone else's… Even an idiot calling his number…

OFFICER: No meat on this fucking animal…

LVOV: Yet no one wishes to be responsible for the condition of the world. That is very understandable. Who would accept the charge?

OFFICER: (*Impatiently.*) Fuck this…!

LVOV: All the dictators are dead. They could not stand the accusation. The accumulation of evidence shamed even their relentless egos, the deserts of their enterprises, the corpses of their epigones, their cardres stinking in the sun, all their little RED AND GREEN BOOKS!

OFFICER: (*Throwing down the carver.*) FUCK THIS, I SAID.

LVOV: No meat?

OFFICER: No meat.

ANNA: (*To OFFICER.*) Come outside, I'll show you something.

OFFICER: What you could show me, I have seen before.

ANNA: All right, I'll fall in love with you as well.

OFFICER: You wouldn't be the first.

> (*ANNA smiles.*)

I like your body, and I like your face, but even love could not undo my orders.

> (*He turns to LVOV.*)

Lvov –

> (*He goes to arrest LVOV, but ARNOLD swiftly takes him by the throat. Everyone watches as he slowly bears the OFFICER to the floor, throttling him. The OFFICER's knees fold under him. He is lowered. ARNOLD walks to a chair and sits, his hands hanging at his sides.*)

LVOV: He was wrong. Love can.

> (*They don't move, but look at ARNOLD. ARNOLD weeps, his shoulders heaving.*)

Arnold, since you were already a murderer, how can I praise you? – You did no more than Anna might have done in fornicating by the shed.

ARNOLD: For a fiction…! For a fiction…!

IVORY: We are all murderers here.

LVOV: Exactly. So a killing is no sacrifice.

ARNOLD: (*Standing.*) IT WAS A SACRIFICE! IT WAS A SACRIFICE.

GISELA: My wrists are like reeds.

> (*She looks at them.*)

Reeds!

ARNOLD: WHY DO I REQUIRE YOU? WHY DO I NEED YOU? I HATE YOU.

GISELA: You couldn't hurt a fly with these…

ARNOLD: I could so easily – I could –

LVOV: Yes.

ARNOLD: SO EASILY.

THE FOURTH PARABLE
The Consolations of Accumulations

A WOMAN enters dragging a strung bundle. She sits on it. The cloud of laughter passes. The sound of music on an ancient gramophone. A MAN dances to a waltz with an imaginary partner. He stops. The WOMAN blows her nose.

WOMAN: Do you think that's funny?

MAN: My partner is dead. Of an illness I could not diagnose.

WOMAN: What are you, a doctor?

MAN: Yes, but I keep it to myself.

WOMAN: Look at my ulcers, and I won't tell anyone.
(*She pulls up her skirt.*)

MAN: What beautiful legs.

WOMAN: One day your sarcasm will turn round and slap you in the teeth.

MAN: No, your legs are beautiful. Inelegant, but beautiful. However, I've no medicine.
(*He pulls down her skirt.*)
The task before us is not to cure deformity but to describe it differently. That is the function of learning in an age of disease.

WOMAN: Excellent. What are you after? A new dancing partner? You're no help to me.
(*She gets up.*)

MAN: What's in the parcel?

WOMAN: Loot. I go around the monasteries.

MAN: How funny! You have given yourself ulcers dragging loot through thorns and hedges. You will become infected and die of loot.

WOMAN: Let's dance, for old time's sake…

MAN: (*Winding up the gramophone.*) Because I'm undernourished I do a rather slower step, but the gramophone is old and matches my retarded style…

WOMAN: If I am ridiculous dragging loot through a devastated country, you are equally ridiculous dancing when you are dying.

(They do a few turns. The THREE SOLDIERS appear, attracted by the sound. They watch. Suddenly the MAN sinks to the floor. The music ceases.)
I asked him to cure my ulcers and all he did was get philosophical. *(She sits.)*

McSTAIN: Is that loot you're sitting on?

WOMAN: Yes, and what if it is? It is, and so what? Of course it's loot, you boggling fool. I am waiting for the restoration of order and the stability of currency. Then I shall sell the loot and enjoy a comfortable retirement.

McNOY: You might as well lug bricks in a bucket.

WOMAN: How do you know it isn't bricks? Bricks are scarce. It might be bricks.

McNOY: The whole lot wouldn't buy a sandwich.

WOMAN: At this moment, obviously. Now, obviously. And I admit the likelihood I shall die of infected ulcers. But at least I keep one jump ahead. At least. At least. At least I look to the future. At least I am an optimist. At least.

MacATTLEE: We passed a skull with its gob full of silver.

WOMAN: At least he had his faith. *(They turn to go.)* Carry my loot!

MacATTLEE: *(Stopping, cruelly.)* With hopelessness comes the decline of temper. So whereas at one time I might have struck you for impertinence, now I merely smile, a smile of insipid tolerance...

WOMAN: Pick it up then, there's a love.

McNOY: We'll carry you, for your ulcers, but not the loot.

WOMAN: The loot also.

McSTAIN: No loot.

WOMAN: What am I without the loot?

McSTAIN: How would I know?

WOMAN: Nothing. Nothing without the loot, I promise you. *(They drift away.)* Oh pity me! Pity an optimist!
(They stop. The wind blows. Pause.)

McSTAIN: We were ever open to persuasion.

MacATTLEE: We were ever open.

McNOY: We have found education in the strangest places.

WOMAN: You! With the broad back! Parcel! You! With the long arms! Stoop!
(*They obey.*)

END OF THE FOURTH PARABLE

LVOV: Take the food outside and leave it on the pavement.
(*Pause.*)
SLOMAN: What is he –
LVOV: Take the food outside and leave it on the –
SLOMAN: WHAT!
GISELA: You heard what he said –
SLOMAN: I HEARD –
LVOV: The pavement, yes. You will have food, but take that food and leave it on the pavement.
FORJACKS: Wouldn't it be better to –
LVOV: Don't look for the poor. Let whoever finds it, eat it. If it is an extortionist, so be it. Or a plump actor, give it to him. It humiliates to choose between the starving, just as to cure one man's blindness while another passes on the other side is to play the arbitrary among arbitrariness. WHO LOVES ME, THEN? WHAT IS THE PROOF OF LOVE BUT DOING THE UNDOABLE?
(*They watch him, holding their plates and reluctant.*)
You don't believe I shall provide? You want it proved. I don't prove anything. Never. WHEN DID WE EVER PROVE? No, proof's for the mob. We abhorred the command to prove, which is the wall to freedom...
(*They hang back, staring at the plates. He looks to SUSANNAH.*)
How she hates me...! (*He laughs.*) And him! (*He looks at SLOMAN. Some drift out of the door.*)
IVORY: (*To LVOV.*) All my life, I think I wanted to be other people. And seeing you, I wanted to be you. I still do. I move like you. Look, this gesture – my arm like this – is pure imitation. That can't be freedom, can it? Freedom must be ceasing to be you.
(*He goes out.*)

DORA: Have you noticed, how we deteriorate? I saw it,
the moment we came in, the deterioration. We all of us
were – silently, but – actually shocked! We didn't say, but
looked, peering in the oily light for what we had been
once. Only you were still the same. You – shone! You
know, don't you, the shame that fastens to the liver of life
in the presence of the abstentionist? And you licensed
everything, only forbidding yourself, IT ISN'T RIGHT, IS IT?
Coming together and seeing ourselves, well, you've got to
be honest, we have all –
(*She shudders. GISELA comes to her.*)
No, I'm all right, I'm perfectly all right, I am merely being
honest, which is arguably a sign I'm not all right at all…
(*She goes out with her plate, swiftly. Others return, empty-
handed, then DORA returns, boldly.*)
The beauty of Lvov was that he arrived complete. He
sprang from – where I don't know – who knows where
he sprang from – and was COMPLETE. The question is
however, whether we admire completeness. Whether we
might not rather admire – flexibility, growth, deterioration,
alteration, because man must, you see, he must –

APOLLO: Suffer.

DORA: (*She shrugs.*) I don't know. Suffer? Yes.

LVOV: You are betraying me.
(*He sits at the table, alone. They are standing. They look at
one another.*)
Not one of you. All of you. But one.

ANNA: We are very hungry, and to put the food –

LVOV: NEVER MIND THE FOOD. (*Pause.*) Tell me how you will
betray me. Anna.

ANNA: Me?

LVOV: Yes. How?

ANNA: Me – I –

LVOV: Think how.

ANNA: I –

SLOMAN: Yes, think!

ANNA: By marrying a glamorous idiot who will ruin my life.
He will make me his thing. We will dance in the lights

and imitate love. I will trivialize myself – That's betrayal, isn't it?

MARYA: I shall become kind.

(*They look at her.*)

WELL, THAT'S BETRAYAL!

SLOMAN: I, obviously, by going down into the street and preaching the likeness of all men. The commonness of all things. In my heart, I have already begun the elimination of Lvov. I have put his power under the light and seen it to be the desperate clamour of a lonely child…

LVOV: How difficult it is for you… Gisela…how will you?

GISELA: By being happy, I suppose…

ANNA: Yes! Yes! That's what he hates! Isn't it, Lvov?

JUDITH: What happiness?

ANNA: That's what gives Lvov the horrors –

JUDITH: WHAT HAPPINESS.

GISELA: The aching for the absent thing might die…and in its place there might be…a continuing fascination with the existent…

JUDITH: Theory.

GISELA: Theory, yes. Since I am all absence. Since I am made of absence. A theory, obviously.

(*Pause.*)

LVOV: Ivory?

IVORY: By killing mundanely. By being ashamed. By repeating slogans invented by Sloman –

SLOMAN: Oh, all right –

IVORY: BY BEING SKINNED AND COOKED BY SLOMAN –

SLOMAN: All right, all right –

IVORY: Shh, I am as ambitious as you, shh, I am, I am…

(*Pause. Then APOLLO occupies the silence.*)

APOLLO: It's true, that at moments of tiredness I long to sit under a tree with a dog. The dog's feet in my lap and its eyes on the moon. I long to hear the train on the incline, reaching for the villages…

(*Suddenly he kneels to LVOV.*)

Master! Master! The pleasure it gives to call him MASTER!

(*He hangs his head penitently.*)

I come to you because you will not ridicule the hunger that I feel for the woman on the corner of the avenue whose skirt lies flat over her belly like a flag on a corpse. MASTER! I lost the top of my head but I came back, who else would justify the pain? MASTER! And Lvov is inferior to me. Both in language and imagination. I know all Lvov by heart.

FORJACKS: It is impossible to know Lvov by heart.

APOLLO: I do. It's my betrayal.

FORJACKS: It's not possible.

APOLLO: All the same, I do.

FORJACKS: Rubbish, with all respect…

APOLLO: WITH NO RESPECT I KNOW IT. Beg me, I will quote.

FORJACKS: It's beyond the –

APOLLO: BEG ME.

    (*Pause.*)

FORJACKS: On Pity, then.

APOLLO: Which?

FORJACKS: On Pity given at –

APOLLO: You don't know yourself! The titles, even!

FORJACKS: Wait!

APOLLO: He barely knows the titles!

FORJACKS: At Rotterdam.

APOLLO: Noon or Night?

IVORY: Night!

APOLLO: It begins with an aphorism. The aphorism is, 'Pity is Theft'. It continues on the theme of the right to suffering, as follows, 'She who hides her pain conspires in the infliction of the wound that follows –'

FORJACKS: That's not all of it –

APOLLO: Of course it's not all of it, do you want all of it? I will give you all of it.

LVOV: No one admires you. They think you sycophantic and absurd.

APOLLO: I am absurd, and therefore cannot be insulted.

LVOV: You have learned the art of the parrot –

APOLLO: I am a parrot and therefore cannot be insulted.

LVOV: And if I repudiate my words?

APOLLO: They stay.

FORJACKS: (*Heated.*) On Violence!

APOLLO: On Violence, given at the Village on the River San.
(*The CHORUS appears to LVOV.*)

LVOV: How absurd! How contemptible they are!

CHORUS: SOON BE FREE.

LVOV: How could you hope to satisfy them?

CHORUS: SOON BE FREE.

LVOV: They hate me, all of them. But they haven't the
courage to act on their hatred –

CHORUS: SOON.

LVOV: I wound them and they still –

CHORUS: SOON.

LVOV: All right!

CHORUS: EASY TO DIE WHEN YOU DON'T LOVE.

LVOV: That's what you say...
(*The cloud of laughter.*)
They must kill me. I cannot kill myself.

CHORUS: THEY'LL KILL YOU.

LVOV: They will? But they love me, no matter how I hurt
them, they still –

CHORUS: HURT THEM MORE –

LVOV: They won't, they –

CHORUS: THEY LONG TO, YES!

LVOV: I am not afraid of death only oblivion!
(*Laughter again.*)
Do you think I lived this terrible life to be forgotten?

CHORUS: WE MARCH ACROSS THE LANDSCAPE SINGING

LVOV: Shut up –

CHORUS: WE TAR THE WOMEN IN SHORT SKIRTS AND
BLIND THE MEN IN GLASSES

LVOV: I defy your power of forgetting!

CHORUS: CHILD OF THE PEOPLE
LVOV
SON OF THE PEOPLE
(*Pause. Sound of the landscape.*)

ELLA: (*From under the table, where she has hidden herself.*) I
killed my child. Is anybody listening? I did it in a railway
carriage. It had no ticket. It should have had a ticket,

shouldn't it? I think the way this war has made people cunning is the most sickening thing and never paying your debts and scrounging and skyving is the rule not the exception, the pleasure in settling one of them I could not begin to tell you no ticket well that's your. SCROUNGING, WELL THIS TIME YOU. I had one, of course. I, who have not two halfpennies to rub together, I got one at some sacrifice and if more people did the same then.

(*Pause.*)

It was obvious, Lvov, you would attract to you all those for whom the normal state of life was nauseating, the mad, the critical, the lawless, the impatient, and that this very following by its character, would discredit you with those who form the mass of our society. Can you explain how you intend to move from the minority to the majority?

(*The cloud of laughter.*)

Years you have been years and still we're twelve. Forjacks was a torturer and there are several murderers among us, it is an unappetising clique and rather dirty. The women are whores and if they're not whores they wish to be –

DORA: I have no wish to be –

ELLA: You would with him –

DORA: I deny –

ELLA: YOU WOULD WITH HIM –

DORA: Oh –

ELLA: Kiss me! Kiss me, do!

(*She throws her arms round DORA.*)

Life was, and ever shall be, of no significance! And yet, desperately, we will discriminate! For example, in the doling out of charity, I fill the spoon more fully for the beautiful orphan. This seems to me not only inevitable, but correct. (*She sits neatly on the floor.*)

SUSANNAH: Are we going to eat?

IVORY: He said –

SUSANNAH: I SAID ARE WE GOING TO EAT.

THE FIFTH PARABLE
How the Child was Lost

The THREE SOLDIERS enter.

ALL: We thought we had a child. We thought we were pregnant.

McSTAIN: How this thought came about.

MacATTLEE: For six weeks we saw nothing but the dead.

McNOY: Perhaps because we walked in circles.

MacATTLEE: This was a suspicion. But coming again upon the dead, such was the speed of their deterioration you could not say –

McSTAIN: With any certainty –

MacATTLEE: With any certainty, this cadaver I have seen before.

McNOY: What with the seasons changing, wild grasses and heathers struggling through the limbs forced them in new positions so –

McSTAIN: This remains hypothetical –

McNOY: Nevertheless, the thought occurred –

ALL: WE THREE ALONE SURVIVED.

(*Pause.*)

McNOY: A sort of ecstasy.

McSTAIN: Terror at our great inheritance but also –

MacATTLEE: Ecstasy!

ALL: WE ROLLED UPON THE BOSOM OF THE EARTH!

(*Pause.*)

McSTAIN: Until there came upon us a cry of mortality.

McNOY: In me especially.

MacATTLEE: In him the cry called loudest.

McNOY: I ached for love beyond the mundane obligations of the squad.

MacATTLEE: He particularly ached.

McSTAIN: And subsequently suffered.

McNOY: A stirring in my lower parts I could not identify.

McSTAIN: The old male anger…

McNOY: No, not that!

MacATTLEE: The hammer of old John…

McNOY: I said not that! (*Pause.*) Then at a cruel hour of the
 night, a cold, dead hour, it began, and neither of these
 could be roused, I at my extremity and they in deathly
 kip, mouths all slobbering the black-toothed bastards…
 I ripped! I ripped!
 (*A CHILD enters.*)
 Oh, gently, gently, little one!
 (*He puts his hands on the CHILD, and caresses her. An
 extensive silence. The others wake.*)

MacATTLEE: We woke, and disbelieved!

McNOY: Look, the comfort of our solitude…!

McSTAIN: What rip?

McNOY: (*Showing his flesh.*) There.

McSTAIN: Rip? Where?

McNOY: I SAID THERE.

MacATTLEE: Let's not quarrel, we are so few. But your gut is as
 smooth as the marble on a tomb –

McNOY: RE – JOICE! RE – JOICE!

MacATTLEE: Just establishing the fact –

McNOY: Re – joice!

MacATTLEE: The fact – purely for the record –

McNOY. (*Furiously.*) RE – JOICE!

MacATTLEE: Must – hang on – to – the –

McSTAIN: No criticism –

MacATTLEE: No criticism, but –

McNOY: RE – JOICE YOU BAS – TARDS –

MacATTLEE: There is no mark on your tummy and I will not
 pretend there is, all right?

McSTAIN: Oi.
 (*He looks at the CHILD. Their eyes travel. McNOY's chanting
 dies. The CHILD has wandered and picked up a bomb. She
 examines it, tosses it in the air and catches it again.*)

McNOY: (*Horrified.*) I ripped…

MacATTLEE: You did…you did rip…yes…
 (*She throws it up again.*)

McNOY: I RIPPED…!

MacATTLEE / McSTAIN: ALL RIGHT!
 (*The CHILD throws it up again.*)

McSTAIN: (*Crawling towards the CHILD.*) What's little baby got there, then? What's baby's lovely thingammy?

McNOY: (*Lying on his back.*) I dream of fields and swings, I dream of cots and snow white coverlets…

MacATTLEE: Mac's ill…

McSTAIN: What's baby do-da doing den?

McNOY: (*Delirious.*) I dream of apple blossom falling on the sunshade…

MacATTLEE: Mac's got childbed fever…

(*The CHILD throws up the bomb again. McSTAIN falls to the ground, covering his head. The CHILD catches the bomb, is entertained.*)

McSTAIN: Show whatsit to old thingammy –

(*The CHILD tosses it up again. McSTAIN cringes to the ground.*)

McNOY: Its tiny fingers grope towards my lips, my breasts ache with milk yet unexpressed, wake! Wake!

MacATTLEE: Oh, Mac, our comrade of so many fallen bells…

McSTAIN: (*Undeterred.*) Teeny weeny turn for palsy, teeny –

(*He sees a WOMAN from the corner of his eye.*)

WOMAN: (*To CHILD.*) Oi. Scraparse. Told you not to play with soldiers. In.

(*She jerks her thumb. The CHILD gets up, goes off, past her.*)

McNOY: (*Sitting up.*) We thought we were alone in the world…

WOMAN: You are.

(*She goes off. The SOLDIERS pick up their bags. MCNOY hangs his head, foolishly. MCSTAIN goes to him, puts an arm round him. They go to leave, when an explosion is heard. They stop. They continue.*)

END OF THE FIFTH PARABLE

LVOV: (*To GISELA.*) The way your eyes hang on me. As if I were the first made man.

GISELA: Oh?

LVOV: Hunger or no hunger. You wash me with desire.

GISELA: I don't notice it any more.

LVOV: Yes. I lather in your fascination. It soddens my clothes.

GISELA: (*She shrugs, sarcastically.*) You don't miss a thing.
(*She goes to a chair, and sits, looking at him.*)

LVOV: Sticky and uncomfortable.

GISELA: Too bad.
(*He stares at her. She returns his stare.*)

JUDITH: (*Breaking the silence.*) You are not as charming tonight as you can be. Is he? Hardly charming at all.

LVOV: You see everything.

JUDITH: It's obvious.

LVOV: And feel nothing.

JUDITH: Yes. I admit that

LVOV: (*Still looking at GISELA.*) Nothing but ambition. Which is not a feeling.

JUDITH: You should know.

LVOV: Not a feeling but a lack.

JUDITH: You should know.

LVOV: Gisela.

JUDITH: Charm of a different order, perhaps

LVOV: Ask Dora.
(*Pause.*)

GISELA: What?
(*Pause.*)

DORA: Yes, I think you should.

LVOV: Dora knows! Without the least articulation, Dora knows! I have not spent so many bitter hours with this woman for her to fail me now.

DORA: Go with him, if it is what he wants.

LVOV: We sat, and the bitterness ran out of our mouths. We might have bitten the iron rims off tables, Dora and I.
(*DORA snatches a laugh.*)

GISELA: Don't play with me.
(*JUDITH laughs, peeling.*)
SHUT UP. SHUT UP.

JUDITH: (*Shaking her head.*) The sentiment... I'm sorry...the sentiment...of course he will play with you...

LVOV: (*Inspired.*) I thought of life as a basket! And in the basket, fruits! Name the fruits!

IVORY: Love.

LVOV: Love.

ANNA: Laughter.

LVOV: Laughter – of a sort –

FORJACKS: Years!

LVOV: Years! Years!

MARYA: Ecstasy.

LVOV: Ecstasy.

DORA: Melancholy.

LVOV: Melancholy, or there could be no ecstasy.

JUDITH: Pain.

LVOV: Pain. But –

APOLLO: Death. (*Pause.*) How you love death. And you have never seen it.

LVOV: Is death bad, then? How bad?

APOLLO: Lvov has never stood under fire. Lvov has never seen the meat. Lvov has never smelled the blood. Lvov has sat in a wooden chair. I say this without the whisper of a criticism. Lvov has never felt the surgeon's. Lvov has never seen the widow's. Lvov has slept in a wooden bunk. I say this without the whisper of. Lvov has never worn bowel as garland. Lvov has never scraped brain. Or watched boys jerk on strings. And yet I listen to him with respect. Because it is hard to go where Lvov goes. Cold there, I think.

LVOV: (*To GISELA.*) If you will see me naked, I'll see you…
(*She gets up. They all stare at her. She glares at them boldly.*)

FORJACKS: (*With gathering clarity.*) I know what you do! I know what you do! You make all things equal, all categories! You make evil good by removing the description! But its essence remains the same. Is anybody listening? That's his method! It's all very well saying his thought is not exactly thought at all but – something else – that's all very well, maybe it's not thought but it still requires two things – consistency and – I AM FREE OF LVOV, I AM FREE, I AM FREE OF LVOV!

ANNA: Be quiet or I'll stab you.
(*He stops. GISELA goes out with LVOV.*)

BE QUIET. (*JUDITH looks at ANNA.*) Lvov – has no
communion with women...
(*She looks round.*)
What's the use if he –
HE DENIES HIMSELF IT IS A PRINCIPLE!
And she –
IT'S A PRINCIPLE HE NEVER –
What's –
He has no –

JUDITH: Cock?

ANNA: It's there but –
It exists but –
The power is not used it only – (*To IVORY.*)
Don't laugh at me, I'll –

IVORY: Was I laughing? I was discerning the contrast between
the shadow and the substance –

ANNA: That's laughter, you male slag –
HOW CAN HE BE TRUSTED?

SUSANNAH: (*Who has watched this icily.*) Lvov is killing Lvov...

ANNA: Gisela!
What's she –
She hangs her education out like some – GREAT TIT – and
as for her – did you read that – her FORMIDABLE MIND –
I read it in the paper – the formidable mind of Gisela
Rust – what's she – (*She sits on the floor.*) I ask a lot of Lvov.
I ask him to be unlike. Utterly UNLIKE. And he said, you
must ask more of me, always more. HE MAKES ME FEEL A
PROSTITUTE.
(*She jumps up.*)
Where are they? (*JUDITH looks at her. Coolly.*) Gisela wears
learning like a strip of chiffon over her arse, who's fooled?
Anybody fooled? (*To DORA.*) You're her – what are you to
her?

DORA: I protect her.

ANNA: Do you?
She is a valve.
A valve with learning smeared. With learning dolloped.
(*Pause.*)

Protect her, then.
(*Pause.*)
My sexuality is thank you perfectly.
I have no sexuality.
Lvov also has none.
(*ARNOLD goes to her. She looks at him, touches his face.*)
Arnold, I'm not hungry any more…
(*She sits at his feet. GISELA enters. She returns to her chair, sits. Pause.*)
GISELA: 'There is no such thing as sin. Merely violence to the self.' Lvov. (*A train comes. MARYA rushes to the window.*)
MARYA: They're coming back – alive!
(*Train wheels.*)

THE SIXTH PARABLE
The Fleeting Appearance of an Idealist

A SOLDIER appears holding wild flowers.

THE GUNNER: Going home.
We picked a certain flower which grew in abundance. A flower as common as men. We pushed the flower down our guns, and walked West. Going home.
LVOV: (*Entering.*) He was not tired of killing. He was tired of killing meaninglessly.
THE GUNNER: I have a child, and an old mother in a room…
LVOV: He is not tired of killing. He requires a better excuse.
(*The CHORUS appears.*)
CHORUS: STILL ALIVE?
STILL ALIVE, LVOV?
LVOV: Yes, and out of my time.
CHORUS: NEW WORLD, LVOV.
LVOV: I notice.
CHORUS: AND WE SHALL BE
ALL IN ONE LINE
ARMS LINKED
THE SHRILL VOICE OF

THE POPULAR AND
(*The cloud of laughter.*)

LVOV: Who could they follow but the one who is not human?
Could you worship a human? Follow me, says the messiah.
And they chuck away their tools. This way, says the
messiah. And they abandon their children. They lock up
their rooms and leave their gardens to the weeds. Could
you do that for a HUMAN?

CHORUS: STILL HERE, LVOV?

LVOV: It's time, it's time, and now they hate me more than
ever they loved…

THE GUNNER: (*About to throw away his gun.*) Away, gun!

LVOV: No, bury it in oiled rags…

(*The GUNNER thinks. The THREE SOLDIERS enter. They see
LVOV and kneel.*)

You only kneel because you do not know me well
enough…

THE MACS: We kneel because we are so tired of being upright.

LVOV: (*With a laugh.*) Excellent! Listen I was not born with this
face, no, I made it. Underneath it lie such long forgotten
qualities as charm and mischief, humour, lechery, like
tumuli in ancient landscapes, who would stoop to excavate
them now? I MADE MYSELF TERRIBLE. I am Lvov, do you
dare to murder me?

THE MACS: We kill no – body!

LVOV: Why not? I never forbade it! IT IS REAL POWER WHEN
YOU ARE NOT AFRAID TO DIE.

THE GUNNER: We put flowers down our guns and
commandeered the train. Home James, we said! The
harvest is due and I have a child to kiss. Home James!

LVOV: You were not tired of killing. You required a better
excuse.

(*A WOMAN enters, holding a CHILD.*)

WOMAN: I told him, take your tunic off and let me hold your
naked body, my thin love, my emaciated love who held
back hundreds, tell me in this bed to the sounds of our
babies sleeping how you held back hundreds with your
gun my thin love, my body aches to hear, my vastness

opens to hear how you held back hundreds, poets,
criminals, tutors, lathe-turners who fell under your gun
you grey-faced thin one, tell me of your concrete and your
wire, oh, my own rear-guard…

GISELA: How extraordinary to achieve clarity from sheer
unhappiness.

But it happens.

How amazing.

You have made me hate my own flesh.

That is – really, that is – criminal – isn't it?

That is surely the very limit of horror?

I terribly hate you and naturally, being an intellectual I
have to know the causes – no, don't piss over my need to
articulate – YOU COMMON BASTARD – there – you have
elicited from me the most appalling abuse – and all this
because I saw you naked and –

YOU COMMON BASTARD –

You saw me –

How I adored you saying no, your eyes saying, and your
closed nature, always no, and how quickly I hated you
when you said yes, how rapidly you appeared in your
authentic COMMONNESS.

LVOV: Yes.

GISELA: What did any of us share? You, was it? Just you? I
hate you because you held us in contempt.

THE MACS: Can we get up now?

GISELA: And your coldness was only contempt

THE MACS: Can we get up?

GISELA: AND YOUR SEX WAS ONLY CONTEMPT.

THE MACS: We will, I think…

WOMAN: We formed a party to protect the land. And a party
to protect the peace. But –

THE GUNNER: Where did you hang my tunic? And my gun,
with the withered flower down its spout? Where did you
put my gun?

WOMAN: Speaking as a party woman I said, much as I
enjoyed your body, now the time has come –

THE GUNNER: Make the flower into a badge. Simplify it. Make a badge.

THE MACS: So we stood up.

(*They stand, nervously. LVOV laughs.*)

GISELA: I have a choice. If I don't hate you, I have only myself to hate. And I am not going to gnaw myself to naked nerve and bone.

(*JUDITH enters.*)

JUDITH: Trust me.

(*LVOV looks at her.*)

You want to do this all on your own, but I know it's beyond you, Lvov. The dying. Beyond you.

(*She sits.*)

They've fallen asleep. Not one of them was your equal. And they've fallen asleep.

LVOV: You are my equal, then…

JUDITH: Yes. Only me.

LVOV: How did you know? How did you know I intended to die?

JUDITH: You must. It is impossible for you to continue. And if all you have done is not to be turned into dust, and error, yes, you must. They have got the measure of you, Lvov.

LVOV: I know.

JUDITH: They parody you. The clever ones.

LVOV: I thought as much.

JUDITH: Yes. They do you very well. And the ones who are not clever complain at your ingratitude.

LVOV: They are only human.

JUDITH: They are human, and you are tired.

LVOV: Am I? Am I tired? Yes, I am tired. Terribly tired. I AM SO LONELY, HOLD MY HANDS.

(*She kneels by him, holding his hands.*)

What do you want?

JUDITH: To know.

LVOV: Yes…

JUDITH: I alone of all of them, I truly want to know. I alone, prefer knowledge to peace. You taught me everything. Everything. But one thing you cannot teach me is what it

is to live without you. And that I have to know. I want to
help you to die, so that there is no one left and after you
there won't be. Anyone at all. Only cacophony. And then
I shall be solely responsible. The sole proprietor of my
mind. So you see, I have to know. That is real, and pure,
and utter curiosity. It was inevitable, wasn't it, that one of
us would take your words to heart?

LVOV: DON'T FALL ASLEEP!

JUDITH: I won't… I won't fall asleep…
(*She holds him.*)

THE MACS: (*To the GUNNER.*) Off we go then… (*Pause.*) Do
we…?

THE GUNNER: I came home, to a new world…

THE MACS: We always do.

THE GUNNER: No, this was newer, though it contained the
old…

THE MACS: It always does.

THE GUNNER: And this world. This world, belonged to me.

THE MACS: This one. Definitely, this one.

THE GUNNER: For this one I will die. And if necessary, make
others die.

THE MACS: Which way?

THE GUNNER: For this, I take up the loathed gun.

THE MACS: THE LOATHED GUN.

WOMAN: No longer loathed.

THE GUNNER: Defender of my child. I oil its parts with such
reverence…

WOMAN: Come back victorious, or not at all.
(*He kisses her. Shoulders his gun, sets out.*)

THE MACS: Erm… (*THE GUNNER stops.*) Erm… (*He looks.*) The
bell order, is it still in force?

THE GUNNER: Bell order?

MacATTLEE: The compulsory unslinging of all bells.
(*THE GUNNER looks confused.*)

THE MACS: (*Crossly.*) THE BELL ORDER.

WOMAN: And seeing him, his loved hands, for fear of calling
him and cradling him and hiding him inside myself I
RESOLUTELY TURN MY BACK…

LVOV: I was shallow. I was juvenile. I said things others had said before me.

JUDITH: I remember.

LVOV: It was only slowly I came to perfection.

JUDITH: Briefly. Wonderfully.

LVOV: And now I decline again.

JUDITH: Inevitably.

LVOV: Decline, yes. And I want to see it.

JUDITH: What for?

LVOV: Witness it.

JUDITH: What for?

LVOV: Autumnal –

JUDITH: What –

LVOV: Etcetera –

JUDITH: What!

    (*LVOV winces. Hides his head.*)

    Fear talking.

LVOV: Fear, obviously

JUDITH: Lvov –

LVOV: I shall never know what it is to bite a peach and lose a tooth –

JUDITH: Lvov –

LVOV: Or see the brown skin hanging off my knee caps –

JUDITH: (*Sarcastically.*) Terrible deprivation –

LVOV: I AM ENTITLED TO THAT ALSO.

JUDITH: Are you?

    (*She gets up.*)

    Are you entitled to the mundane satisfactions of the common life?

LVOV: Yes!

JUDITH: You spit on common life.

LVOV: Yes!

JUDITH: Spit on it.

LVOV: All right, I spit!

    (*Pause.*)

    For one weary moment, I longed for friendship, simple, open-handed friendship...

JUDITH: The charismatic have no friends...

LVOV: Judith, how you force greatness on me…and I would love to swerve…be kind –
(*He reaches out.*)
JUDITH: Kindness!
MURDERED WORD.
(*His hand drops.*) Die tonight, or I shall…sicken…do you understand me? Sicken.
LVOV: Yes.
(*Pause.*)
They will kill me. You must orchestrate it.
JUDITH: Yes.
LVOV: But more.
JUDITH: More?
LVOV: More, yes.
JUDITH: What more?
LVOV: (*Triumphantly.*) HA! YOU ARE GREATER THAN ME AND YOU CANNOT IMAGINE!
JUDITH: What more?
LVOV: SHE IS GREATER AND SHE CANNOT THINK!
JUDITH: What? What more?
LVOV: Lvov! Lvov! The Great Imaginer! Lvov
(*The cloud of laughter roars overhead.*)
CHORUS: Lvov was born the son of a bricklayer and his first language was
DIALECT
Lvov looked at his father's house and experienced
DISGUST
He stood on the railway station looking
ASHAMED
LVOV: What's knowledge! It is prejudice grinding on the conscience…
CHORUS: And when the train came he climbed always into the compartment reserved for
WOMEN
MARYA: (*Pause.*) It rains on all the graves, so what? It rains on all the widows, so what? And the ill-fucked women, it rains on them. Lvov, I only liked you because you were not kind. You were not considerate, or gentle. You had

immaculate manners but without charity. How I liked
that! How I responded to that! You were not casual, nor
carefree, keeping yourself at a cold distance, and touching
no one. How I liked that! You did not tell me I was gifted.
You never praised my poetry. How I liked that! How I
responded! You never told me we could live at peace. Or
apologized for acts that had no justification –
(*She opens her blouse.*)

Goodbye you male scum! (*She laughs.*)

LVOV: (*To JUDITH.*) When I am dead – when –

CHORUS: LVOV

THEY'RE HUNGRY

AND THEY WANT THEIR SUPPER

(*Cloud of laughter.*)

LVOV: If I wish to live forever, I have to die.

CHORUS: FEED THEM!

LVOV: But more than die...they must consume me...
(*Pause. JUDITH sways.*)

JUDITH: Why –

LVOV: To live in the memory.

JUDITH: Yes...it's perfectly true... I have no imagination... I
am cleverer than you but with no imagination HOW DARE
YOU. Come up with such a HOW COULD YOU INFLICT
SUCH

LVOV: Do you think I'd die like anybody else?
(*Pause.*)

JUDITH: And if we don't? If we revolt? If we say ENOUGH
MANIPULATION FROM BEYOND THE GRAVE? If we
just chuck you on the tip? Another bit of old Europe?
ANOTHER CORPSE, WHAT!

LVOV: Obviously I place great faith in you.

JUDITH: Liar. Faith! You liar.

LVOV: You'll do it.

JUDITH: Why?

LVOV: Because you will want it finished. You will not settle
for anything less. It's the investment the servant makes in
servitude. (*Pause.*)

JUDITH: Kiss me.
    Kiss me.
    (*He kisses her cheek. The sound of desolation.*)

THE SEVENTH PARABLE
The Authentic Madness of a Redundant Class

McNOY enters.

McNOY: McStain is dead
    McStain
    McStain
    How he
    His awful
    Unforgettable McStain
    The way he
    And that habit of
    Indelible McStain
    (*Pause.*) With two our role is impossible to play. With two,
    no bell can be unslung. The officer who gave the order
    knew the necessity for three pairs of hands. The officer
    who is buried in the village square knew the subject.
    How well he knew! Which is rare among the givers of
    instructions. And now McStain is dead! Already McStain is
    fading. Indelible McStain!
MacATTLEE: (*Entering.*) I buried McStain. And burying him, I
    interred all memory. Who was McStain?
McNOY: I couldn't help, I was too moved.
MacATTLEE: No, I like digging. I like to dig alone.
McNOY: And now we.
    And so we.
    Where does that leave.
    (*Pause. They instantaneously engage in a cruel and relentless
    fight, pushing each other this way and that. IVORY appears.
    They cease, exhausted.*)
IVORY: Who was McStain?
    I passed his grave in the Avenue of Poplars.

(*The MACS look bewildered.*)

I saw his crossed sticks on my return from the Knot Garden.

(*Pause.*)

I was coming from the Temple of the Four Winds when I saw –

Please do not piss yourself laughing I am sorry you are sweating embarrassment at every pore but I lived and loved here

OF COURSE THE LANDSCAPE'S DIFFERENT

(*Pause.*)

The hamper spilled and her shoe came off, the label still inside. HOW CLEAN SHE WAS, OH, CLEAN. A shallow laugh however. Adorable shallowness. And I talked volubly. I, educated and in possession of three thousand books. THERE!

(*He points to a barren spot.*)

No one came near. The walls of the estate were higher than two men.

McNOY: I saw a wall…

IVORY: That was the wall –

McNOY: I saw a fragment of a wall –

IVORY: That was the wall.

(*Pause. MCNOY and MACATTLEE, by tacit agreement, get up to leave.*)

Pity the man who has no wall.

Pity his limitless choice of.

(*The MACS are about to walk away when bells are heard. They stop, by instinct. Pause.*)

IVORY: (*Darkly.*) Shall I become McStain?

(*They look at him.*)

McNOY: How could his way of –

His habit of –

IVORY: I shall become McStain –

McNOY: His old trick of –

IVORY: I am McStain. (*McNOY looks at him.*)

McNOY: You are nothing like what I recall McStain to –

IVORY: I am sufficiently McStain to be McStain. Later I will
be all that he consisted of.
(*They are afraid of him. The bells continue faintly.*)
This is the way.
(*He starts off. Stops.*)
MacATTLEE: (*Cunningly.*) The wall. (*He winks at McNOY.*)
Unfortunately the wall…
IVORY: (*Taking it from his pocket.*) I have the key.
(*He smiles.*)
When she came, laughing shallowly, I locked the gate
behind her, and as we tussled on the lawn the key fell out
of my pocket. I looked all day for the key. Then the war
came, passing and repassing. Today I found the key, flung
up by the gravedigger.
McNOY: Well, then…
(*They shrug.*)
MacATTLEE: McStain carried the ropes.
(*He tosses a coil.*)
And me the hammer.
(*They set off.*)
IVORY: Already, I feel his nimbleness!

END OF THE SEVENTH PARABLE

The sleeping guests stir.

ANNA: (*To LVOV.*) They talked about you! They said – I did
too – what has made Lvov like this? They were – I was
too – full of criticism and called you, for example – a sham.
And said – me too – we were taken in by Lvov, who is a
sham. Are you a sham, Lvov?
LVOV: Yes. Wake them up now. Kick them with your whore's
heels. Drive them out their kip you frilled object.
ANNA: Lvov –
LVOV: You orphan of a bitch and a thin lout.
ANNA: You want me to hate you and all I feel is love! I was
so angry with you and now I understand your loneliness,
your –
GISELA: We talked.

ANNA: We hated you and then –

GISELA: We talked and we decided –

ANNA: We decided –

GISELA: The cruelty you did me no man could do were he not himself in AWFUL AGONY. I saw how shallow my anger was. Nothing is lost of my terrible bond with you. Only more so. It is bound in nakedness and pain now, too…
(*He stares at her.*)

ANNA: That's what I wanted to say! You said it beautifully!
(*She hugs GISELA.*)

LVOV: But you must murder me.
(*Pause. He looks around them.*)

SLOMAN: I have seen through you twice. The first time, I saw through your message. Second, I saw not only was your message failing, but that your provocations were an attempt to save your message. The message must die, and be seen to die. You must not be permitted to obscure the collapse of your teaching by a flamboyant death.

APOLLO: We said, Lvov is rude today, and sullen. Today we like him less that ever. But hate him?

LVOV: Listen.

I am the supper.

SLOMAN: (*Triumphantly.*) You see! You see!

LVOV: If you don't hate me enough, love me enough!

SLOMAN: You see!

LVOV: I AM THE SUPPER!
(*A train passes, fast.*)

ELLA: The war is over! Now it'll be hell!
(*Its lights and sound fade.*)

IVORY: I ate a woman once, who came to picnic on the terrace. It's not impossible. She sat in a cloud of finery and all the time the ribbons on her hat went twitter, twitter. How perfect she was clothed, and how perfect unclothed. How perfect her skin, and how perfect her inside. Her exterior, and her interior…

LVOV: I surrounded myself with murderers. Not knowing this. But what is accidental? I drew you all to me not planning this but who is better? HELP ME I AM CAPABLE OF SUCH

COWARDICE. I could so easily run in the dark crying love and love and kiss the wheels of filthy wagons, HOLD ME DOWN, THEN!

(*He kneels. They are still.*)

JUDITH: And the bones will be relics. And sterile men will plead upon them, make me fecund!

SLOMAN: Anyone who goes near him, I will stab.

(*He takes his carving knife.*)

IVORY: But we are so hungry, aren't we? So very hungry.

SLOMAN: Anyone, I'll stab! (*Pause.*)

JUDITH: Sloman, who fears the immortality of one man…

SLOMAN: No one to help his vanity to flourish. CAN'T YOU SEE IT'S A TRICK!

ELLA: Of course it's a trick. Don't you want to be tricked? Oh, don't you ever long to be properly tricked?

(*SLOMAN looks at JUDITH in horror.*)

JUDITH: We have to kill Lvov, because he is ceasing to be Lvov.

SLOMAN: Yes…! Rejoice! Under the ballgown, the scab! And the rat on the wedding cake! Rejoice!

ELLA: I will kill him rather than hear him utter a trivial thing. Me, Ella, alone.

SLOMAN: WHAT ARE YOU, A SLAVE?

(*LVOV bursts out laughing, ceases.*)

WHAT ARE YOU? (*He looks around them.*)

FORJACKS: When Lvov is dead, I shall be the archivist, does everyone agree with that? I am the scholar, so it's obvious I.

DORA: It's true, in every sense, that Lvov is no longer necessary to Lvov. It's even possible, Lvov is an impediment to Lvov, and to our – adoration of him. I think now, we own Lvov, and Lvov is in danger of becoming an embarassment… – And I speak as one who loves him –

ANNA: You don't need to say that –

DORA: I don't need to say that, no –

APOLLO: (*Walking forward to LVOV.*) Climb on my back.

LVOV: To gallop off? To break out of encirclement?

SOME DO! SOME HAVE!

SUSANNAH: I killed my husband and buried him in the marsh. In three parts. I rowed him. How my arse ached, and how happy I was! And Lvov praised me. He sang me a song…

APOLLO: Climb on my back. Die on my back.

SUSANNAH: What a song. The words came automatically to him…!

MARYA: Lvov never sang.

SUSANNAH: He did sing. He sang that once.

MARYA: Lvov abhorred all singing.

(*LVOV lets out a cry.*)

APOLLO: Many men died on my back. I carried them, like a mule. So much carrying, and the telling of comforting anecdotes. And at the dressing station, putting them down, found them unworthy of the effort. Found them, ungratefully, expired. Climb on.

(*LVOV utters a horror.*)

(*No, you, the offer's serious.*)

ANNA: To die among friends. To die at the hands of friends, is, surely, the mark of the divine…

(*APOLLO crouches.*)

SLOMAN: I insist on describing the nature of this madness, I insist on exposing this irrationality, I will reveal to you notwithstanding your intoxication the appalling fraud which is being perpetrated!

LVOV: Oh, I a little baby! Oh, I a little thing, mother! (*APOLLO locks arms in LVOV's and hoists him on his back.*) Judith!

ANNA: He calls Judith. I was his love but he calls Judith…!

LVOV: (*Voluble, in a panic.*) I tell a story of a boy a lonely boy who never smiled except to please and never laughed except to hide from those already laughing – JUDITH!

(*JUDITH takes the knife from SLOMAN, who is watching, transfixed.*)

JUD – ITH!

(*She approaches him.*)

It's not what I want! IT'S NOT WHAT I WANT!

(*She thrusts the blade with determination.*)

ANNA: Me! Me!

(*She takes the blade from LVOV's body and plunges it in.*)

CHORUS: WE EXPRESS THE COMMON MAN'S
    THE MAN IN THE STREET'S OBJECTION TO

LVOV: Changed my mind… !

CHORUS: THE ARROGANCE OF
    AND THE SPECIAL PLEADING
    (*DORA goes up, and stabs LVOV.*)

DORA: Oh, that, how unconvincing!
    (*She goes to LVOV again.*)
    How tentative and unconvincing!
    (*She stabs again.*)

CHORUS: WE DON'T ACCEPT THE INNOCENCE OF
    WE WILL NOT TOLERATE THE MOCKING OF
    OUR
    (*As MARYA stabs LVOV.*)
    LONELINESS

JUDITH: Lvov? Is the light going?
    They say the light goes, is the light going?

MARYA: I do it!

DORA: WE WANT
    WE WANT
    A ROOM WITH A VIEW

APOLLO: (*As others stab.*) I feel him going…

JUDITH: He can't be, he promised to describe it, whisper me,
    Lvov – (*She goes near to him.*) Whisper!
    (*They begin, in an intoxicated way, to hop up and down.*)

CHORUS: WE WANT
    WE WANT
    SEX IN A BEDROOM

ARNOLD: (*Stabbing.*) You are not better than me! No one is
    better than me!

CHORUS: WE WANT TO BE ASHAMED
    WE WANT
    WE WANT TO BE ASHAMED
    WE WANT
    (*The door flies open, the crash acting like a bell in a boxing
    ring. The MURDERERS are still, hands in their mouths.*)

FARMER: Is that Lvov?
    Obviously, Lvov…

He's killed himself in order not to speak to me.

(*He takes a grubby book from his pocket, flings it at the wall.*)

Message of Lvov…

SLOMAN: The master's dead.

Eat the master. The master's dead.

You'll never be free now.

(*He looks at the FARMER, who has a penknife out.*)

What are you doing?

FARMER: (*Sawing at LVOV.*) Taking a finger, he won't need –

SLOMAN: WHAT ARE YOU DOING!

FARMER: Taking a –

SLOMAN: WHAT FOR!

FARMER: (*Sawing.*) I can show this.

FORJACKS: Show it?

FARMER: Show it, yes –

(*He waves the knife.*)

GET AWAY

I got nothing from Lvov, so Lvov can serve me now. There are places where they revere him. (*He cuts off the finger.*)

FINGER OF LVOV! AUTHENTIC!

Don't stand in my way, I have a living to make.

(*He goes out.*)

APOLLO: I shall put him down, now. Put him on what, though? Someone speak…

(*They are silent.*)

Or should I carry him my whole life? Is that what you want? Through wind and sun? I could do.

ELLA: We have to save Lvov. From the Lvovites.

SLOMAN: You see! Once you begin! You see! He governs you!

DORA: I found the stabbing easy. I don't think stabbing him was any sacrifice.

Did you?

IVORY: Easy.

DORA: Easy, yes.

SLOMAN: (*To the dead LVOV.*) MANIPULATOR!

GISELA: His ordeal is over. Ours now. Or they will carry him to every corner of the earth.

SLOMAN: (*With a sickly laugh.*) I really think, I really, really
    think –
JUDITH: Knife, then, and basin…
SLOMAN: THERE IS NO CONTROLLING YOU.
    (*He shudders, then with decision.*)
    I'll eat Lvov. I will partake.
IVORY: Thank you.
SLOMAN: I will because this scheme of his is nothing but a
    plot to bind you in mystification. I will call the CORPSE'S
    BLUFF. Butcher! I will swallow and be not less but a greater
    cynic. Butcher!
    (*He drags the knife from LVOV's body. He stands, holding it,
    defiant. The wind of desolation.*)

THE EIGHTH PARABLE
The Complex Origins of Domesticity

*McNOY and MacATTLEE are carrying IVORY in a chair. They stop. The
cloud of laughter passes.*

McNOY: Who is cheering?
MacATTLEE: I've heard cheering before, but this is
    disembodied.
IVORY: It is the irrepressible expression of solidarity which
    has become detached from humanity and drifts over the
    landscape. Why have you stopped? Did you think it was
    for you?
    (*MCNOY shrugs.*)
MacATTLEE: He thought –
McNOY: No, no –
IVORY: He thought it was for him!
    (*MCNOY shakes his head.*)
    He thought it was gratitude!
    (*MCNOY shakes his head.*)
    Yes!
    He still yearns for appreciation!

(*He smiles. MACATTLEE shakes his head with amusement. A
WOMAN appears, holding a pair of trousers.*)

SEAMSTRESS: (*To IVORY.*) Aren't you McStain?

IVORY: I am, I think, entirely McStain.

SEAMSTRESS: I ask because I have been darning his trousers.
(*She holds them out.*)
He paid in advance, so I knew he must come back.

IVORY: He has. As you say, it was inevitable.
(*He reaches for them.*)

MacATTLEE: She is lying, despite her wonderful breasts. We
never came this way before.

SEAMSTRESS: I never forget a face.

MacATTLEE: She is looking for a husband and this is a trick to
demonstrate her needlework. Don't believe it, McStain.

IVORY: But I can see these are a perfect fit.

MacATTLEE: You are fascinated, and that has nothing to do
with the truth or otherwise of what she says.
(*᠎ ᠎ ᠎᠎᠎᠎᠎᠎᠎᠎᠎᠎᠎*)
If you are a needlewoman, show us other trousers.
(*She pulls out other pairs.*)
You see! She is a consummate liar!

IVORY: Put the chair down. I want to examine her.

MacATTLEE: No! You are as smitten as the crew of Odysseus in
the locality of sirens. Don't put him down, or we shall be a
bellman short.

SEAMSTRESS: You're quite right. I am looking for a husband
and I've never heard of McStain.

MacATTLEE: You see! This is what we have to guard against!
And her breasts are forever pleading their case. Look
away, McNoy…

IVORY: (*Persisting.*) I am a landowner. Do you find me
attractive?

SEAMSTRESS: From my first glance.

McNOY: It's all up with us…

IVORY: (*Hopping down.*) This is the parting of the ways.

SEAMSTRESS: (*To IVORY.*) When I look at you I feel no
shyness. We shall join together, and I will see clouds over
your shoulder, and you will see grass under my head.

MacATTLEE: McStain, I have to warn you, is a murderer and a cannibal.

SEAMSTRESS: Let him murder me. He is beautiful and a landowner. I would be happy to be murdered by such a man.

MacATTLEE: How she simpers! And what is that on her mouth? It's the stain of some wild berry which in my opinion utterly fails to enhance her appearance. Come on, McStain, the world is full of belfries!

IVORY: (*Eyes on the SEAMSTRESS.*) Leave the chair. It is the beginning of our home.

MacATTLEE: It is the beginning of delusion.

IVORY: (*Taking down the chair.*) Sit, sit my love…
(*As she does so, McNOY strikes a fatal blow on IVORY's head. He falls.*)

McNOY: I'm sorry! I'm sorry! I'm sorry!

MacATTLEE: We kill nobody!

McNOY: (*Hopping about in horror.*) I'm so sorry! I'm so sorry!

MacATTLEE: (*Beside IVORY.*) Oh, McStain, what could she have given you?
(*They all look at the dead figure of IVORY. The SEAMSTRESS turns to go, then stops. She looks at the trousers she is holding.*)

SEAMSTRESS: Is one of you McNoy…?

END OF THE EIGHTH PARABLE

The DISCIPLES are distributed over the stage. They are stooping on all fours, or sitting with their knees drawn up, still and silent as in a tableau. An appalling silence. A single sound. Silence.

ARNOLD: We did it and –
(*A cacophony as everyone launches into speech.*)
Shut up!
(*Silence, long, still.*)
And then –
(*Cacophony breaks out again.*)

MARYA: SHUT UP!
(*Silence, long, still. At last SLOMAN rises to his feet.*)

SLOMAN: Hold hands.

We mustn't part.

Hold hands.

(*He extends his hands. No one moves. He cries out in despair.*)

HOLD HANDS!

(*Silence. The door opens. The FIRST OFFICER enters. He wears a sash.*)

OFFICER: The war has ended and I have come to claim Lvov.

(*No one moves.*)

To settle with those whose statements were not clear. The ones who failed to simplify. And the wearers of glasses.

(*Pause.*)

Are you hiding Lvov?

(*Pause.*)

Some of you will be hanged. And the women given medicines. Where is Lvov?

JUDITH: Gone.

(*Pause. He looks at them, turns to go.*)

APOLLO: Was it hard out there?

OFFICER: Hard? You couldn't call it hard. And yet, if I say it was not hard, you will think it was easy, so I don't know what to say. Accuracy is impossible. We abandoned accuracy in the first few days. Without accuracy, things become tolerable... Report, if Lvov shows up.

JUDITH: He won't.

OFFICER: What makes you certain?

(*Pause.*)

The certainty of you people! When everything shows that nothing is certain.

(*He turns to go, treads on something. He disdains to look down.*)

What is that?

JUDITH: Spectacles.

OFFICER: He is here, then. He could not travel without spectacles. (*Pause.*)

SLOMAN: Yes.

He's here.

(*The cloud of laughter passes.*)

ANNA: He wanted praise, but not from us. He thirsted for
    applause, but the applause of the select.
JUDITH: Who this select was, he never said.
    (*The cloud again.*)
OFFICER: Show me Lvov.
SLOMAN: HOLD HANDS!
    (*They hold hands. The OFFICER is poised. wary. Pause. Voices
    are heard, singing badly. The TWO MACS enter.*)

THE SONG

THE MACS: How skilful we have been
    To make sure we were seen
    RELUCTANT
    How tactful we behaved
    At the palace or the cave
    ABJECT
    And playing cards we choose
    Invariably to lose
    INOFFENSIVE
    We took the long way round but we arrived
    And if the pub has disappeared
    Where we watched girls slyly
    In the grip of the sexually proud
    WELL
    And if the bed's been commandeered
    Where we kipped late in the morning
    And the mothers are all lying in their shrouds
    WELL
    The thieves have shit my sheets
    And my one and only suit
    Is on the back of a dog that's going mental
    But we arrived
    AND IF WE KILLED IT WAS PURELY ACCIDENTAL
OFFICER: (*Seizing the opportunity.*) Rope them!
    (*THE MACS are momentarily dumbfounded.*)
    Rope them!

(*Their instinct returns. McNOY casts off the bell ropes and they run around the DISCIPLES, pulling them into a tight noose. They knot the ropes. Pause. The sound of a distant celebration. THE MACS sit on the floor and smoke. The OFFICER drifts towards the sound.*)

SUSANNAH: He had the flavour of –

ALL: Don't mention it!

SUSANNAH: He had the texture of –

ALL: Don't dare describe it!

(*The knot of DISCIPLES drifts, first one way, then another. The cloud passes overhead.*)

SEVEN LEARS

The Pursuit of the Good

'The best and soundest of his time hath been but rash…'
Goneril, *King Lear*

Characters

LEAR
A Child, later a King

GLOUCESTER
A Vagrant, later an Earl

LUD
His Brother

HERDSMAN

ARTHUR
His Brother

CORDELIA
A Princess

THE EMPEROR OF ENDLESSLY
EXPANDING TERRITORY

BISHOP
A Teacher

EMPRESS

PRUDENTIA
A Widow

FIRST MAN
Servant of the State

CLARISSA
Her Daughter, later a Queen

SECOND MAN
Servant of the State

HORBLING
A Minister, later a Fool

DRUMMER

KENT
A Soldier

THE GAOLED
A Chorus

OSWALD
A Soldier

THE TERRIBLE SOLDIER

BOY

THE SURGEON ASSISTANT

GONERIL
A Princess

REGAN
A Princess

THE INVENTOR

FIRST LEAR

Darkness. A Pit in the Kingdom of LEAR's father. A child's voice, full of apprehension.

LUD: Let's play football! Let's fly kites!

ARTHUR: Let's build castles on the beach!

LEAR: Something bad is happening here…!

LUD: Something horrible!

ARTHUR: I dropped my stick!

LEAR: Something rotten, can you smell?

ARTHUR: My stick! My stick!

LUD: Horrid smell!

LEAR: Something's alive, but only just!

ARTHUR: Oh, let's build castles on the beach!

LEAR: Someone's in pain…!

LUD: Let's play football! Let's fly kites!

ARTHUR: I want my stick!

LEAR: That smell is pain! Be careful where you tread!

LUD: A hand! A hand! I trod on a hand!

THE GAOL: WE ARE THE DEAD WHO AREN'T DEAD YET
    EVER SO SORRY
    NOT DEAD YET
    (*The CHILDREN cling together.*)
    WHATEVER WE DID
    WHATEVER IT WAS
    HOW COULD IT JUSTIFY THIS?

LEAR: Are you the bad, then? That you smell so badly?

ARTHUR: We are clean children and our mother loves us.

LUD: Are you our father's enemies? If so, however bad this is, it can't be bad enough for you!

THE GAOL: WE NEVER SAID THAT WE WERE INNOCENT
    WHAT'S INNOCENCE?
    WE NEVER CLAIMED WE HAD NO HATRED
    WHO HAS NONE?
    WE NEVER CLAIMED THAT THIS WAS ARBITRARY
    WHAT ISN'T?

LEAR: They have no light…!

LUD: We are the royal children, shut your mouths!

LEAR: They have no sheets…!

ARTHUR: FOOT-BALL…!

LUD: Die, you horrid, stinking criminals!

ARTHUR: FOOT-BALL…!

LEAR: Oh, you poor, wet things, I never knew the ground was full of bodies, and you've got no sheets…!

LUD: All horrid things deserve to die…!

ARTHUR: FOOT-BALL…!

(*He tears out followed by LUD. LEAR hesitates.*)

LEAR: I shan't be king, because I am not the eldest but…if I were king…for one thing… I'd stop this!

(*He runs out. A ball bounces in a field. A bright sunlight fills the stage. The CHILDREN wander, apart.*)

No criticism of our father, but I wonder is it necessary that –

LUD: DON'T TALK ABOUT OUR DOINGS.

LEAR: I wasn't, but I find my mind –

LUD: DON'T REMIND US OF IT, POSTS!

LEAR: (*Taking off his shirt.*) If people were good, punishment would be unnecessary, therefore –

LUD: (*Pointing.*) Penalty spot.

LEAR: The function of all government must be –

LUD: We kick that way.

LEAR: (*Placing ARTHUR's shirt as second post.*) The definition of, and subsequent encouragement, of goodness, surely? (*LUD prepares a flying kick-off.*) Perhaps by making goodness easier, fewer people would – (*LUD boots the ball with terrific violence. It sails high and away. LEAR follows it with a look of incomprehension, shading his eyes.*) You've kicked it so hard it's – (*LUD puts his arm lovingly around ARTHUR's shoulder.*) gone right over the cliff… (*Linked together, LUD and ARTHUR walk slowly upstage. LEAR sits on the ground to wait.*) You would define goodness in such a way that ordinary people – who at the moment are so horribly attracted to bad things and immoral actions – would find it simple to appreciate and consequently act upon – (*He stops. He is*

inspired.) No! No! That's wrong! The opposite is the case!
That's it! You make goodness difficult, if anything. You
make it apparently impossible to achieve! It then becomes
compelling, it becomes a victory, rather as acts of badness
seem a triumph now! What you need to do – (*He turns.
His BROTHERS have stopped at the very edge of the cliff and
look down.*) I think, Lud, when you are king, the correct
approach to punishment would be – (*They fall out of sight,
together. LEAR stares, fixedly. A thin wind blows. He utters a cry,
terrible and deep. At last, a BISHOP enters.*)

BISHOP: I am your education.

LEAR: I am hard to educate because I was born wise.

BISHOP: That's something everybody knows.

LEAR: I will be relentlessly critical and nothing you say will I
take on trust. Why should I?

BISHOP: Why should you, after all?

LEAR: This is not arrogance on my part.

BISHOP: No, indeed.

LEAR: On the basis of mutual study we may answer some
questions that have haunted me since birth.

BISHOP: My imagination is at your disposal.

LEAR: I must warn you I am peevish at times and come out in
rashes, I suppose you know that.

BISHOP: I know everything about you.

LEAR: Everything? No one can know everything.

BISHOP: I know your brothers killed themselves. I know you
think of death yourself. I know you cry for animals but
harbour hatreds you yourself do not yet understand.

LEAR: Yes. How will you educate me?

BISHOP: I will educate you by showing you how bad I am.
Because I am a bad man you will learn much from me. I
will tell you nothing but what accords with my experience,
which is not a happy one. Hope, for example, I have
dispensed with entirely. There will be no books because
you know the books and have digested them. I detest all
untruths, but especially those which are sentimental, and
I will beat you sometimes, for which I have authority.
Almost certainly, these beatings will appear to you

unjustified. I will explode in rages and then fawn on you. I may kiss your body and then ignore you for days on end. You will detest me and your innate sense of justice will cry out for satisfaction. When one day, that cry ceases, your education will be over. God alone know why your father appointed me.

SECOND LEAR

The CHORUS is disposed about the stage. LEAR, a youth, comes among them as if between trees. He drops to his knees. He shudders. He laughs. He clasps his head.

LEAR: I'm in such
    I'm in such
    I WON'T SAY ECSTASY
    I WON'T SAY
    (*He shudders with emotion. A WOMAN enters. She extends a hand to him.*)
    Don't touch!
    (*He rests his forehead on the ground.*)
PRUDENTIA: Oh, you bastard, you mistreat me, and I a woman of distinction. Oh, you shallow and temperamental manipulator of emotion, do you think I can't see through you? And your love is rough. Your love is ROUGH.
LEAR: Yes. Go back to your books now. You are a lawyer, aren't you? Study the laws of infatuation.
PRUDENTIA: Our next meeting, will it –
LEAR: Next?
PRUDENTIA: Meeting, yes, will it be –
LEAR: NEXT MEETING? NO SOONER HAS SHE, NO SOONER HAVE WE THAN. WHAT OTHER MEETINGS? (*She looks at him.*) Memorise me. Store my touch. (*She turns to go.*) SHE WANTS A MEETING! (*She starts to walk away.*) Please come back! (*She stops.*) I am so thin, and boastful, and poor-minded, I am so empty and shallow as a tin bowl, ping! Love my emptiness, and don't run to men of quality and honesty, I will execute all men of character if you do, all those of deep soul who command the loyalty of women,

the bearded and the bald, the calm-eyed and the knowing, love your tin bowl or it's a massacre. Ping! (*He extends a hand. She goes to put it to her lips.*) Not there. (*She places it on her belly.*)

CLARISSA: (*Off.*) Mother...!

(*A GIRL enters.*)

Mother...! (*PRUDENTIA turns to face her daughter.*) You are everywhere these days except where you should be! That sounds silly but. And you smell strangely. Now look at you! This was the last place I expected to. But now I think, where is the last place she might be, go there! And that is always where I find you! (*She laughs.*) And you smell strangely... This is such a miserable corner. No sun! Your law books are quite dusty. What is attractive about these sunless corners? And you smell strangely.

LEAR: I am a tin bowl. Ping!

PRUDENTIA: Do you know, there is a law in life –

LEAR: A law in life!

PRUDENTIA: Which says, she who habitually absents herself is best left undiscovered?

LEAR: Ping! Remember the law! Ping!

CLARISSA: Why does he say that so often?

PRUDENTIA: I smell oddly because I have been in Heaven.

LEAR: (*Standing.*) I met a poet, and he said –

PRUDENTIA: Heaven clings.

LEAR: Very gravely, very portentously –

PRUDENTIA: It stains.

LEAR: His eyes on mine, how I detested him, how I hate the gravity of poets. 'GREAT LOVE LASTS THROUGH WINTERS.' (*He pulls a face of contempt.*) I, of course, shrank at the wisdom. I, being a tin bowl, shallowly vibrated at his profound bass notes. I tinkled on the table. Do you not feel oppressed by the wise, their laws and their shuddering complacency, the fact is I am girl-mad, which is shallowness itself, and most becoming in a tin bowl! Ping! (*He looks at CLARISSA.*)

CLARISSA: You are funny, for a prince. I think you can't command yet, much respect, can he? But here is my

mother with him! So there is respect, of some kind,
obviously. (*She turns to her mother.*) I came to tell you what
no longer seems significant.

PRUDENTIA: Why? Tell me.

CLARISSA: I can't. It no longer seems – it has no –

PRUDENTIA: But all the same.

CLARISSA: I would feel humiliated, since it so obviously lacks
significance. What delighted me for half an hour suddenly
seems pitiful. I suppose because you have been in Heaven
and I only thought I was… I DON'T SEE WHY HEAVEN
NEEDS TO STINK. (*Pause.*) My bird is found.

PRUDENTIA: Bird… (*Pause.*)

CLARISSA: You don't remember my bird.

PRUDENTIA: Yes, I –

CLARISSA: No, you have entirely –

PRUDENTIA: No, I don't think I –

CLARISSA: You have entirely obliterated my bird from your
memory, and why shouldn't you?

PRUDENTIA: Yes. I had. I'm sorry, Clarissa, yes.

CLARISSA: Yes. I am not you, and you are not me, it is futile
we rehearse an intimacy which no longer exists, I am not
critical, you understand, I only –

PRUDENTIA: Clarissa –

CLARISSA: I only want to be honest. From this moment I
mark the closure of my childhood. I am sixteen, this is
farewell and a dismal corner is correct for it. Shake hands.
(*She puts out a hand.*)

PRUDENTIA: Of course not.

CLARISSA: Very well. Thank you for your love. I am most
grateful.

LEAR: Ping! I remember your bird very well!

CLARISSA: Why does everybody lie?

LEAR: I don't lie, I exaggerate.

CLARISSA: You think you are amusing, but you are an
exhibitionist.

LEAR: I think I am the most melancholy and degenerate
character, so sunk in contemplation of myself I walk
with stooping shoulders and lids half-draped over my

never-sparkling eyes, white-skinned with horror of the sunshine and prematurely bald, incapable of friendship and though wealthy, inclined to theft. I steal the clothes of women and insinuate myself in wardrobes listening to their acts of love. Poverty disgusts me, but equally does wealth. I listen to old men, at least for seven sentences and go early to bed, but your bird has red feathers and was brought from China.

CLARISSA: Yes. But I am looking for a friend now, not an idiot.

(*She turns to go.*)

LEAR: If you fuck with a greybeard, I'll – If you go down on quiet streets and bed with a musician, I'll –

(*He kicks a stone. PRUDENTIA goes out with CLARISSA.*)

THE GAOL: WE ARE THE DEAD

WE ARE THE CRUEL

WE NO LONGER NEED

TO MOUTH FIDELITIES

FIRST VOICE: I AM THE TORTURER

SECOND VOICE: I AM THE VICTIM

BOTH: WHAT BROUGHT US INTO SUCH PROXIMITY?

THIRD VOICE: I AM THE PHILOSOPHER

FOURTH VOICE: I AM THE PEASANT

BOTH: WHAT BROUGHT US INTO SUCH UNHEALTHY INTIMACY?

(*A peal of laughter. They depart.*)

LEAR: How proud I was, when she did not resist my hand. How its smooth gliding to her heat was uncontested. YOUTH – ITS PIQUANCY! How she forgives me everything. How she is tolerant of my dog's paws in her liquidity. YOUTH – ITS INTRANSIGENCE! She loves me not for what I am but for what I will be. To what I will be she believes herself a SIGNIFICANT CONTRIBUTOR. Oh, the vanity! And she complains if I turn her too swiftly on her face. Ow, she says. Some arthritic. Some rheumatic. Ow! (*He covers his face with his hands.*) I must recover. I must shed. I must emerge from this – cruelty…!

(*The BISHOP enters. LEAR hurries to him.*)

I have seen a girl I want! (*The BISHOP puts his arm around LEAR.*) Of course this may be a passing feeling. It may be slight. It may be trivial. Her hair is gold and her mouth far from luscious but. And gold is not a colour I much care for. It is tangled. Naturally, it's tangled. NOT HER HAIR THE EMOTION. I don't think anything should stand in the way of my desire, do you? On the other hand, what good can come from it? I think what I want I should have. To be deprived, what good is it? And pain, yes, obviously pain will be experienced, but it is tangled. I am fucking with the mother.

(*Pause.*)

BISHOP: Have the mother murdered.

LEAR: I considered that! The moment I saw the daughter I considered that. The thought leapt to the very forefront of my mind, it knocked against my skull demanding my attention, one look and I thought, the mother has to die! But no, I love the mother.

BISHOP: Abduct the daughter.

LEAR: Abduct her, yes! Would you help with that? No, it's not what I want…

BISHOP: You change, my son.

LEAR: I do! I do change! Hourly! The surface of my mind is like the boiling tar vat, God knows what may bubble from the bottom, tar in the eye! (*Pause.*) I think I must adore this child Clarissa. I think this is religion. What else is it? Do you recognise religion? My considerateness, my solicitude – what else is it?

BISHOP: I want to show you cruelty.

LEAR: Yes.

BISHOP: I want to teach you indifference.

LEAR: Yes.

BISHOP: Because you are in danger.

LEAR: Am I? Yes, I am.

BISHOP: From your own brilliance.

LEAR: Yes!

(*A lamp is lowered on a chain, a cold wind.*)

Hold my hand!

(*THE GAOL murmurs.*)

BISHOP: Look, the gaol is full! Which is excellent!

LEAR: Excellent? Why excellent?

BISHOP: If some are to be free, others must be unfree, or they could not know freedom.

THE GAOL: DON'T TURN OFF THE LIGHT

WE LONG FOR THE LIGHT

HOW ELSE CAN WE LODGE IN YOUR MEMORY?

LEAR: Are they guilty or innocent?

BISHOP: They are all guilty of something, even if it is not the cause of their punishment.

LEAR: But so are we all!

BISHOP: That's perfectly true, but it alters nothing.

THE GAOL: LEAR!

TEN YEARS SINCE YOUR LAST INTRUSION AND YOU ARE NOW A BIGGER PRINCE!

LEAR: Yes, and how ugly you are! I may have changed but you have not...my brother could not bear your ugliness...!

BISHOP: The suffering are the least objective, they are swamped in sentiment as they are by sewage. They think, if only others knew our pain, they would cry out, end it! But not so! First error of the conscience-ridden!

LEAR: But isn't this injustice?

THE GAOL: INJUSTICE YES

THAT IS THE WORD FOR IT

REMEMBER THE WORD WHEN YOU GO BACK INTO THE LIGHT INSCRIBE IT ON YOUR LIFE

BISHOP: We can go to dinner now. We eat. We drink. We lie on clean mattresses.

LEAR: No, no, that is unthinkable!

BISHOP: Think it! You must think it! (*He seizes LEAR.*) Boy, you must think and swallow it!

LEAR: Can't eat!

BISHOP: Must hold these in your head and still pick up the crystal glasses!

THE GAOL: LEAR

SOON

LEAR

SOON

THE KING DIES

BISHOP: You see, their inextinguishable optimism!

LEAR: I'll act! I'll act, I promise!

BISHOP: (*Drawing LEAR into an embrace.*) I am trustworthy.

LEAR: (*Trying to escape him.*) Yes –

BISHOP: I am utterly and wholly trustworthy.

LEAR: All right –

BISHOP: And I love you.

LEAR: Yes –

BISHOP: No one more.

LEAR: Yes, yes! My loved one. My true father. But all you say
I can't take heed of. And one day, possibly I'll kill you.
Loving you just the same. Loving you undiminished.

BISHOP: (*Freeing him from his arms.*) Yes.
   (*The lamp is drawn away.*)
   What's a life?
   (*He goes out.*).
   What's a life…!
   (*LEAR is alone on stage. He sits.*).

LEAR: The poor are not the same as the rich. The poor have
   got no money! (*He claps his hands.*)
   That's an untruth! The truth is, they are not the same as the
   rich. Having no money, they became different.
   (*TWO FIGURES enter, equipped.*)
   The innocent are the same as the guilty! They were merely
   looking the other way! (*He claps his hands.*)
   Untrue! Another untruth! The innocent exerted themselves
   to be innocent. Difficult. Difficult.
   (*THE FIGURES cross the stage, he calls to them.*)
   Is there a war on?
   (*He gets up and scuttles to them.*)
   I know nothing! I'm told nothing! On the other hand, I
   don't enquire.
   (*They gawp at him.*)
   Take me. It's unnecessary I know the details, the causes
   and so on. And stabbing you can teach me on the way. Do
   you know who I am?

SOLDIERS: Prince Lear.

LEAR: Me, yes. Soon to be. Imminently, your master. What war is this? My father takes a long time dying. Are you making for the frontiers? DEFEND THEM WITH YOUR LIFE. No, run away if you want to. I permit it. There. Permission.

(*He slaps their hands with his own.*)

Fleeing licence. (*He laughs.*)

I talk gibberish because I'm not the monarch. Come monarchy, all statements I recant. All oaths, in the bin.

(*They turn to go.*)

He's dying, but so slowly. So laboured his departure it is miserable to watch. DON'T GO.

(*They stop.*)

I know what you're thinking. You are thinking – fuck this for an heir apparent.

(*They laugh, frankly. So does LEAR. HORBLING, a minister, enters.*)

HORBLING: Your father is sinking.

LEAR: Sinking? Still? How farther can he sink?

HORBLING: I inform you. I inform you, merely.

(*He turns to go.*)

LEAR: I THINK YOU SHOULD ENJOY ME. (*HORBLING stops.*)

I think you should luxuriate in my infantilism, which undoubtedly must have its rim, the comic preface to unmitigated cruelty. THE HEADS WILL MAKE A PYRAMID TO THE STARS.

(*HORBLING goes out. The SOLDIERS prepare to march.*)

Listen, I am barmy for a skinny girl and infatuated with her mother –

(*They bow and march off.*)

Yes. I respect that. Yes.

I WISH I HAD A BROTHER!

(*FIGURES appear, carrying a body on a bier. LEAR turns his back on it, shrinks.*)

Listen, I am playing tennis! Don't attempt to dissuade me because youth needs exercise, it must be flexed about the

muscles and I have sat about so long DON'T BRING HIM
IN I CAN'T –

(*They progress. They put down the bier.*)

My sense is I shall not do this job well. Is that your sense?
(*He climbs to his feet, and goes towards the body with a
resolute movement. Suddenly he stops and points.*)

Red bird!

(*He follows it with his eyes. CLARISSA enters, with a cage in
her hand.*)

CLARISSA: Gone again…!

LEAR: The first thing is I go to bed early. Please make a note of
that, and second –

(*He stops, rushes to his father's body and seizes it in his arms,
rocking it to and fro and moaning. CLARISSA puts the cage on
the floor and walks to him.*)

CLARISSA: You should not do that. Whatever the feeling.
You should not do that because in governors extremes of
emotion are not liked. (*He continues to sob.*) And anyway, I
think you are pretending. (*She sees the bird.*) There it goes!
(*She follows it off. LEAR releases his father's body.*)

LEAR: Bury him. I shan't attend.

(*He walks away. They carry away the bier. HORBLING
attends on LEAR, patiently.*)

HORBLING: I was your father's minister.

LEAR: I know the face.

HORBLING: And gave ten years of good advice.

LEAR: Excellent. And yet he died.

HORBLING: On finance, planning, and on policy towards the
rival states.

LEAR: We still exist, so excellent.

HORBLING: I had particular regard to harvests, which in all
my years were poor, and yet there was no famine.

LEAR: I think –

HORBLING: And land reform was something of a speciality.
The draining of the marsh beyond the river yielded fifty
thousand acres. Here I propose a settlement for landless
peasants.

LEAR: I think –

HORBLING: You ask me how this can be managed? Treaties of friendship with the Irish and the Cornish will reduce the need for soldiers, which will release the necessary labour and save the expense of weapons. Furthermore –

LEAR: I think –

HORBLING: I have prepared in detail plans for the ten years hence which I should like to show you, but in the meantime, this is the summary.

(*He extends a sheaf of papers, crisp. LEAR looks at him, without taking the papers.*)

LEAR: You are so good at things. Obviously, so good at things. And yet I have no fool.

HORBLING: Fool?

LEAR: Have I? Lando is senile. Whoever laughs at Lando now?

HORBLING: Well, this is not my field of expertise but Lando could be pensioned and the post advertised, of course.

LEAR: Lando did nothing but make ridicule of women. Their fat arses and so on. So they have fat arses.

HORBLING: Yes… I was never greatly amused by Lando…

LEAR: You do it. (*Pause.*)

HORBLING: Do –

LEAR: Why not? Bring to it the same invention as you bring to drainage or economy. And give those to your successor. (*HORBLING's face is aghast.*) Oh, but this is promotion! (*HORBLING is unconsoled.*) And this way, I will have your best, surely? You will, in this function, be unconstrained by duty, conscience, or whatever drives you to make such squiggles on the paper…

HORBLING: MY SKILLS ARE ALL IN GOVERNMENT!

LEAR: No, that's false modesty and impossible to credit…

(*HORBLING looks at the floor, then bows and starts to withdraw.*)

Careful…! And be funny…!

(*HORBLING goes out, passing PRUDENTIA, who, alone with him, opens her arms. He runs to her.*)

Men hate me!

PRUDENTIA: No, no…

LEAR: Hate me, yes!

PRUDENTIA: No, but bury your father –

LEAR: No!

PRUDENTIA: Think of the people, the people will deduce –

LEAR: I DECLINE, I DECLINE, AND ALL DEDUCTIONS, POX! Listen, I think I am alive for one reason, and that is you. But listen again. The you must be as I create her. The you gives no advice. That comes by volume from old men and clerks. Kiss me. Oh, hot and thick skirts, hide me, woollens, linens, silks, hide me, the odour of deep cloths and waterfalls of shift, do you have a centre, hide a mad child there!

PRUDENTIA: My genius. My rare thing. Do not die.

LEAR: Shan't die...

PRUDENTIA: My magician, my liar, don't be murdered...

LEAR: Shan't be.

PRUDENTIA: Promise!

LEAR: Can't. Nothing will I promise, and never anything on oath. (*He detaches himself.*) Why call me a liar?

PRUDENTIA: Did I? I must long to be lied to. (*Pause.*)

LEAR: Yes... That also might be a sign of love...go now... (*She goes to leave.*) I must fuck your daughter. (*She stops.*) I must. And someone will. It must be better it were me.

PRUDENTIA: That would so injure me.

LEAR: I'd best not tell you, then.

(*PRUDENTIA grapples with the idea. LEAR watches her.*)

PRUDENTIA: This feeling...your feeling for...my daughter... can be explained...can only be explained by...my daughter being...

LEAR: Your daughter, yes. I dare say.

PRUDENTIA: So in one respect at least...it's...profoundly tied to me...and yet another manifestation...of our intimacy... couldn't that be said...?

LEAR: It could be said.

PRUDENTIA: It could be, yes. I see your point.

LEAR: My point? But you made it.

(*She goes out, thoughtfully. He watches her.*)
Oh, kindness...! Oh, decency...!

THE GAOL: LEAR
    CAN WE ADDRESS YOU
    LEAR
    THE TESTAMENT OF TORTURERS AND VICTIMS
    OUR STRANGE COLLABORATION
    THE FIRST AND TERRIBLE DISCOVERY
    WHEN ONE LIE FAILS
    WE ARE IRRESISTIBLY ATTRACTED TO ITS OPPOSITE

LEAR: I was born ancient, and I must discover infancy. I was born wise, and I must find ignorance. Or I will suffer...
(CLARISSA enters, pristine.)

CLARISSA: I think you want me to admire you. In many ways I do but it would be no compliment if I praised things merely to please you. That would not be friendship, would it? Don't you agree? So I will say – as best I can – only the truth. You will say, of course, what's truth, you do that all the time, but where does that get us? Not very far, I think. *(He smiles at her.)* I am glad to be invited to your house, but also wonder why. I am not very fascinating. I am sixteen. How can I be fascinating?
(LEAR goes uneasily towards her.)

LEAR: Well...it's...well... I...well, now you... *(He smiles, stops.)* Speechless!
(He throws up his hands. SERVANTS appear, carrying a lavish table.)
Do sit!
And feel –
The absolute and uncommon pleasure of knowing nothing secret exists between us!

CLARISSA: *(Accepting a chair.)* I do feel that.

LEAR: You do? Excellent!
(Pause. He taps his fingers. Food is transported to the table.)
Commonly I find, alone with a woman, so much unsaid. Much speaking but so much unarticulated. Now, with you –

CLARISSA: I say whatever comes into my head!

LEAR: Excellent! This is an Irish fruit. Don't you feel a long way from me? Not a very sweet fruit but should all fruit be sweet? I don't see why. I can hardly see you! (*The SERVANTS are active.*) Don't you love table cloths? This one is Dutch and took the woman eighty weeks to manufacture. Am I boring you? When my father died he left three tons of linen. I do not exaggerate. Give her some wine.

CLARISSA: No alcohol!

LEAR: Of course no alcohol. This is a Scottish thing, no grape has been within a mile of it. Why no alcohol, it is not prohibited.

CLARISSA: I like to be myself.

LEAR: Well, she is the one I invited. Isn't this pleasant, and you are excellent company.

CLARISSA: That can't be true.

LEAR: It is true.

CLARISSA: It can't be true, I've said nothing and now I feel foolish. Please don't lie even for kindness. Where is the virtue in it?

LEAR: Do you like this room? It was decorated by Persian gardeners. (*She laughs.*) It was! (*He smiles at her.*) It was! I love to see you laugh. I love your teeth, which are not even, but who likes even teeth? My father brought them here to plant the oriental garden but –
  (*CLARISSA suddenly stands, terrifyingly.*)

CLARISSA: THIS IS FATUOUS.

LEAR: They were surplus to requirements…
  (*She glares at him.*)

CLARISSA: You do not want to lunch with me.

LEAR: No.

CLARISSA: It's something else you want and this is just –

LEAR: Yes. And conversation is a screen. A futile screen in your case, since you are so –

CLARISSA: You are going to flatter me and I hate –

LEAR: I was! I was! All part of my conspiracy to –

CLARISSA: IF YOU LOVE ME SAY SO. (*Pause.*) Or. (*Pause.*)
  What do you want to do with me? Undress me? I find this difficult but however difficult it is vastly preferable to lies, fruitcake, table cloths and so on. What do you want to do? Handle me down below? There, I said I would

respect you more if you simply told me what it is you want. Now I'm blushing but that is preferable to. Oh, I'm vilely uncomfortable and I have homework to do!
(*GONERIL and REGAN enter.*)

GONERIL / REGAN: We are the children of the union! Oh, father, oh, mother, spare us the sights and sounds of struggle!
(*LEAR gets up.*)

LEAR: I want to see you naked.

GONERIL / REGAN: Oh, father, this is the spectacle that brought you daughters! Do you not know even a look has consequences?

CLARISSA: I think that is probably the first honest thing you've said to me! I think we can be friends if you are honest. It isn't difficult, is it? Honesty? (*He looks at her.*) But of course you can't see me because –

GONERIL / REGAN: Only a look!

CLARISSA: A look would only –

GONERIL / REGAN: Give him a look!

CLARISSA: And that would hardly be the end of it so –

GONERIL / REGAN: We want to be born! We want to be born!
(*Pause.*)

LEAR: I must see you and the door is locked.

GONERIL / REGAN: WE ARE GOING TO BE BORN! WE ARE GOING TO BE BORN! INSIST ON IT!

CLARISSA: Is that expression meant to frighten me? It really is a rather silly face and – (*LEAR slaps her. She shudders, and then masters herself.*) I want to go home now.

LEAR: Impossible.

CLARISSA: I said.

LEAR: And I denied.

CLARISSA: THEN YOU ARE AN IDIOT. (*She glares at him.*) Nakedness can be so cold. Can be so granite. Do you want granite? Here's granite! (*She drags up her dress violently. Her belly is revealed. Her manner humiliates him.*) You foolish man. What use is it? Unless I feel? Unless I want? Dead iron on a mountain. (*She drops her dress.*) Give me the key now, Lear. (*He shrugs.*)

LEAR: Not locked.

(*CLARISSA starts to go out.*)

We must be married. (*She stops.*) It's obvious to me. The pain and. The grinding and. The punishment. Clarissa. (*A wind.*)

THIRD LEAR

A battlefield following a defeat. Figures drift over the stage. HORBLING, in a filthy greatcoat, shaking a bellstick.

HORBLING: Humour.

LEAR: (*Offstage.*) Kill the prisoners!

HORBLING: (*Sitting.*) Humour is the grating of impertinence upon catastrophe.

LEAR: (*Entering, supported by KENT and OSWALD.*) Burn the villages!

HORBLING: Am I academic? I was made that way.

LEAR: And all the infants, massacre!

HORBLING: I bring to foolishness the erudition of a scholar, which is an obstacle, I admit.

LEAR: (*As they help him onto a tarpaulin.*) Hang all the citizens! Are the prisoners dead yet?

KENT: There were no prisoners, sire.

HORBLING: But he is tolerant. I have yet to make him laugh.

LEAR: I love to kill! Throat high in killing!

KENT: (*To others off.*) Brandy, over here!

LEAR: Who panicked, then? Who fled?

OSWALD: We did.

LEAR: No, surely, we haven't passed this way before?

OSWALD: We fled wrongly.

KENT: The army fled in one direction, and we fled in the other. They fled home, and we –

OSWALD: Deeper still into the enemy's territory.

HORBLING: Humour! Humour is the consolation of impotence! Am I academic? I don't intend to be.

(*A SOLDIER enters with a brandy flask. They nourish LEAR.*)

KENT: Four thousand miles, if we can make it.

LEAR: Put the lights out! Don't tread on twigs! And make yourselves earth colour. Be clay! This is only the first of my many victories.

OSWALD: We have been warned...

LEAR: Pity the dead, though...pity the common and the uncommon also...there was a singer in the bodyguard who –

OSWALD: Dead –

LEAR: Call him anyway!

OSWALD: Jack! (*Pause.*) No Jack.

LEAR: Extinguish all lamps! Is no one listening?

KENT: They are the lamps of the enemy, they are seeking us to kill.

LEAR: Understandable, we have burned their country. But let me talk to them. I don't see grounds for malice.

OSWALD: We have spoiled their peace and happiness!

LEAR: Admittedly, but someone would have done so. So many buildings, such fertile crops. Jealousy alone ensured someone would have put them to the torch. Let me talk to them.

KENT: I shan't stop you.

LEAR: (*Staggering to his feet.*) I'll say Lear's army was no more than fate, no more than hurricane.

KENT: Yes, try saying that.

LEAR: And therefore temper is as appropriate as bawling at the weather, and vengeance as absurd as stabbing wind.

KENT: Do try that argument.

LEAR: As for the dead, they would have died in any case, complaining, sick and senile, which is a burden on the state.

OSWALD: (*Pointing.*) They're over there...

(*He points to small lights moving. LEAR pulls his greatcoat round him, begins to move off.*)

HORBLING: Majesty! (*He looks back.*) Stay with me.

LEAR: They'll miss us if we don't accost them. They'll pass us by.

HORBLING: Stay, and write your wisdom in a letter. You see I think its truth will numb them, as if, when standing too close to a bell, its boom is staggering, and then they might misuse you. But from a distance, in the quiet of contemplation, the bell is music. Write it in a letter, and then your truth might have a chance. (*Pause.*)

LEAR: Yes. That's good.

(*Suddenly he lets out a terrible cry, and covering his face with his hands, shudders with the horror. HORBLING embraces him, rocks with him.*)

I saw so many corpses!

HORBLING: Yes.

LEAR: I saw so many eyes!

HORBLING: Yes.

LEAR: Eyes hopped! Eyes wriggled! BANG! And out came eyes!

HORBLING: They do…

LEAR: Clang goes the club!

HORBLING: Out come the eyes…

(*Pause. They wait for LEAR to recover. He adjusts himself. He looks around him.*)

LEAR: Thank you for your patience. It's obvious I am not yet in all departments fit to govern. (*They look at the floor.*) I say, demonstrably, I am not, and this disaster is the proof. I say you would be well within your rights to put your daggers to my throat and end it. All of you. Now. Not legitimate, but right. Rush me if you will and quickly, I shan't lift a finger. Leave me tongue-stiff in the dark, who'd stoop to call it murder, I wish I had a brother. (*Pause.*)

His body lay in Asia, what a clown… (*He indulges.*)

Stabbed by his lieutenants in the Caucasus, this monarch little known… (*He watches.*)

But. (*Pause.*)

Lear now has this thing in his heart which no successor owns. A treasure. An ingot, hard beneath the bone.

(*He looks from one to the other.*)

ERROR.

Oh, the heat of error, and its light…come, warm yourself at error, who else has this? All this dead, and all these eyes, are waste if I'm not used for further government. I'm grown. (*He shrugs.*)

Of course, this argument is difficult, when you're knee-deep in clot and vein.

(*HORBLING breaks the silence with a compulsive shaking of his bells, a bitter, fury of ringing. He stops.*)

KENT: Lear is shit. Lear is vomit.

LEAR: Yes.

KENT: Oh, my dead loves out there!

LEAR: Yes.

KENT: Oh, my better-than-any-woman things, my lovelier-than-cunt brigades, all flat, all pulp!

LEAR: Yes. (*KENT stares at LEAR, but does not move. HORBLING in a paroxysm, shakes the bells again.*)

OSWALD: I should kill you now, and scraping home in rags from fifteen months of vagrancy, say honour me, for I struck down the thing that piped us into swamping death, YOU CHOSE THAT GROUND!

LEAR: Yes.

But that was another Lear.

Already I don't know him. He also lies among the reeds.

(*OSWALD wavers. HORBLING exclaims.*)

HORBLING: Stab him now! I have the policies! I have the plans of reconstruction! Stab him now! New currency! New industry, clothes for the starving, dinner for the naked. Stab him, then! I predict a marginal increase in taxes, but silent buses, I've got the documents, why don't you stab!

(*He tears off his cap and holds out the plans. KENT stares.*)

OSWALD: (*Lying flat.*) Lights…!

(*They all duck, but for LEAR, who climbs to his feet. Pause. Lights flicker.*)

LEAR: Death will either occur, or if not, I shall be better for having been exposed to it. In any event, it can't be meaningless…

(*He walks offstage towards the lights which bob, and then are stationary. Pause.*)

CLAR-ISSA!

(*A cheer from offstage. CLARISSA enters with new troops,
LEAR draped about her. HORBLING immediately begins
hopping about, ringing the bells febrilely as if to demonstrate
his innocuous character.*)

She!

She!

God's own if there is a God!

Perfection if perfection is!

KENT: (*Kneeling.*) Oh, Christ in ecstasy, how did this come
about?

CLARISSA: We are the Second Army.

OSWALD: Second?

CLARISSA: Who came here by a different route, and found
a swamp of corpses, all our colour. Through these we
searched for Lear.

LEAR: I was not dead!

CLARISSA: This army will cover your withdrawal.

LEAR: Withdrawal? But we have new troops!

KENT: Withdrawal, yes.

LEAR: WHO SAYS WITHDRAWAL! WHO! (*KENT is silent.*)

CLARISSA: The enemy is also tired, and will let us out the
country, which this time we should not burn, but tread
with exaggerated care, like men who were once drunk,
but in the morning rather shamefaced, replace the broken
fence posts in the gardens.

(*LEAR looks at her, conceding.*)

KENT: (*Rising.*) We'll wash, if you've the patience, and when
you say so, march.

(*He and OSWALD go out.*)

LEAR: Kent likes me. He says I have kind eyes. And when I
said destroy me, he hung back…

HORBLING: And me! I said things so ridiculous it made
execution improbable. Improbable! What more can you
hope for!

(*He smiles, weakly. LEAR falls into CLARISSA's arms.*)

LEAR: Hold me…! I'm real…! I do exist, don't I? Hold me…!

(*THE GAOL appears to LEAR.*)

I've not forgotten you…! I have you very much in mind…!

120

Time to unlock the gaol! Or maybe not!

CLARISSA: Ssh... I came for you...

LEAR: It is not the circumstance, it is the exposure, it is not the subject but the experience which –

CLARISSA: Shh... I'm here...

LEAR: I mean –

CLARISSA: Shh –

LEAR: (*Feverish.*) Oh, let me think – oh, let me – disaster was not the failure – but the purpose of the war!

(*He stares at her. She wipes his face.*)

HORBLING: It's hard to be a fool with this monarch. I meet many fools now and they say, the job is not what it was. What was it, then, I say, I am not a trained fool, I am a novice. They tell me you could do well at one time saying out loud the first thing that came in your head. Any shit. Any trivia. This was called Fool's Wisdom. But now...you see...there's no future in that one. (*He looks to CLARISSA.*) Take me home, Miss, I have a longing to sit in a garden...

(*He goes out. LEAR looks at CLARISSA.*)

LEAR: You are going to criticise me...

CLARISSA: Who else will, if I don't... (*He shakes his head.*) I must, Lear... (*He nods.*)

I must because to swallow criticism in the interests of false harmony would be –

LEAR: False?

CLARISSA: It is my nature and impossible to –

LEAR: Oh, look, your knee! Through all the filth of campaign, KNEE! I was ready to die – no – more than ready, yearning to die – and that knee reminds me – THE MOMENTOUS LOSS. (*He extends his hand slowly.*) I dare not touch it. How I want to but I won't. I'll torture my already flogged imagination. FINGERS WAIT! (*He slaps one hand with the other.*) I won't say I've missed your sex exactly. It was stiff and – it was board on sand if I remember, us – a strange collision, grit not fluid, glass not dew, but I thought again and again, I want what we can not, I want what we do not, the possibility of you, more than the plunging pleasures

I have on occasions – needless to relate – indulged elsewhere. Let me touch. (*He kisses her knee.*)

CLARISSA: You must be sensible, and hear advice. (*He kisses it again, kneeling.*) You must regard the judgement of others as equal to your own. I think if this is to be a happy kingdom you must study good, which is not difficult, and do it. I will help you. I will criticise you, and I will say when you are childish or petulant, and you must try to overcome the flaws in what is otherwise, I am sure, a decent character! (*LEAR stares at the knee.*) You are often amusing, which is surely a sign of goodness!

(*LEAR does not meet her eyes.*)

LEAR: How far I've come. They say three thousand miles of marching, and the villages all roofless where we trod. I am no longer what I was. But you, equally travelled, are more yourself than ever.

CLARISSA: What was good in me, through seeing, is now more good. What was less good, there is less of.

LEAR: WHAT IS THIS GOOD?

(*He sways, seized, pained. She looks at him. He uncurls, like screwed paper. Pause.*)

And is your mother –

CLARISSA: Yes. She's well… (*He stands.*)

LEAR: Clarissa, if I am a child, it is because a child must know. Its ravings are the protests of the uninstructed. It thinks the sky is a false barrier, and the floor, pretence. It raves less, year by year, as all the barriers are demonstrated to be real, and insurmountable. I am still in my pen, and so I squeal. But thank you. And now I must see you undressed, look at your taut belly and think, childlike, it must be a fruit and a squirming animal, both.

(*Darkness. A drum taps. In the light of morning SOLDIERS and FOLLOWERS assemble in a ragged line, shouldering their packs. CLARISSA enters, overcoated, a general. She walks among them, making her address.*)

CLARISSA: I am a queen, and you are peasants. There is the first thing. I am not like you, and cannot call you brothers. So you know me as I am, and never falsely. The second is, when we are home, nothing will reward you but home itself, and this may be poor recompense, or even brutal. I promise nothing, except to be truthful. And the third thing is, many will die on the return as many died in coming. These will have no monument. Lastly, I am pregnant with the King's child. I hide nothing from you, not even the fact I shall eat better, and sleep warmer than you on these freezing nights. When you see my camp fire burning, you will say, she burns the last wood for herself. I am the Queen, and that is so.

(*They cheer her.*)

LEAR: How well she speaks! And I said such dishonest things! How well she stands! And I was all gesture and false movements. My friends, I said, my darlings, my brothers and such bollockry, no, she is exemplary, she is, and I should commit suicide!

BISHOP: Never say –

LEAR: I should, and she should govern! What's wrong with suicide? More should contemplate it.

BISHOP: You are a great king.

LEAR: Be careful! Such hyperbole leads to further horror.

BISHOP: A great king and she is shallow.

LEAR: She lacked the benefit of your teaching, which only threw my mind into worse chaos. My head's a sack of clocks, all keeping different hours. A SACK OF CLOCKS. I blame you for this, love and blame you, look at her, she sees through me!

BISHOP: She sees nothing.

LEAR: She sees my incurable sophistication! (*He goes to her.*) I'll speak, shall I? Or not? I thought you exemplary for brevity. No need, I think just –

SOLDIERS: LEAR! DON'T GO! WE SAVED YOU, LEAR! WE CROSSED A THOUSAND MILES OF DESERT AND DRANK FOUL WATER.

LEAR: I burned the houses. I poisoned the wells.

SOLDIERS: OUR GUTS ROARED LIKE THE DRAINAGE OF THE DUNGEON AND SOME WERE SLICED BY TRIBESMEN. HORRIBLY SLICED.

(*They stare at him. With an inspiration, he jumps onto a chair to address them.*)

LEAR: Was going to say –

But won't now.

Was going to exaggerate –

But not now.

Had planned such a speech but now won't give it.

Plaster you with gratitude and effusiveness...

But who requires it?

(*Pause. They look at him.*)

Or do you...?

When I see a crowd I think –

OH, HORROR, THEY EXPECT BANALITY! (*Pause.*)

Which you don't, surely? Grey eyes? Bloody paws, and stitched-together?

GROWN OUT OF FUTILE COMPLIMENTS, SURELY?

(*Pause. He searches their faces.*)

Or not?

DON'T WANT MY WET-EYED EXHORTATIONS, SURELY?

Want my tiny thanks, great murderers? (*Pause.*)

I am certainly the cleverest king that ever lived and this cleverness I wish I had not, I promise you, but there it is, as some have moles or a sixth finger I have appalling sight, so you must be patient, SAY WHAT YOU WANT AND I'LL SAY IT!

(*They start to drift away, unhappily.*)

WHO SAID YOU COULD HE DISMISSED? (*They stop, reluctantly.*)

TERRIBLE SOLDIER: Praise us, Lear. (*Pause. They look at him.*)

LEAR: I pat the dog for bringing me my slipper. And hounds who fetch dead birds. Pat. Pat.

TERRIBLE SOLDIER: But for us you'd be a skin in the enemy's museum.

LEAR: Ask more of me than thanks. That's easy to give and since I don't love life –

TERRIBLE SOLDIER: YOU DON'T LOVE LIFE? (*The shout is violent. The pause also.*) HE SAYS HE DON'T LOVE LIFE. (*He*

124

looks around.) MY MATES HAVE THINGS STUCK IN THEIR
EYEBALLS AND HE SAYS HE DON'T LOVE LIFE.

BISHOP: (*Sotto voce.*) Thank them. In any words. But thank
them.

TERRIBLE SOLDIER: I buried lovely friends and foes alike and
this one DON'T LOVE LIFE.

BISHOP: Quickly, satisfy them.

LEAR: I merely meant my nature is too philosophical for –

TERRIBLE SOLDIER: I CRAWLED THROUGH BURNING
SCHOOLS AND AM ONE-EYED FOR HIM. AND HE TELLS
ME HE DOES NOT LOVE HIS LIFE.
(*LEAR looks with a profound hatred at the TERRIBLE
SOLDER.*)

LEAR: If you hate me, fight me.

BISHOP: No, no, he is ten times your –

LEAR: Then at least I can keep pure in my language, which is
the heart of me.
(*The TERRIBLE SOLDIER unpacks his kit, which falls
to the floor along with his packs. Taking a knife from his
collection, he flings one to LEAR.*)

BISHOP: He knows nothing of killing…!

TERRIBLE SOLDIER: Then why does he make wars?
(*The CROWD roars, and forms a ring of curiosity.*)

CLARISSA: My husband is a child. Tell me if he lives, I refuse
to watch…
(*She sweeps out. The TERRIBLE SOLDIER stalks LEAR.*)

LEAR: First, I held my ground…
And then…
I RAN IN CIRCLES! (*He runs. He stops.*)
I thought, I must resort to stratagems. I thought this
morally dubious and yet, was not all life likewise dubious?
For some seconds I was paralysed by the futility of the
ambition to continue to exist. And then –
(*Suddenly he lets out a cry and runs, through the watchers.
The TERRIBLE SOLDIER pursues him offstage. The watchers
follow the figures with hand and eyes, groaning or applauding.
HORBLING squats, not following.*)

HORBLING: The Condolences of History. (*A roar. They point.*)
A belief, the holding of which one day appears sheer
mischief or eccentricity, on another, shimmers with, rings
with, the light of perfect truth. (*They groan.*)
An individual, mocked for his misfortune, acquires,
through patience, the attributes of holiness,
notwithstanding he hates men. (*They cheer.*)
Your enemy, however great his suffering, and justified in
his revenge, will spoil his victory by excess. (*They groan.*)
The oppressor will be pitied, too. (*They cheer.*)
It is a matter of sitting around. (*He cannot contain himself.*)
KILL HIM! STRING HIS BODY TO THE TREES! I HAVE THE
PROGRAMME! BURY LEAR AND ALL HIS MEMORY!
(*He waves the papers. A silence. He has his back to the
direction in which LEAR enters, wearily. The silence is
suggestive. His hand falters. He slips the papers back under his
hat. Pause.*)

BISHOP: My son... Oh, my son...

LEAR: Shh...

BISHOP: Oh, my one son...

LEAR: Shh... (*He is still, allowing no one near him. The TERRIBLE
SOLDIER, dying, enters, falls. LEAR turns to the body.*)
Oh, awful face, how fate has made a fool of you.
RIDICULOUS JOURNEY OF A SIMPLE MAN.
(*Suddenly he falls beside the dying man.*)
I want to be good! Get up! I want to be good!
(*The watching crowd drifts away as CLARISSA returns. She
looks at him.*)

CLARISSA: Now we have the child I think...
Now you are soon to be a father it must be time. SUPPOSE
HE'D KILLED YOU.

LEAR: You're right. Everything you say is true. Such a clear
mind you have, what I wouldn't give for it.

CLARISSA: You congratulate me all the time.

LEAR: Do I?

CLARISSA: Then persist with your –

LEAR: Yes, I do – I –

CLARISSA: So why admire? What's admiration without imitation?

LEAR: What is it, yes, that's indisputable.

CLARISSA: I believe you have a good character but something is obscuring it.

(*He nods. She takes his cheeks in both hands.*)

Now, call your armourer. We must set off.

(*She leaves. The BISHOP is alone on the stage with him.*)

BISHOP: How did you win?

LEAR: I appealed to all that was good in him.

BISHOP: Excellent.

LEAR: Which weakened him.

BISHOP: It does.

LEAR: Which made him – anybody's fool.

(*The BISHOP takes him in his arms. They embrace. A BOY enters with armour. The BISHOP goes. LEAR looks at the BOY. Then he stretches his arms.*)

If we are to be friends you must be truthful with me,

(*The BOY begins to armour him.*) I mean by this, keep nothing back, even offensive things you must articulate because secrets are the rot of friendship, aren't they, don't you find? And I will burden you with mine, that is the price of love, it shoulders all else out the road, it's selfish, it is petulant, it rubs the lovers raw. Do you agree?

BOY: Yes…

LEAR: You are so like me! How you love to care for me. So beautiful the way you tie that sleeve. I think of you a lot. I say a lot, but what's a lot? Always I think of you! What's your name?

BOY: Gary.

LEAR: Oh, I don't like that! Of all the names you might have had, I like that least, but I MUST MAKE MYSELF.

BOY: I could call myself another –

LEAR: No. We cannot turn the world over. We must love it as it is. The helm now.

(*The BOY puts LEAR's helmet on, then runs off. The army begins passing over the stage in its retreat. LEAR is quite stationary. The BISHOP passes, stops.*)

BISHOP: I found five candlesticks in a burning church. But we must loot. How else can we assuage our impotence? And I'm a bishop! Why do I need candlesticks?

(*He goes out. The others pass. At last, KENT. He stops.*)

KENT: You want to be the last. But I am. (*LEAR doesn't move.*) They say sacrifice is worthless if the object of the sacrifice is itself unworthy. But they who say that don't understand sacrifice.

(*Pause. At last LEAR moves off. KENT follows, the last to leave a devastated country. LEAR's Kingdom.*

PRUDENTIA alone.)

PRUDENTIA: I wanted my daughter back. Oh, my little daughter. I wanted my daughter dead. Oh, my excellent daughter. I wanted none of them back. Oh, my perfect solitude. I don't know why I like the law so much, I think because it's bottomless, I think because it's interminable, and absolute in five hundred volumes. THERE A PAIN CAN BE ASPHYXIATED. (*LEAR enters, almost on tiptoe.*) A man can lose his hand for theft on Tuesday but not on Saturday. DON'T THINK THAT'S RIDICULOUS. On Tuesday he has had time to weigh alternatives, but by Saturday his morality is tired. You're not dead, then? (*LEAR stops.*) To be honest I would not care if you – and she too – alive? If you were three bones in Asia – and I like libraries, they contain on average one truthful book, but finding it! That's the nightmare, and truth's a thing you can grow out of, I – (*Pause.*)

LEAR: Any other men?

(*Distant sound of parades and rejoicing.*)

PRUDENTIA: My health has been good. Every day I walk. And eating simple food, which is in any case the easiest to find, the shortages have been most exasperating to a scholar but – (*Pause.*)

LEAR: Any other men?

PRUDENTIA: And I plant roses. Only white. Though white is never white. My little garden has a dozen whites, all white and yet –

LEAR: No others, then. (*Pause.*)

PRUDENTIA: Take off your shirt. Obsessionist. (*He removes it, slowly.*) I knew this would be the style of your return. The banners dragging in the dust. The shuffling feet of the humiliated. And your grin.

LEAR: I burned five towns!

(*She looks at him, at last.*)

I poisoned all their rivers!

And dragged ploughs through their palaces.

PRUDENTIA: Oh, Lear... I thrive on your insanity.

(*She reaches out, touches him with the tips of her fingers.*)

LEAR: Tell me I can do no wrong.

PRUDENTIA: All wrongs are right with you.

LEAR: Tell me my excellence.

PRUDENTIA: All you are is excellence.

LEAR: My sin, even?

PRUDENTIA: Even that is grace.

(*He laughs, shuddering with relief. They embrace. GONERIL hurries in.*)

GONERIL: My birth! My birth was far from easy!

(*CLARISSA enters, holding her belly.*)

CLARISSA: My child comes!

(*LEAR and PRUDENTIA skip apart. A pandemonium of doctors and midwives. A couch.*)

GONERIL: I was reluctant. No, that's understatement. I was recalcitrant. Even that won't do! I FIXED MY HEELS IN HER BELLY AND STUCK!

LEAR: (*Horrified by CLARISSA's pain.*) I hate this...! (*She cries.*) I hate this...!

SURGEON: Turn her on her side and throw cold water on her back!

ASSISTANT: (*Calling off.*) COLD WATER!

GONERIL: I sensed – out there – was vile.

LEAR: (*Wringing his hands.*) I hate this... I hate this!

SURGEON: A dead cat on her stomach!

ASSISTANT: (*Calling.*) DEAD CAT!

LEAR: Is it always like this?

PRUDENTIA: (*As a MAN enters with a bucket.*) Why a dead cat?

GONERIL: I clung – and yet – hearing my father, thought – how kind his voice is…

(*A bucket of water is thrown over CLARISSA. She gasps.*)

PRUDENTIA: A dead cat, why?

SURGEON: WHY NOT A DEAD CAT! DIDN'T YOU REQUIRE A DEAD CAT?

PRUDENTIA: Never.

SURGEON: That is your tragedy.

ASSISTANT: Dead cat!

(*An animal is carried in.*)

LEAR: I am to blame! I am to blame!

CLARISSA: (*In throes of pain.*) YOU ARE TO BLAME!

LEAR: I said so, didn't I!

SURGEON: Face down, now!

PRUDENTIA: FACE DOWN?

SURGEON: You talk too much! You create a most unhelpful atmosphere in which the miracle of birth can be enjoyed by –

LEAR: NO MORE LOVE. NO MORE LOVE.

SURGEON: SHUT UP, YOU ARE NOT CONTRIBUTING.

PRUDENTIA: (*Holding his hand swiftly.*) Go into the garden.

LEAR: Yes.

(*He turns to go.*)

SURGEON: We'll save the child.

(*He returns to the patient. LEAR is struck, his mind races.*)

LEAR: Save the child – then –

PRUDENTIA: GET THIS CAT OFF!

LEAR: Save the child? You mean –

SURGEON: (*Grappling with PRUDENTIA.*) YOU ARE SABOTAGING THIS DELIVERY!

GONERIL: (*As they fight over the birth couch.*) A FIGHT AT PARTURITION! HOW COULD I HAVE BEEN ANYTHING BUT SAVAGE? And yet… I heard my father… Suffer… (*She skips out.*)

SURGEON: I TAKE NO FURTHER PART IN THIS, I RETIRE FROM ALL, PLEASE WITNESS, I WITHDRAW FROM ALL, AND DENY RESPONSIBILITY FOR ALL. Collect my bag, John we are going home.

ASSISTANT: (*Going out.*) You can easily remarry...
(*The thought penetrates LEAR.*)

LEAR: Obviously I can remarry... An Asian princess,
possibly... I like their eyes...
WHAT IS TO BE DONE WITH ME? I THINK I AM EVIL!
(*CLARISSA and PRUDENTIA deliver the child. It gives a first cry.*)
Evil because...
Evil accommodates every idea...

PRUDENTIA: (*Bringing the child over.*) I think the child
wants you...

LEAR: Me?

PRUDENTIA: Look. It does want you...!
(*He holds it.*)

CLARISSA: Lear...

LEAR: How beautiful it is! But only beautiful because it owes
its life to me...

CLARISSA: Lear...!

LEAR: The nature of beauty, as of goodness, rests in its power
to substantiate the self... Which is not goodness at all, is it?
(*He wanders off, thinking, still holding the child.*)

CLARISSA: Lear...!
(*CLARISSA alone with PRUDENTIA and a SERVANT.*)
Bring my red bird!

PRUDENTIA: (*At her side.*) Rest, now...!

CLARISSA: I think I am living with a murderer!

PRUDENTIA: Shh, now...

CLARISSA: All kings are murderers, BUT I THINK I AM LIVING
WITH A TORTURER, BRING MY RED BIRD!
(*The SERVANT hurries out.*)

PRUDENTIA: Shh... shh...

CLARISSA: All kings are torturers, but WHY DO YOU ALWAYS
APOLOGIZE FOR HIM? (*Pause.*) That is suspicious, though
I hate suspicion. And yet it will occur to me no matter
what I.

PRUDENTIA: You are so –

CLARISSA: Delirious, of course I am, HAVE HIM IF YOU WANT
TO. NAKED AND.

(*The SERVANT brings the cage and places it by her. He goes out.*)

That is a terrible accusation, mother. And I uttered it.

PRUDENTIA: Yes.

CLARISSA: Crossing the desert I felt once – so clearly – no one will ever love me.

PRUDENTIA: That's silly, that's –

CLARISSA: No, don't pity me! I don't mean I wept. I was not desolated, I felt – a quality in me forbids it. A good quality, perhaps.

PRUDENTIA: I want to hold you, and yet I can't.

CLARISSA: That's funny.

PRUDENTIA: Yes. Believe me when I say I want to hold you.

CLARISSA: Yes, but it makes no sense. (*Pause.*) I should sleep now! Perhaps when I wake up I shan't suffer this oppression…

(*She sleeps.*)

PRUDENTIA: I also want a child…are you asleep? I also want a child…

(*She goes to leave. Semi-darkness, out of which a white plane suddenly descends.*)

FOURTH LEAR

THE GAOL: LEAR
    WE ARE FAMILIAR WITH THE LIES OF POLITICIANS
    THEIR GRINS AND HANDSHAKES WE DESPISE
    AND THE FREEDOM FIGHTERS
    WHO TRUSTS THEIR PASSIONATE EMBRACES?
    THEIR CLENCHED FISTS WHICH DON'T UNCLENCH
    LOOK OUT FREEDOM'S FIST IN YOUR EYES!
    LEAR
    OUR CALLS MUST REACH YOUR BEDROOM
    ON STILL NIGHTS WHEN YOU SLEEP ALONE
    THE LOCKS LOCKED
    THE BOLTS BOLTED
    AND THE SHUTTERS TIGHT
    THE MOON IS WALKING IN THE GARDENS
    AND WE SAY

LEAR IS THINKING OF OUR PAIN TONIGHT!

(*The white plane descends, in the opposite direction. The* BOY *runs in. Dogs bark.*)

BOY: Fell there! (*He runs off.*) Fell there!

(*LEAR enters, with an INVENTOR.*)

LEAR: Is this with God's permission? Or is it against God?

INVENTOR: He gave us word. He gave us paper. And he gave us curiosity.

LEAR: But not wings.

INVENTOR: Not wings, no.

LEAR: He did not intend us to be birds, or we should be thick with feathers. But does he resent us becoming birds? There is the question.

INVENTOR: He is eager for us to be so. But he requires we ourselves furnish the means. He says, I give you intelligence. Employ it, therefore. The means I will provide, the will you must discover.

LEAR: I have the will.

INVENTOR: He says the earth is a most imperfect place, go forth and tidy it.

LEAR: Yes.

INVENTOR: After all, did He not have a mere seven days to make it?

LEAR: No time at all.

INVENTOR: He knew even the infant would place his finger in the caterpillar's path. Why? To observe how it altered its behaviour. So every man inflicts himself on his terrain. The horse is placed in shafts. The peasant turns the water's course to his advantage. And even in the death cell the prisoner tutors the mouse. God smiles at this. God claps.

(*The BOY appears holding the damaged plane.*)

BOY: Busted.

LEAR: Correct its faults.

(*The INVENTOR bows.*)

Then make the full-sized version. (*He bows again.*)

I'll fly myself. (*He goes out.* LEAR *seizes the BOY in an embrace.*)

Here's peace! Here's goodness, surely? Here's truth without contradiction?

BOY: You're hurting me… (*LEAR looks at him. Pause.*) Yes…
    (*KENT enters. The BOY runs out.*)
LEAR: Ah, I do so hate to see you sometimes. Always grave.
    Always responsible. I never had an uncle but you must be
    what uncles look like. I never had a friend, but you must
    be what friends aspire to. You are going to reprimand me.
    (*Pause.*) Or shall I make the speech? I could.
KENT: Everything is neglected.
LEAR: Yes.
KENT: To take a single example, the roads are pits.
LEAR: The people move too much. Look at all these accidents.
KENT: I beg you to be –
LEAR: PEOPLE MUST KEEP STILL.
    What connection is there between movement and
    knowledge? None, I promise you. Anything else?
KENT: The river burst its banks.
LEAR: It's the rain does it.
KENT: Obviously, but –
LEAR: If we control the river, we shall control the lake.
    If we control the lake we shall control the weather.
    If we control the weather we shall abolish rain, for no one
    likes to get his head wet. Then we shall starve. No, it's
    better we endure floods.
KENT: We? The castle's on a hill.
LEAR: It is much closer to the lightning.
KENT: ALL THESE UNNECESSARY DEATHS!
LEAR: Unnecessary deaths? And what is a necessary one?
KENT: YOU IRRITATE MY LOYALTY WITH SUCH FATUOUS –
LEAR: And you my patience with inanity! (*Pause.*)
    No, we must be friends. Mustn't we? If friends we are.
KENT: I think, Lear, in your case, there is no fitting the hand
    of intelligence into the glove of government.
LEAR: None. And I gave you the chance to kill me in the
    desert… (*KENT walks away.*) They say you are a nice man!
    But wouldn't a nice man kill me, in order to be nice to
    others?
    (*A thin bell rings. A pair of BEGGARS enter, one mute.*)

Hey! Two of my happy subjects! What, brothers, no clinic?
No warm house? No hot dinners? There's the man! Protest!
(*He points to KENT.*)
He says you should not die – unnecessarily!
(*KENT goes out in disgust.*)
I feel you ought to live to ninety, but what's ninety? No,
that's unjust, seven hundred would be better, UGH, THAT
SORE IS VILE…!
(*He turns in horror, then slowly, turns back and compels
himself to examine it. The BEGGAR rings the bell.*)
You have the sore… I have the coin… I give you the
coin…you still have the sore… (*He holds out money.*)
BEGGAR: Give you the sore with pleasure.
LEAR: (*As the BEGGAR pockets the coin.*) Do you believe in
    anything?
BEGGAR: Yes. Tomorrow.
LEAR: Is that so? I fear tomorrow. I fear tomorrow I may
    doubt the few things I succeeded in believing in today.
    (*The BEGGAR sets off.*)
DON'T GO I'M THE MONARCH.
(*The BEGGAR stops.*)
I do think it's funny, that you and I have nothing in
common. Less even than a cow and a crow. Or a worm
and a horse. Less than them, even.
BEGGAR: They share the field, at least.
LEAR: They share the field, yes.
(*The BEGGAR sets off with a ring of his bell.*)
DON'T GO I'LL STAB YOU!
(*The BEGGAR stops.*)
BEGGAR: I'll starve to death if I must listen to your logic –
LEAR: (*Cruelly.*) I NEED IT. AS YOU NEED BREAD, I NEED IT.
    (*Pause. The BEGGAR shrugs.*)
BEGGAR: At least give us another coin. (*LEAR spins one.*)
LEAR: I'm sure we must have one thing in common. Don't we?
    ONE THING?
BEGGAR: I shit.
LEAR: Yes, well there is a beginning.
BEGGAR: And piss.

LEAR: There's another, but don't be coarse I'll have your tongue out. This is a polite society.

BEGGAR: I was born, and I must die.

LEAR: The first yes, the second we don't know yet.

BEGGAR: Must die, obviously.

LEAR: What's obvious about it? (*He spins another coin.*) All we know is that all others die. From that it cannot be deduced we also shall. Perhaps you are immortal. It would be like immortality to bestow itself on something so grotesque and unbenign as you. DON'T RING THE BELL, I'M TALKING. (*Pause. The BEGGAR is patient.*) How greedy you are. I have already given more than you could hope to beg in seven days and far from creating in you a sense of gratitude you are ringing now from pure avarice!
(*Pause. The BEGGAR is so uncomfortable under LEAR's examining gaze that he fumbles for the money in his pockets and flings it down.*)

BEGGAR: I can't stick this! Take it! Can I go now, monarch?
(*The coin rolls over the floor. The BEGGARS get up to go.*)

LEAR: A duke has died without an heir. Of some place known as Gloucester.

BEGGAR: Tramped there…

LEAR: Good. You are his successor.
(*The BEGGAR stares at LEAR.*)

BEGGAR: What is this? Torture?

LEAR: YOU THINK YOU ARE THE ONLY ONE WHO'S TORTURED? (*A smile comes over the BEGGAR's face. He grasps his mute companion.*)
Not him.

BEGGAR: I've tramped with him eleven years.

LEAR: This is a journey you must make alone.

BEGGAR: He has no tongue and –
(*LEAR, mocking dumbness, shakes his head. A pause of sufficient brevity. Then the BEGGAR disburdens himself of his bags and satchels and drapes his companion with them. He kisses him swiftly on the cheek and gives him the bell. The CHORUS enters.*)

LEAR: Let no one say I hide things from myself.

THE GAOL: LEAR

LEAR: Let no one say I do not see all sides of the argument.

THE GAOL: LEAR

LEAR: All consequences and connections.

THE GAOL: LEAR

LEAR: Ramifications and –

THE GAOL: LEAR

LEAR: I had not forgotten you. One whim could liberate you. So small an action on my part. And yet. (*An effect of sound and light. An airplane is revealed.*) For this a hundred children starved. For this, four thousand went without arithmetic. And groves of soft fruit perished…
(*The BOY enters holding LEAR's flying kit. LEAR extends his hands for the gloves. PRUDENTIA enters. She looks at him.*)

INVENTOR: The wings rotate at seven revolutions to the minute, the mean average of the herring gull. The thickness of the air will cause the craft to float as boats do on water and possibly you may effect a landing on the clouds, the upper sides of which it is believed by us contain estates of lush cultivation.

PRUDENTIA: My body is a better medium to move in, did I not praise you enough, I am forever praising you, this is an affront to me, this is a criticism, or rather a pique, a little criticism worthy of an infant and not a solution.

GONERIL: (*Entering.*) Do go, and hurry, I love you!

PRUDENTIA: The things you have called me, the abuse and the superlatives, my coarse hound, you raised me up against the factory gates one night, there was flight if ever flight was.

GONERIL: And bring me something!

PRUDENTIA: HAVE I NO POWER OVER YOU!

GONERIL: Something big and lovely!

PRUDENTIA: I shan't plead! I shan't wheedle! If you fall dying to the ground I'll put up my skirts and piss your face with anger, do you hear me? Do take the gauntlets off you look an idiot but I'm the only one who'll tell you, it takes love to properly humiliate, die for all I care, but not absurdly, please, it mocks me also…! (*CLARISSA enters, pregnant with REGAN.*)

CLARISSA: Don't fly.

PRUDENTIA: He flies because he hates us.

GONERIL: Be quiet, I want a present!

CLARISSA: Don't fly.

LEAR: If I discover paradise, I shan't come back. At least until I discover paradise is wanting. Kiss me all those who loved me, and the rest, pretend.

(*The COURTIERS gather round, but PRUDENTIA and CLARISSA remain still.*)

LEAR: Clarissa, always you make me feel ashamed. And to escape shame, I try to rise above it…

GONERIL: Oh, do go and hurry!

(*The INVENTOR goes to a wing, the BOY to another. A drum is tapped. LEAR, in the pilot's seat, cranks a handle to the rhythm. GLOUCESTER, the elevated beggar, appears resplendent. He goes to HORBLLNG.*)

GLOUCESTER: On Thursday I was a tramp, on Friday I fucked rich women. There's a joke, surely? Don't tell the other tramps! (*He goes to PRUDENTIA.*) Have you a lover?

PRUDENTIA: I am learning to go without one.

GLOUCESTER: Excellent. (*He goes to CLARISSA.*) And you?

CLARISSA: I led an army into Asia…

GLOUCESTER: I saw them. They were on the bridge and I was underneath it.

CLARISSA: I led an army into Asia…

GLOUCESTER: So you said, but I would love to see your belly.

CLARISSA: FOR THIS…! (*The drum beat rises. LEAR cranks faster.*)

HORBLING: The king became a bird, have you heard this one? The king stuck feathers on himself. And the queen said – I SO HATE COMEDY IT MAKES MEN CRUEL! (*The cranking and the drumming reach a climax at the end of which LEAR falls exhausted over the handles. The drumming slows, the wings cease to flap. In the stillness, GLOUCESTER goes to the DRUMMER, takes his sticks, and tosses them onto the floor.*)

GONERIL: Oh, he is not perfect, my father…!

(*CLARISSA goes to her child. She puts her hands on her shoulders.*)

CLARISSA: Lear wished to fly, and could not. And I wish to be happy, and cannot. Always less. Less always. In lessness we must discover plenitude. Less always. Always less.
(*LEAR climbs off the plane and flings himself to the ground. He flattens himself, as if struggling to be drawn into the earth. He writhes. He moans.*)

INVENTOR: It's weight.

CLARISSA: IT IS NOT WEIGHT IT'S PURPOSE.

INVENTOR: The king, though much reduced by fasting, also reduced his energy, thereby demolishing the ratio of power to wing area –

KENT: Shh…

INVENTOR: The necessary combination can be achieved by –

KENT: Shh… (*He goes to usher the INVENTOR away.*)

LEAR: My boy is light…
(*They stop. LEAR rises onto his knees.*)

CLARISSA: Lear, accept the sign.

LEAR: (*To the BOY.*) You're light, aren't you?

CLARISSA: Accept the sign, that also is a proof of wisdom.

LEAR: SIL-ENCE! (*He blocks his ears.*)

BOY: I'll go. But I'll be late for dinner!

LEAR: (*Rising to his feet.*) We'll keep some back.

INVENTOR: (*Moving to the wings.*) Drummer!

CLARISSA: Oh, you are intolerable to a kind mind!

LEAR: AND YOU ARE A GUILLOTINE ON LIPS OR FINGERS!
(*CLARISSA takes GONERIL out.*)
STEEL MOUTH AND STEEL BODY!
(*The BOY climbs up on the plane.*)

BOY: Ready!

INVENTOR: Drum!
(*The DRUMMER beats the cranking rhythm. The INVENTOR and another return to the wings. A wind. The BOY cranks. LEAR hurries forward as a torrent of feathers descends over the stage, obliterating the plane.*)

LEAR: Oh, who loves kings!
Oh, who loves thrones, somebody must!

THE GAOL: HA, HA, HA, HA, HA, HA!

LEAR: Oh, kneel before his severed head, it was so full of passion once!

THE GAOL: HA, HA, HA, HA, HA, HA!

LEAR: The temper of the underdog has its own beauty, but so has the firing squad!

(*Silence. The last feathers fall. Sound of the wind. Nobody moves. Their eyes scan upwards.*)

HORBLING: If ever there was need for humour this is. Since no one else will I.

At certain times only an idiot can find the words so.

His ineptitude uncannily fills the need of.

For example, at Golgotha, there was an idiot. This idiot danced under Christ whilst.

(*Pause. The clothing of the BOY falls out of the sky at LEAR's feet.*)

LEAR HAS KILLED HIS ONE LOVED BOY! (*He points at LEAR.*)

THERE IS THE CAUSE OF ALL OUR DISCONTENT SO.

ACCUSE HIM!

OVERTHROW!

(*No one moves. HORBLING rubs his face ruefully. LEAR picks up the clothing.*)

LEAR: He did not love me. But when I instructed him, he repeated the words. (*He looks around.*) What more can you ask?

GLOUCESTER: (*Coming to him.*) Let's adjourn to a silent room, and ask an old woman to dance naked...

LEAR: Why...?

GLOUCESTER: Or row a skiff to the madhouse on the rocks...

LEAR: Why...? (*GLOUCESTER shrugs.*) It is not life that's sacred. It is death.

INVENTOR: (*Picks up a fragment.*) The structure of the rudder seems –

LEAR: Did he have time to make his death?

INVENTOR: If anything, too flexible, which is not difficult to –

LEAR: His lost years are nothing but could he make his own death, or did you deprive him?

(*The INVENTOR looks uncomfortable.*)

INVENTOR: It is the story of our progress. Grief, and after grief, design. The graveyard and the drawing board.

LEAR: Yes. But we must live our own deaths, and not be cheated. You robbed him with your accident. (*The INVENTOR looks to KENT, anxiously.*) Lock this criminal away, and keep him pencilless. For if he has a pencil, he will invent. And no twigs either, or he'll make charcoal. It is a disease, this rabid invention. (*KENT goes, reluctantly, to arrest the INVENTOR.*) You shuffle, which is a mute criticism of instruction.

KENT: Perhaps you know things which a simple man like me –

LEAR: Come, come, you, simple?

KENT: A man of rather plain intelligence –

LEAR: You, plain? Never. Why this incessant apology, you bolt apology to yourself like armour, and you love my wife. (*Pause. KENT drags the INVENTOR offstage.*)

PRUDENTIA: (*clinging to him.*) Make love to me, you wretched, lonely man.

LEAR: Tuck up your skirt for Gloucester, he has more appetite.

PRUDENTIA: Have you no love for me? I AM SO GLAD YOU ARE NOT DEAD.

LEAR: It's shallow…

PRUDENTIA: Let it be shallow. SO GLAD.

LEAR: It was a lake, and now it is a pool. Soon, it will be a puddle, and the sun will boil it to a dark stain on the pavement.

PRUDENTIA: I have been too loyal.

LEAR: Who knows?

PRUDENTIA: I have made myself a casual possession.

LEAR: Who knows? And once I lay all night on a roof to watch you dressing.

PRUDENTIA: I have no dignity. Come with me. I have no pride.

LEAR: And that's a freedom… (*He puts a hand on her.*) I am waiting to be killed, and no one does it. (*She takes him in her arms. He clings to her.*)

INTERLUDE

The sea shore. The BISHOP paddles, lifting his robe.

THE GAOL: HOW EXCELLENT
   TO BE THE EXECUTED
   HOW EXCELLENT
   TO KNOW YOU CAUSED OFFENCE
   HOW PAINFUL TO BE JUST
   THE VICTIM OF AN ACCIDENT
   A PIECE OF HISTORIC INCONSEQUENCE

   HOW GOOD TO BE AN EXECUTIONER
   THAT ALSO IS A SKILL
   ASK THOSE WHO SUFFERED FROM THE INEPT
   HOW GOOD TO BE AN EXECUTIONER
   HE WALKS HOME WITH A CIVIC SENSE
   (*KENT enters, and watches the BISHOP from a distance.*)
BISHOP: (*Sensing him.*) I have these feet.
   And salt relieves them.
   Sometimes the feet are twice the size.
   Pity me. I do. (*He paddles.*)
   The sea!
   Sometimes it kills, and sometimes it cures.
   Pity me I haven't long to live.
KENT: Nobody likes you.
BISHOP: It's true. I always seem to be thinking something else.
   Behind good-morning even, there is an altogether different
   sentiment. No one likes this, naturally.
KENT: They say you spoiled the king.
BISHOP: Yes, and what are you, the vessel of opinion or do
   you have a –
   OH YOU HAVE A KNIFE
   HE HAS A KNIFE FANCY
   FANCY
   HE HAS A KNIFE
   And look at me, too far from anyone, oh, I have chosen a
   silly time to bathe, no, what is your view, or are you just
   the vessel of opinion? Chuck us a towel.

KENT: Unnecessary.

BISHOP: What, the towel?

KENT: Unnecessary, yes.

BISHOP: Oh, dear, never to have dry feet again. This is the last time I shall get near a vessel of opinion. Who are you doing this for? Everybody? I do love that! You are smothering your personal dislike of violence in the interests of the community. I do love that. Give us a towel.

KENT: No towel.

BISHOP: Time to get rid of the Bishop. Ask Kent. He's free. Seen Kent? I know someone who can stick a knife in. Kent, you mean? Yes, him, but say it's for the people. Oh, Kent, you're in, everybody hates the Bishop, got ten minutes? KENT YOU HAVE NO INTERIOR SIGHT AND YOU PASS THAT OFF AS GOODNESS. (*KENT takes out his knife.*)

KENT: You have to die.

BISHOP: Only me?

KENT: I think so, yes

BISHOP: Only me. Relax, you other criminals. Only me...
    (*Two children appear, GONERIL and REGAN.*)

GONERIL / REGAN: 'ello, 'ello! 'ello!

KENT: Go away. Your mother wants you.

GONERIL / REGAN: 'ello, 'ello 'ello!

BISHOP: COME HERE, DEARIES!

KENT: Oh, you loathsome man...

BISHOP: Yes, but I must be consistent.

GONERIL: What are you doing here?

BISHOP: Not a lot.

REGAN: You don't go to the beach, do you?

BISHOP: No, this is my final visit.

GONERIL: Mummy says steer clear of you.

BISHOP: Difficult, up till now. But from tomorrow, easy. THAT'S ENOUGH WIT, THIS MAN IS OUT TO MURDER ME! (*The CHILDREN stare, open-mouthed. Then they hold hands.*)

REGAN: Swim, then. That way.

KENT: How loathsome, to drape yourself in children.

BISHOP: Yes, how loathsome I appear to want to live. I appear to be prepared to annex anything to hand to

143

perpetuate my miserable life. How loathsome. I really need examining.

GONERIL: Swim for a day and you get to an island.

BISHOP: I haven't a day, unfortunately.

(*Swiftly, he grabs REGAN, thrusting her body in front on him.*)

REGAN: Ow! Mummy!

KENT: Oh, you nauseous and –

GONERIL: (*Rushing off.*) Mummy! Mummy!

BISHOP: Oh, vile thing I am, vile bag of wicked thought and physical corruption, I am so ashamed!

(*Gulls cry. REGAN is stiff and white.*)

KENT: If I doubted the rightness of this murder, this action must confirm it.

BISHOP: Hilarious. Your logic. Hilarious.

REGAN: He'll kill me by mistake!

BISHOP: Well, yes, I think he will. He is a man of real convictions, DON'T MOVE. (*The CHILD stares. At last, the BISHOP pushes her away. She wanders, then runs off.*) How magnificent the gestures of the bad... I did that, not out of love of infants, who are nothing, but because one day I think she will hunt you...

(*KENT goes to him, kills him. The BISHOP sinks into the water. CLARISSA appears, controlling her horror.*)

CLARISSA: I never thought I would give thanks for murder, but I must not hide behind the fiction that all life is good. How simple that would be. How simple and intransigent. Such absolute moralities are frequently the refuge of misanthropy...

KENT: (*Roping up the body.*) Any thought that Lear produced, this man legitimised.

CLARISSA: WE MUST PROTECT THE WEAK AGAINST THE CUNNING.

(*Pause. KENT stops, looks at her.*)

KENT: Yes...

(*The CHILDREN call, off, she goes, swiftly.*)

THE GAOL: OH KENT

YOU EXCELLENT AND PERMANENTLY SERVILE MIND

KENT: The tide...

THE GAOL: EVEN YOUR WORST ENEMY YOU BURY

KENT: How swift this tide is!

THE GAOL: YOUR MOTHER TAUGHT YOU MANNERS AND
YOU CAN'T FORGET
YOUR FATHER SAID TO TELL THE TRUTH AND OPEN
DOORS FOR WOMEN

KENT: Hey! (*A high wind lashes the stage.*) He floats! His corpse
is a balloon of gases!
(*He clings to the body of the BISHOP. Music, which stops with
a burst of sunlight. KENT climbs off the body.*)
God help me... I am on a rock...a fucking rock...and oh...
NOBODY!

BISHOP: There's me...

KENT: No sticks to burn... no fruit to eat... OI! I RAILED OI! I
railed, and then I sat, for standing was pointless. And then
lay, for sitting was pointless...
(*He lies. The sun beats down. His hand goes to his crotch.*)
Clarissa... If three matrons stood between you and my
cock I'd savage them ANYBODY LISTENING! (*The sea.*)
Clarissa... I would bend you across my knee and stare into
your cavity... ANYBODY LISTENING!
(*The sea.*)

BISHOP: Sun...surely?

KENT: I would walk over the mouths of the world's poor to
grasp you by the –

BISHOP: Salt water, obviously...

KENT: (*Prodding the body.*) Get back! (*The BISHOP laughs.*) Get
back. (*Pause.*)
I pushed it away, but back it came, on every tide...my
superior in perception...

FIFTH LEAR

*A hammering at a door. LEAR, bearded, on a bed. A window, with
a number of kites outside, flying, indicating the height of the room.
HORBLING enters.*

HORBLING: I knock. But that's a formality. I have permission.

145

Permission, and more permission. For what? What's
permission if imagination's dead? (*He goes to LEAR.*) Are
you asleep? I bring petitions. From the inventor, asking
for his sentence to be halved. And the rest are from the
inveterately cruel. They give them to me because Kent's
missing. By the time I reach the top of the stairs I am
carrying my own weight in paper.
(*He drops a pile of petitions on the floor. He watches the kites
move.*)
Why don't you give them bread? I don't understand it.
There is enough bread. You get the loaf and you go – (*He
pretends to break it.*) Two people fed! And you take the
two halves and you – (*He mimes breaking them again.*) Four
people fed! I really do not understand –
(*PRUDENTIA enters.*)

PRUDENTIA: Weren't you the minister under the old king?

HORBLING: Me?

PRUDENTIA: Yes. Horbling, wasn't it?

HORBLING: I don't think so. Or was I? Oh, yes, but briefly!
(*LEAR sits up. The sound of metallic footsteps outside.*) What's
that? (*They come nearer.*) Your assassins, I presume...?
(*Two armoured FIGURES appear in the door. HORBLING
rushes to them.*)
There he sits! Eliminate the bloody oppressor of widows
and orphans! Strike and.
(*He stops. He sits. LEAR comes to the FIGURES, and looks at
them. They begin to shake, with laughter.*)

GONERIL / REGAN: Oh, Dad, our hearts ache for you!
(*They throw off their helmets.*)

REGAN: Such trickery to reach our father, so immured is he in
his tower!

GONERIL: But love will always find a way!

REGAN: Love does!

GONERIL: Love will!

GONERIL / REGAN: Love always –
(*They revolve in an embrace, stop.*)

REGAN: Why is our mother's mother here?

GONERIL: We reach our non-existent dad and –

REGAN: Why is our mother's mother here?

(*PRUDENTIA moves to the bed, and sits.*)

GONERIL: (*Bursting with pleasure again.*) We were going to sing you a song!

REGAN: We learned a song!

GONERIL: But now we're too happy to sing! Do you admire us?

REGAN: We're women of EXCEPTIONAL INITIATIVE you must admit!

(*She kisses LEAR.*)

GONERIL: We're giggling!

REGAN: We're frothing!

GONERIL / REGAN: How clever to get past the guards!

REGAN: Do we embarrass you!

GONERIL / REGAN: PAIR OF IDIOTS!

(*LEAR holds them to his chest.*)

GONERIL: I passed my exams!

REGAN: And I learned archery!

GONERIL: I can swim the rivers both ways!

REGAN: Boys we hate

GONERIL: But horses!

REGAN: We're giggling!

GONERIL: We're frothing!

GONERIL / REGAN: WE EMBARRASS HIM!

(*A pause. LEAR examines them.*)

REGAN: How warm your hands are, like loved garments…and the smell… (*She kisses his hands.*)

LEAR: Every moment I yielded up to love…has lost to my own struggle…

GONERIL: (*Peering into him.*) What struggle…?

REGAN: Look, his feet point inwards still…!

LEAR: Every excellence of intimacy broke the thin wire of my concentration…

GONERIL: Yes…?

LEAR: I wish to be a saint, and all your charm, and love, and small, round voices, washed like a babbling stream the mortar from the joints of my great arch, I want to be a saint and more so than a father…

GONERIL / REGAN: Yes, yes! And that is why we love you!

REGAN: We said that together!

GONERIL / REGAN: DO IGNORE US IF YOU WISH!

GONERIL: And that, too!

PRUDENTIA: I encouraged him. In every thing, I encouraged him. Because he is a great man.

HORBLING: She says so, but where's the evidence? She asserts it, but where's the proof? If he is great why are the poor poor? This tower is so tall their dying groans don't reach him.

PRUDENTIA: Yes, he is a perfect man, and you screech like a duck drowned by its companions.

REGAN: Why is our mother's mother here?

GONERIL: She cleans does she?

REGAN: She makes the beds?

HORBLING: Makes the beds untidy, yes, by manoeuvring upon her arse. DON'T PUNISH IT'S ALL IN THE PAST, as the killer said to the widow.

GONERIL: Why does the king like you?

HORBLING: Good question. He brought me up this tower and gave me a spoon. That may be fondness, that may be not. If A is sent to gaol and invites B to join him, is that friendship? Ponder. Ponder. If B refuses, is that bad manners?

LEAR: (*To his daughters.*) Leave us now. You've grown, that's obvious. Whether you're beautiful is for other men to judge, and whether you're intelligent is insignificant, for if you're not, others will be.

GONERIL: You once ran with me the length of the sea-shore. I've never forgotten that.

LEAR: I loved you insanely. But in loving you insanely, I only loved myself.

REGAN: Come out and govern the world.

PRUDENTIA: He had a teacher, but now he teaches himself.

GONERIL / REGAN: WHAT IS OUR MOTHER'S MOTHER DOING HERE?

(*The ground. The CHORUS are seen holding the kite strings and staring up to LEAR's window.*)

THE GAOL: FOR EVERY CHILD THAT DIES WE FLY A KITE
   LEAR
   ARE YOU NOT BLIND WITH KITES?
   FOR EVERY SUICIDE THAT LEAPS INTO THE RIVER
   WE FLY A KITE
   LEAR
   HOW DARK YOUR ROOM MUST BE!
   (*CLARISSA enters, holding a loud-hailer. She puts it to her lips and addresses LEAR.*)

CLARISSA: I most tenderly wish to see you.
   I most anxiously want to touch you.
   I married you.
   I saved you from your enemies.
   I will not be dissuaded from you no matter what indifference you show.
   My bird is dead but I have learned his patience.
   And if you hate my voice it is no more than I hate it myself.
   (*The strings move in the wind. She gives the loud-hailer to a MAN. He proceeds to reiterate her speech.*)

MAN: She most tenderly wishes to see you. She most anxiously wants to touch you. She married you. She saved you from your enemies. She will not be dismissed from you no matter what indifference you show. Her bird is dead but she has learned his patience And if you hate her voice, it is no more than she hates it herself.
   (*He walks to a new spot to repeat the message.*)

CLARISSA: Every day I'm here. Every day the message seems less true. But it is not less true merely from being repeated.
   (*REGAN and GONERIL appear, elated.*)

GONERIL / REGAN: WE SAW HIM!

GONERIL: And he is beautiful!

REGAN: He wears black!

GONERIL: Aged a little –

REGAN: Considerably aged!

GONERIL: Considerably aged yes –

REGAN: But silent!

GONERIL: Almost –

REGAN: Almost silent, yes –

GONERIL / REGAN: AND THERE IS A WOMAN THERE WHO LOOKS AS IF. (*GLOUCESTER enters.*)

GLOUCESTER: I go to the brothel. I do not expect to be happy in the brothel. But there at least I am able to suffocate the question whether I am happy or not. (*He looks up.*) What does he do up there? (*He goes out.*)

CLARISSA: (*To her MAN.*) When she comes down, my mother, hood her, and in the hood, bring her to me. Do it if she cries or struggles. But hood her. (*He bows.*) I MEAN HOWEVER PAINFUL DO IT.
(*He goes out. She looks to GONERIL and REGAN half-afraid. But they are bland.*)

GONERIL: What kind of grandmother was that?

REGAN: She never played with us.

GONERIL / REGAN: AT THAT AGE YOU SURELY SHOULD BE NICE!
(*They run out. CLARISSA looks at the CHORUS of the poor, as they pluck their kite strings, moving together like tillers of a field.*)

CLARISSA: I so hate lies. But, look, the poor! (*She looks at them silently moving.*) I so hate subterfuge. But, look, the destitute! (*She looks. She hurries away. PRUDENTIA hooded is brought in by TWO MEN.*)

PRUDENTIA: It's all right, I can walk! Oh, let me walk! Why drag me when I have –

FIRST MAN: LEGS!

PRUDENTIA: Legs, yes –

SECOND MAN: WE SEE YOUR LEGS!

FIRST MAN: And wonder –

SECOND MAN: WHERE HAVE THEY BEEN, THOSE LEGS?

FIRST MAN: WHERE HAVE THEY THRASHED THE SKY, DON'T WE? (*They place her on a stool.*) The pleasure it gives us to grab a lawyer. We were so abused by you in courts. You and your vocabulary. You and your wit.

BOTH MEN: YOU CALLED US THINGS AND IT STUCK LIKE SPIT TO OUR EXPRESSIONS. ADMIT OUR PLEASURE. NO HUMAN COULD RESIST.

(*They stand back from her.*)

PRUDENTIA: Do you know who I am?

FIRST MAN: Yes.

PRUDENTIA: Do you realise the perilous position you have placed yourselves in?

SECOND MAN: We realise your legal language is quite dead.

FIRST MAN: Oh, immaculately exercised legs. Grandmother...
(*They creep away, silently. CLARISSA appears.*)

CLARISSA: Oh, mother, thank you for years of love...
(*She collapses onto another stool, holding her head in her hands.*)
I must leave you hooded because if your eyes meet mine, no thing that is correct could be articulated...

PRUDENTIA: Take it off.

CLARISSA: Your eyes would make all crime like passing showers.

PRUDENTIA: Remove it, then.

CLARISSA: Precisely what I cannot for the reasons I have just –

PRUDENTIA: Excellent reasons.

CLARISSA: Are they, though?

PRUDENTIA: Yes, it's truth which burns out argument.

CLARISSA: I WILL NOT HAVE YOU UNCOVERED ALL MY LIFE I HAVE BEEN DOMINATED. WORDS. AXES. LOOKS. CLUBS. (*Pause.*) Pity me, because this is so difficult.

PRUDENTIA: I pity nobody.

CLARISSA: NOT EVEN THE POOR.

PRUDENTIA: Not even them. (*Pause.*)

CLARISSA: You have been seized because – (*She stops, shakes her head.*) No, I seized you. I did. Because things can't go on.

PRUDENTIA: They can if no one puts an end to them.

CLARISSA: They can't go on and –

PRUDENTIA: NO ONE HAS TO ACT. (*Pause.*) This acting. This intervening. This putting stops to things. Who obliges you, Clarissa?

CLARISSA: My conscience.

PRUDENTIA: Put it to sleep, then. Strike it with a shovel. Like a senile dog, one swift and clean blow kills it. I was spun by conscience like a top. And when it died I came to life. The top ceased spinning. Look how you shiver. Look how manifestly you are inferior to me. Do I shiver? You are in the blindfold.

CLARISSA: I THINK YOU LIE IN BED WITH MY HUSBAND AND –

(*She shakes her head like a cat in a bag.*)

No!

No!

Do what you wish, I am not censorious, do what comes to you, but out there is all starvation and mismanagement and you encourage him!

PRUDENTIA: I could have read this diatribe off any wall.

CLARISSA: Yes.

PRUDENTIA: When a child dies they fly a black rag.

CLARISSA: Yes.

PRUDENTIA: And for every suicide a white.

CLARISSA: You notice, then?

PRUDENTIA: You think the recitation of their agony could alter his pursuit? The sky could be thick in kites and the sun dead. (*Pause.*)

CLARISSA: I think your passion, which was magnificent, perhaps, has gone misshapen with obsession, and your love has failed, for love must also be correction –

PRUDENTIA: Ha!

CLARISSA: Yes, love says because I love you I forbid you this or this –

PRUDENTIA: Ha!

CLARISSA: Ha! as much as you like, I am not deterred – a proper love is a matter of fine balances –

PRUDENTIA: FINE BALANCES.

CLARISSA: And equilibrium –

PRUDENTIA: EQUILIBRIUM!

CLARISSA: Yes! And how you hate those things, how you strangle the clean things in yourself –

PRUDENTIA: THIS IS CLEAN. (*Pause.*)

Shh!

That's him! He calls me from the tower!

(*She stands, head tilted.*)

CLARISSA: I think you are guilty. Of smothering your self.
Which also is a murder.

PRUDENTIA: He is a great man, and I gave him birth. More so
than his mother. (*CLARISSA sobs violently.*)

CLARISSA: How your reproaches twist my stomach, and pulp
my little heart…

(*LEAR's distant cry is heard. In a spontaneous gesture,
PRUDENTIA reaches out her hands to CLARISSA. CLARISSA
does not accept them.*)

NO LOVE WITHOUT CRITICISM!

(*She looks at her mother. PRUDENTIA's hands fall.*)

And I must see you. I must not hide.

(*She pulls away PRUDENTIA's blindfold. She stoops in front
of her, looking into her eyes.*)

How hard this is.

But I.

And I.

Can.

THE GAOL: OH, GOOD!

SHE'S EVIL IF THE WORD HAS MEANING

OH, GOOD!

WE DO HATE PUNISHMENT BUT SOME IT MUST BE SAID

DESERVE

OH, GOOD!

IN THIS CASE HUMAN DIGNITY CRIES OUT FOR

ONE OR THOSE RARE OCCASIONS WHEN EVERYBODY

MUST

AGREE

COLLECTIVELY WE MUST RESPOND

MUSTN'T WE

(*An effect of sound.
LEAR runs in to an empty stage, bright as day. GLOUCESTER
is shambling.*)

LEAR: Hey!

GLOUCESTER: Shh, I'm depressed…

LEAR: Have you seen a woman?

GLOUCESTER: I'm so depressed…

LEAR: In a red skirt and –

GLOUCESTER: I'M TOO DEPRESSED. (*He sits. LEAR sees another.*)

LEAR: Hey! (*The FIGURE stops.*) Have you seen a woman?

HERDSMAN: What do you want a woman for?

LEAR: I want her because – (*He ponders.*) I no longer have her.

HERDSMAN: But when you had her –

LEAR: None of your peasant wisdom. I am Lear. Nothing you can tell me I did not already know at birth. She wore a red skirt.

HERDSMAN: I could have been a monarch. I was born in the wrong room however. (*He laughs coarsely.*)

LEAR: (*Going close to him.*) I said none of your profundity you ambling and complacent self-regarding parcel of banality, if she's dead I also wish to die. (*Pause.*)

HERDSMAN: She is.

LEAR: She is, is she?

HERDSMAN: The king's whore's dead.

LEAR: The king's whore, yes, that is the one I am referring to. The slag. The man-lover whose parted limbs are ridiculed in public places.

HERDSMAN: Dead yes, what more can I say?

LEAR: No more. Now murder me.

HERDSMAN: I would, except it's treason.

LEAR: I give you permission, here. (*He scrawls on a scrap of paper.*) Command, it says, and that's my signature.

HERDSMAN: I'd rather not.

LEAR: Piss your preference, do it, here's the knife.

HERDSMAN: Look, there's Jack over there –

LEAR: Fuck Jack, you are the chosen –

(*He thrusts the knife into the HERDSMAN's hand.*)

HERDSMAN: There are more women than –

(*LEAR seizes him by the throat.*)

LEAR: LIAR! HE TELLS ME THERE ARE MORE WOMEN THAN ONE! LIAR! THERE WAS ONLY ONE!

(*The HERDSMAN drops the knife and runs.*)

Thrash him for lying! Break him on some wheel for lying!
I never lie! Every word I look at, both from the front and
the back…! (*Pause.*)

GLOUCESTER: I go to the brothel. I say to the girl, act
naturally, as if I were repulsive to you. 'You, repulsive?',
she says. YOU ARE SUCH A BAD INTERPRETER OF MY
NEEDS, I say, with an artificial grin. I do detest you. I do
resent your ignorance. If I wanted love, I'd find it…
(*KENT enters, slowly. He looks at LEAR.*)

KENT: I have been six years on a rock.

LEAR: And I six in a tower.

KENT: I thought of a woman. This kept me sane.

LEAR: And I through one. This maddened me.

HERDSMAN: (*Returning.*) Changed my mind. I thought, I'll do
this. How my neighbours will congratulate me. Michael,
they'll say, it is a privilege to shake your bloody hand.
Wash it never.

LEAR: Too late.

HERDSMAN: No, surely? (*LEAR goes to him, and retrieving the
knife, swiftly kills him.*) Hey…!
(*LEAR goes out.*)

KENT: THE THINGS WE QUARRELLED OVER NOW SEEM
THE THINGS WE STABBED FOR SUDDENLY AREN'T
THE BOOKS WE CARRIED HIGH
ARE ONLY
FIT FOR ARSE PAPER

THE GENIUS WE THOUGHT HAD UNDERSTOOD REALITY
HIS EIGHTY VOLUMES NOW I SAY ARE
HIS BEARD I WISH
HIS TOMB I COULD

THE LITTLE MAN FROM CHINA WITH THE ANSWERS
WAS A TORTURER I NEVER KNEW
I NEVER KNEW
I NEVER KNEW
DID YOU

AND THE POET IN THE TOWER WHO WE CALLED A
FUCKING SNOB
HAS RELEVANCE

SIXTH LEAR

A table. CLARISSA, GONERIL, REGAN seated. LEAR enters.

LEAR: Nearly stupid. (*Pause.*)
But not quite. (*Pause.*)
I am shedding thought as a lout shakes scurf. (*He scratches his head violently, stops.*) Nearly fit to govern. (*CLARISSA extends a hand to him across the table.*) I killed a man and Kent's back.
(*Ignoring her hand he sits. The table is an image of domestic silence. CLARISSA's hand remains until it agonises her.*)

GONERIL: Oh, take back that hand…!

REGAN: Mother!
(*It stays, until at last CLARISSA falls into her chair, her eyes on the floor.*)

CLARISSA: I can't apologise for what was proper. Or that's madness. But for pain, I share that.
(*She looks at LEAR, who extends his arms over the table, so his hands reach for his children, his cheek to the table. They take his hands. They look at their mother. A sound of martial music, light and popular. A BOY DRUMMER enters, drumming, and goes out, followed by LEAR, REGAN and GONERIL. The music fades. KENT appears, behind CLARISSA. He is still.*)
Dear friend, it must be you. And thinking, as usual, how excellent my nature is. (*She shakes her head ruefully.*) At least you are not dead, and anything else is tolerable.

KENT: No one ever gave me a greater compliment.

CLARISSA: No?

KENT: You are truth itself and never need embellishment.

CLARISSA: I bask in your respect but don't make my life more painful.

KENT: How could I do that?

CLARISSA: By showing kindness, which cracks my armour.

KENT: You need not wear armour.

CLARISSA: No? What's life without armour?

KENT: I was on a rock. I travelled to this rock on the corpse of a bad man, bloated by his gases. So there I was, a good man, saved by putrefaction. Every day he came back, on every tide, viler and viler to behold. And then one day, he did not.

CLARISSA: He sank?

KENT: Inevitably, he sank.

(*She senses his movement.*)

CLARISSA: DO NOT UNDRESS. (*Pause.*)

KENT: I entertained such thoughts of you, which if I described, would make you shrink. These thoughts absorbed whole days, and kept me sane, though they were insane thoughts.

CLARISSA: How? Love's kindness.

KENT: Love's not, love never was, and if I'm vile you also are responsible – (*She goes to move.*) DON'T TURN LIKE THAT YOUR HIP –

CLARISSA: (*Amazed.*) What

KENT: YOUR HIP –

CLARISSA: (*Horrified.*) What –

KENT: DOES SUCH

CLARISSA: I cannot help my hip – (*KENT covers his eyes.*) I must have caused this and forgive me, or how could you be so bad? (*He lets his hands fall.*) Your eyes are narrow with a cruelty that distorts your normally kind features, dear friend…

(*He shakes his head laughing.*)

KENT: Oh, words, oh, words kill words…!

(*LEAR returns. He looks at them.*)

LEAR: I spend whole days with Gloucester. He shows me the other kingdom. YOU THINK THERE IS ONE KINGDOM ONLY? Under the kingdom, the kingdom…

KENT: (*Going to him.*) Take your wife, and love her.

LEAR: Why, don't you?

KENT: Yes!

LEAR: Then she's over-loved, because you love her and I am occasionally kind, which is more than most get.

KENT: I love and suffer her.

LEAR: Good! Now have a picnic on the hill! Take some poems and a rug.

KENT: You ought not to…!

LEAR: She reads classics – in translation – at least, the minor
works –

KENT: OUGHT NOT TO.

LEAR: And sings a bit to the guitar, a sort of wail she learned
in adolescent solitude –

KENT: OUGHT NOT TO PISS ON INNOCENCE.

(*LEAR stares at KENT.*)

LEAR: What word is that? I'm nearly stupid now, what is that?

(*The DAUGHTERS enter. They are impatient.*)

GONERIL / REGAN: Our picnic with our mum and dad!

LEAR: Not me! I have a headache!

GONERIL / REGAN: Oh, not another headache!

LEAR: Yes!

CLARISSA: Yes, we need some air!

LEAR: Indeed, take Kent! (*A pause.*)

CLARISSA: I think it's better if we three –

LEAR: Yes, and take Kent!

CLARISSA: The three of us merely –

LEAR: In case of wolves.

GONERIL / REGAN: (*Disbelief.*) WOLVES?

LEAR: Cats, then.

GONERIL / REGAN: WHAT CATS?

LEAR: Angry ones who once were petted. You know, or
hawks with debts to settle. (*He smiles.*) Do. I hate to think of
danger from the wild.

(*Pause. They go out. KENT following. LEAR is left alone.*)

THE GAOL: LEAR...!

OH, LEAR...!

MAY WE DISTURB YOU?

SO MANY PROBLEMS BUT WE HAVE SUFFERED BEYOND
MEASURE.

LEAR: (*Kneeling to them.*) You say this often, as if pain had
measure.

THE GAOL: WE HARP ON JUSTICE HERE

UNTIL THE WORD

EATS TUNNELS THROUGH OUR BRAINS

LEAR: The word's abolished, then, since it grieves so many.
It must be cut out of the dictionary. SCISSORS!

THE GAOL: OH, LEAR
YOU WERE SO MUCH KINDER AS A BOY!

LEAR: Yes, but he was so intelligent, that boy. And he knew
philosophy.

THE GAOL: WHAT IS PHILOSOPHY UNLESS IT DISSOLVES
PAIN? (*LEAR sits, contemplatively, among them.*)

LEAR: Surely, it is melancholy...be assured, I think of you
often...and need you...oh, how I need you...
(*He gets up. The picnic party returns. They look at LEAR.
KENT flings himself to LEAR's feet.*)

KENT: Execute me, then!
(*GONERIL and REGAN go to LEAR.*)

GONERIL / REGAN: We found these flowers! Leaving them
with poems, we found you flowers!

KENT: Execute me, then!

GONERIL: Execute you?

REGAN: Why is he so silly?

GONERIL / REGAN: Execute yourself!
(*LEAR runs his fingers through KENT's hair, absently. The
DAUGHTERS drape LEAR with the wild flowers, and skip off.*)

LEAR: When people loved me – and many have – I felt
burdened. When they ceased to love me – I felt cold...

CLARISSA: I can't talk of love because I know so little of
it. So I'll talk of necessity instead. And how – through
so much – silence – I have longed to be clamoured for.
And even how, perhaps, whoever clamoured would have
earned my – YOU ARE SMILING AND I AM TRYING TO BE
HONEST. (*Pause.*) I am pregnant without question, and not
by you. (*Pause.*) Oh, listen, I had a bird once but the bird
died!
(*Music. The DRUMMER appears again. crossing the stage.
They watch him pass.*)

LEAR: What is he...!
Hey!
What is he...!
(*He runs out. A wind and light change. LEAR enters edging
a barrel painfully onto the stage. The barrel is massive. He*

steadies it, stops. A newborn child is heard. GLOUCESTER
enters holding a bundle. LEAR looks at him over the rim.)

LEAR: Gin.

GLOUCESTER: Bastard. (*LEAR lifts the lid.*)

LEAR: Love…!

(*GLOUCESTER holds out the bundle, then drops it in. LEAR*
replaces the lid.)

GLOUCESTER: Cordelia, she calls it.

LEAR: Thank her. I have seen it, say. And add, Lear was not
more arbitrary than rain. Or earthquakes. Or weapons
badly aimed. (*GLOUCESTER turns to go.*) WE CRAWL ON
THE EARTH LIKE WORMS. (*GLOUCESTER stops.*) But she
knows that. Leave the last line out.

(*GLOUCESTER goes. KENT enters, bows.*)

KENT: The Emperor of Endlessly Expanding Territory.

(*He bows as a DIGNITARY enters, robed.*)

LEAR: I greet my visitors in casual dress, which is a
compliment, given my inclination to be naked. (*The*
EMPEROR looks.) I have no throne but this and you must be
happy with a stool, or did you bring your own?

(*He hops onto the top of the barrel and sits. KENT extends a*
stool to the EMPEROR.)

They report you very wise, which I was as a child and now
am merely arbitrary. The difference is of no significance,
the people will substantiate. (*Pause.*) What do you want?
(*Pause.*)

E OF EET: There are not enough bodies in the world.

(*A pause of gathering comprehension.*)

LEAR: My wife sleeps with another man. I do not love my
wife. What then, is the cause of my anxiety?

(*He hops off the barrel, leans on it thoughtfully. A sound of*
tapping from within.)

My wife will tell me everything because she cannot lie.
Her inability to lie is agony to me. If she were a liar I could
tolerate her. I might love a liar. If she fucked secretly in
cellars with bald men I'd applaud her. I cannot help the
feeling her honesty is an attempt on my sanity. (*Pause.*)
What do you mean, not enough bodies?

E OF EET: For the faith. (*Pause.*)

LEAR: What faith?

E OF EET: There is only one faith. (*He looks into LEAR.*) Are you not tired from walking in the dark?

LEAR: Yes.

E OF EET: Are you not weary knowing all you know is false?

LEAR: Weary beyond imagination, yes.

E OF EET: And do you not ache for the solution?

LEAR: The solution's death. (*Tapping on the inside of the barrel.*)

E OF EET: But after death?

(*LEAR stares.*)

LEAR: HOR-BLING!

Oh, be careful, you will explode my skull and send the splinters in your eyes!

HOR-BLING!

(*HORBLING enters, springing as best he can and shaking a bell.*)

HORBLING: I'm getting better!

LEAR: (*To the EMPEROR.*) They say you executed seven hundred in an afternoon, I don't criticise, they say you blind adulterers, I don't criticise!

HORBLING: Better, but still not good! (*He skips.*)

LEAR: HE TALKS OF AFTER DEATH.

(*He stares at HORBLING. Sounds from inside the barrel. HORBLING hears it, amazed.*)

E OF EET: I come to you, when being the greatest power in the world, it was more fitting you should come to me. But I have no pride. I never conquer. I only deliver.

(*HORBLING scrambles to the side of the barrel, listens.*)

LEAR: (*Still reeling.*) AFTER – DEATH? (*REGAN and GONERIL enter.*)

GONERIL / REGAN: Our mother says the baby where is it?

LEAR: This man says there are not enough bodies for the faith.

This man has seven million soldiers on the frontiers.

GONERIL / REGAN: Cordelia, she says, where is she?

LEAR: SEVEN MILLION UNAFRAID OF DEATH!

(*The DAUGHTERS look at the EMPEROR.*)

REGAN: Stab him.

GONERIL: Hang him up by his heels.

LEAR: (*To the EMPEROR.*) Children! Aren't they miraculous? Do you have children? I'VE THOUGHT OF THAT.

GONERIL: He would look different naked. Where's the baby, our mother says.

HORBLING: (*Flinging himself at the EMPEROR's feet.*) Seven million? (*He points to LEAR.*) There is the enemy of the faith! There is cynicism and apostasy! (*He drags off his cap and takes out the now decaying papers.*) This plan requires five years to change the kingdom from a lair of beasts to Paradise! Five years, and I revise it frequently, these corrections are illegible I will admit, no – the wrong way up – here – no, that's smudged, it says – I translate – do you have a minute, I – that's the introduction, skip that – it's – this page goes there –
(*He falters as CLARISSA enters.*)

LEAR: She does not put on lipstick, Clarissa. Or any false thing.

CLARISSA: Where is my baby?

GONERIL / REGAN: We asked and he –

CLARISSA: Cordelia?
(*LEAR chooses to be silent, walking a line in silence, and returning to the spot, thoughtfully. CLARISSA lets out a mournful cry. She falls to her knees and beats the ground with her fists.*)
I'VE DONE NOTHING! I'VE DONE NOTHING!
(*She stops. She straightens herself.*)

LEAR: (*To the EMPEROR.*) Do you do dinners? That is what is wanted here. (*The EMPEROR stares at him.*) I loved a woman. She made death possible, and yet to die would be to lose her, therefore she kept me living... (*Pause.*) Bring your armies. And I'll be burned. Or skinned. Or whatever it is you do.
(*Suddenly, as if on an impulse, LEAR rushes to the barrel and flings off the lid, which rolls. He plunges in his arms and pulls out the dripping bundle of CORDELIA.*)
Gin! Gin!

And she still lives! (*He holds it up, smothers it with kisses.*) Oh, was that good?

Oh, was that a good thing, hey?

(*The EMPEROR, in disbelief, rises to his feet. The baby cries.*)

GONERIL / REGAN: (*Jumping up and down.*) OH, OH, OUR SIS-TER! OH, OH, OUR SIS-TER!

(*LEAR thrusts the dripping baby at the girls, and kneeling at the EMPEROR's feet, tears open his collar to expose his throat.*)

LEAR: Seven million daggers.

SEVEN MILLION KNIVES! (*The EMPEROR stares.*)

CLARISSA: (*To the EMPEROR.*) You see how terrible we find life? How it maddens us? Don't offer us another…

(*Pause. The EMPEROR places a hand on her, in a gesture of profound pity. HORBLING tears up his five-year plan, gazing on LEAR, and withdraws. The light changes, the EMPEROR goes out. LEAR remains in the posture.*)

LEAR: I wanted to die. And you saved me. I was ready to die. THE THIRD TIME YOU HAVE SAVED ME!

(*He stares at CLARISSA in horror.*

A second light change. CORDELIA enters.)

CORDELIA: I think if he had drowned me, I should have forgiven him…!

KENT: (*Entering.*) You are at an age when the agonized seem beautiful. Yet there are thousands curse him every day.

CORDELIA: I call them vermin for it!

KENT: I am not trying to make you hate your father, merely – (*He shrugs.*)

CORDELIA: (*To KENT.*) I do think, when you speak, it is as if each word had weights attached to it which catch your teeth. You are utterly kind to me but. Perhaps you harbour some sex thing for me, in which case I wish you'd say – (*KENT seethes.*) Is that wrong? I'm often wrong. I get that from my father, not from my mother, who is never wrong and can't be, it seems.

CLARISSA: (*Extending her hands as if conducting a walk.*) CHIL-DREN!

CORDELIA: But if it is so, I wish you would admit it. A thought is better born than smothered, THERE NOW I SOUND LIKE HER! (*She grins.*)

KENT: NOTHING OF THE SORT. (*Pause.*)

CLARISSA: (*Enters.*) CHIL-DREN!

CORDELIA: Oh, good. (*She smiles.*) Oh, good!

(*REGAN and GONERIL hurry in.*)

GONERIL / REGAN: We're going to a dance.

CLARISSA: Later.

GONERIL / REGAN: Going to a dance and now we're late!

(*They stare at CLARISSA. LEAR is motionless.*)

CLARISSA: I must show you something I have found.

(*The sound of the GAOL.*)

THE GAOL: WHERE'S LEAR?

NO ONE COMES HERE BUT LEAR

YOU HURT OUR EYES WITH STRANGENESS!

GONERIL / REGAN / CORDELIA: Let's play houses! Let's fly kites! LET'S BUILD CASTLES ON THE BEACH!

CLARISSA: Hold hands, I said!

THE GAOL: HE DOES NOT LICENSE VISITORS!

(*Pause. LEAR at last abandons his posture, and rising, comes to them.*)

LEAR: You have found the one place I can discover sanity...

CLARISSA: Free them.

LEAR: You have trespassed in my garden...

CLARISSA: Garden...?

(*Pause. With infinite slowness. a chain swings twice, like a pendulum, between them. A wind.*)

Free them. Lear.

Free them.

THE GAOL: OUR SUFFERING IS OVER

OUR BODIES ARE RETURNED TO US

DO YOU REMEMBER HOW IT FELT TO OWN YOUR BODY?

(*They laugh madly, uncontrollably, and stop.*)

LEAR: I said to the inmates of the gaol, when I have done a crime sufficient to dwarf not only what you did, but what you have imagined, then daylight's yours. The gaoled are only in the gaol by being worse than their gaolers. How else? (*Pause. The chain swings again and stops.*) OH, WHO WILL CORRECT ME WHEN MY WIFE IS GONE?

CORDELIA: I will...

(*REGAN and GONERIL look at each other with profound realisation.*)

GONERIL / REGAN: Let's go to the dance!

CORDELIA: (*Releasing the hand of CLARISSA.*) How hard it is to say this, but I do not pity you. I think you never did a bad thing in your life. Or let a false emotion slip through your net. Or postured. Or ever were corrupt. And I think – shall I go on?

GONERIL / REGAN: Do go on!

CORDELIA: I have a deep and until today, an unstirred hatred for you.

(*The chain swings again.*)

GONERIL / REGAN: IT'S TRUE! IT'S TRUE! SHE DOES SAY THINGS WHICH WE FIND IMPOSSIBLE TO EXPRESS! (*Pause.*)

CLARISSA: Don't hurt me. Someone must do good. And of all people I've done least to – (*Pause. She breaks into a sobbing laugh.*) What's that to do with anything! (*Pause.*) I've never exaggerated. And I am not going to now.

CORDELIA: DO! OH, DO EXAGGERATE...!

(*CLARISSA shakes her head defiantly. The chain passes again. A cacophony breaks in.*)

ALL: MUMMY/DADDY/WHERE ARE MY/GOING TO A DANCE I SAID/HAVE YOU SEEN MY/COMB YOUR HAIR YOU LOOK/DADDY/SHOES AND SOCKS/CHRISTMAS IS SO/WE LOVE EACH OTHER DON'T WE/MUMMY/LOVE EACH OTHER SO/AND HOLIDAYS ARE/WILL YOU STOP QUARRELLING/AND MY DAD SAYS/I SAID STOP THAT/I SAID/I SAID/GET OUT THE PHOTOGRAPHS!

(*The chain again, observed this time by LEAR.*)

LEAR: God wants her for the comfort of His solitude... We can't be blamed...

(*With a sudden access of energy, LEAR leaps and clings to the chain, usurping it.*)

RAISE ME!

RAISE ME THEN, GOD!
(*He swings to and fro, pitiful and absurd. The light on*
CLARISSA fades. After some minutes, GLOUCESTER appears.)

GLOUCESTER: May I have her, do you think? (*They look at*
him.) I mean, there can be no particular requirement for...
When I was a beggar I made lovers of the dead since I
was...scarcely a proper suitor for the living... (*LEAR swings.*)
And they are – perfectly passionate...

CORDELIA: (*To GLOUCESTER.*) Take me away. To some corner
of the wood. And do whatever you do to young women.
(*The DRUMMER is heard, and the band music. LEAR jumps*
down. The THREE DAUGHTERS crowd to LEAR and embrace
him. The DRUMMER comes nearer.)

LEAR: Hey! (*The DRUMMER enters, passing. LEAR chases him.*)
Who are you?

DRUMMER: Happiness!

LEAR: But I never wanted happiness! Why do I follow you,
therefore?
(*A sudden and terrible wind. Snow falls.*)

SEVENTH LEAR

The CHORUS OF THE GAOL lies heaped and dead. LEAR is sitting in
overcoats on a folding stool. Through the wind KENT staggers on with
a chess table. He places it before LEAR and unfolds his own stool. He
sits. They study. A long time passes. KENT goes to make a move.

LEAR: Erm!
(*KENT stops in mid-movement. Pause. He continues to move.*)
Erm! (*He stops again.*)
If I may say so.
Begging your.
Etcetera but. (*KENT finishes the move.*)
Erm! (*KENT looks resentful. LEAR turns aside.*) I do think
cheating is peculiar, so peculiar, because even when the
cheat might win on skill alone he still prefers to cheat. It is
impossible to satisfy him. I have watched you cheating for
eight years.

KENT: Eight years... ?

LEAR: Eight years to the day and never once protested.

KENT: I admit nothing. But why today?

LEAR: Why, indeed? Yes, why today? If only we were constant, if only we were! But today I felt it necessary to protest – no – not protest exactly – but to announce my knowledge of your cheating, which I had detected on the first day.

KENT: If only you had said.

LEAR: If only I had, but what difference would it have made? Do continue cheating. I merely wished to acquaint you with the fact I knew –

(*KENT suddenly rises to his feet, pointing to the CHORUS and letting out a moan.*)

Now you are trying to change the subject – (*KENT groans.*) I apologize for spoiling what was a perfectly innocuous and trivial practice – (*KENT points.*) I am a pedant! I am a pedant! I admit it!

(*Pause. The world shudders. LEAR turns thunderstruck on the chorus.*)

Please move...

THE GAOL: WE KNEW

HOW ELSE COULD WE BE FREE?

BUT KNOWING

HOW COULD WE BE ALLOWED TO LIVE?

LEAR: Please move...

(*KENT looks at him, then in a spasm of love, reaches out his hand and clasps LEAR's across the table.*)

HATED NIGHTFALL

The tutor of the Romanoffs.
His exemplification of desire and subsequent martyrdom in the
schoolroom at Ekaterinburg 16th July 1918

Characters

DANCER
A Tutor

ROMANOFF
An Emperor

CAROLINE
An Empress

CHRISTOPHE
HELEN
GRISELDA
Their Children

JANE
A Servant

FITCH
ARRANT
DISBANNER
DENADIR
ALBEIT
Officials of the Revolution

A CHORUS
(To include the above)

Part One

A substantial interior space, barren. A single upright chair on which a WOMAN sits asleep. It is the sleep of exhaustion, manifested in her posture. The silence is ruptured by the intrusion of orchestral music, which ceases. In the restored silence, a CHILD passes, dragging a pillow. A MAN enters. He goes to the sleeping WOMAN and places his hands kindly on her shoulders.

ROMANOFF: I'm sorry
    I'm sorry
    I'm so sorry
    So sorry
    So sorry
    (*The WOMAN is not awakened. He goes out. A SECOND MAN enters. He stares at the WOMAN.*)
DANCER: (*Pause.*) This will not be my decision the decision comes from elsewhere rather far away by telephone no not by telephone (*Pause.*)
    By telegram and this decision is irrevocable so please don't entertain hopes of reprieve no messenger will arrive no stained rider on a lathering horse etcetera no and furthermore I am the one who (*Pause.*)
    I volunteered (*Pause.*)
    No one persuaded me or appealed to higher principles (*Pause.*)
    I think with a rifle (*Pause.*)
    No a knife (*Pause.*)
    A rifle or a knife (*Pause.*)
    I have a knife whereas a rifle I should need to borrow so what I can borrow it (*Pause.*)
    It is perhaps important the executioner regards himself as a professional his actions unimpaired by enthusiasm or reluctance in this case however (*Pause.*)
    I confess to very real desire I am immensely (*Pause.*)
    Drawn to the task (*Pause.*)
    My only fear believe me being that another might offer his services and the thing degenerate into a competition short

and long straws the tossing of a coin etcetera no when the
decision is announced over the telephone it will be I and
no other I alone who (*Pause.*)
Or telegraph I think however the existence of the order its
material existence (*Pause.*)
Incriminating bits of paper (*Pause.*)
Caroline (*Pause.*)
Most likely therefore to be the telephone by which
(*He stops, aware he is being observed by a WOMAN holding a
broom and bucket. Pause.*)

JANE: Let her sleep.

DANCER: I'm not stopping her.

JANE: (*Cleaning the floor.*) You're pestering her.

DANCER: Not in the least.

JANE: Muttering and so on.

DANCER: Be quiet you are a servant.

JANE: I am a servant and so are you.

DANCER: A servant and no one cares for your opinions.

JANE: No one cares for them but still they exist.

DANCER: Let them exist but unarticulated.

JANE: Shut up.

DANCER: You shut up.

JANE: No.

DANCER: Do as you are told.

JANE: Of course I won't.

DANCER: Look, her knees have drifted open with that
abolition of all consciousness that comes with sleep and if
I – (*He cranes.*)
Stoop or – (*And kneels.*)
Kneel –
The shadows fall between her thighs and –
WHAT'S THERE
WHAT'S THERE
(*He squirms. JANE looks at him. He gets up, brushes his
knees.*)
No one will ever understand my attitude to women. Never.
(*JANE goes out.*)
So what.

I am never to be understood.

So what.

Let them bury me beneath a tree

An insubstantial tree

Never mind the oaks the urns the obelisks

And when the tree blows down

SO WHAT

SO WHAT

(*He covers his face with his hands. The overture is revived, clamorous. The CHILD passes with a pillow. The music ceases. ROMANOFF appears.*)

ROMANOFF: If we are guilty of anything it is an excess of love.

DANCER: (*Recovering.*) Excellent!

Preposterous!

And excellent!

I do so love the apologia of kings!

I llluɪɪʋ⁄ɪ

Impertinence.

Presumption.

I'm not conducting the trial, someone else is.

ROMANOFF: Love of one another. Consuming love which blinded me to circumstances beyond the wall.

DANCER: Wall? What wall?

ROMANOFF: The wall of love.

DANCER: Is love a wall, then?

ROMANOFF: A wall behind which the most tender flowers of affection, intimacy and –

DANCER: Push her knees together, you are her husband.

(*ROMANOFF glares at him.*)

Her knees. (*Pause.*)

Have come apart. (*Pause.*)

A wall, is it? I am wholly ignorant of love but that is possibly only a reflection of my dissidence, a characteristic of my revolutionary nature which cannot subscribe to platitudes. Perhaps I know more about love even than you, but love of a different kind. Perhaps at this stage I am obliged to be strictly theoretical about this love, but with the changing circumstances of our time, I might –

(*ROMANOFF seizes DANCER by the throat. Comic music accompanies his attempt to throttle him. They move to and fro in a terrible embrace. A CHORUS of shadowy figures laughs as an accompaniment. The music stops, and the CHORUS is silent. Only DANCER's laugh is heard, as he adjusts his collar. ROMANOFF, exhausted, hangs his head. The CHILD is discovered, watching, holding his pillow by its corner. DANCER goes to the CHILD.*)

DANCER: Your father cannot forgive me, cannot, no matter how he tries, and he is Christian, he is devout! (*He looks at ROMANOFF.*) As to whether I am able to forgive him, that hardly enters into it –

ROMANOFF: Forgive for what?

DANCER: No, no –

ROMANOFF: For what?

DANCER: You see, he cannot even conceive of his offence –

ROMANOFF: For what, I said –

DANCER: What am I, after all, a tutor, a servant, a domestic animal –

ROMANOFF: Please –

DANCER: Which whilst possessing the propensity for craven gratitude –

ROMANOFF: Stop this –

DANCER: Is incapable of registering resentment –

ROMANOFF: Stop, I beg you –

DANCER: HATRED OR CONTEMPT (*The CHILD shudders. DANCER holds him tight.*) It's all right, it's all right, don't be frightened, what does it matter, after all, I am a transient phenomenon whose own extinction is already written in the Book of Circumstance, yes, a transient phenomenon, can you say that? (*The CHILD opens his mouth.*) Yes, quite so, that's what I am, remember that and the firing squad, that also is, look boldly in the barrels of the guns, transient phenomenon, shout…!

(*He pushes the CHILD violently towards ROMANOFF.*)

CHORUS: DANCER

DANCER

WE THINK IT POSSIBLE YOU ARE A FRAUD

DANCER: I never rule it out, gentlemen!

CHORUS: AND WE WILL PAY A PRICE TO FOLLOW YOU

DANCER: Yes, why shouldn't you? Pay the price and be
damned!

CHORUS: DANCER
WHAT KIND OF TUTOR WERE YOU?

DANCER: Not nice, obviously.

CHORUS: ALL YOUR CERTIFICATES WERE FORGED

DANCER: Yes, I am without qualifications! On the other hand,
I am blessed with this extraordinary facility for speech.
Words tumble. Words froth. And in the proper order! Now,
stop pestering me, I am expecting a communication of the
highest significance. (*He turns.*)

CHORUS: DANCER

DANCER: What!

CHORUS: IF YOU WERE A LIAR UNDER ONE REGIME
HOW CAN WE TELL
YOU WILL NOT LIE UNDER ANOTHER?
(*Pause. DANCER is patient.*)

DANCER: Listen, the words are moribund. The words are
wasted with disease. They haunt old libraries as sick men
creep the corridors of sanitoria. (*He smiles.*)
New words, please… (*He goes to leave, turns swiftly.*)
YOU WANT ME TO CONFESS!
CONFESSION IS YOUR SOLITARY NEED.
I do not confess. The instinct is missing in me…
(*He looks at them, provocatively.*)
I leapt into the fireplace as a baby, from my mother's arms,
which is why I have this scar on me. Why, I wonder? Did
I think no flame could scorch me? I'll perish, obviously,
and in a ghastly way. Take comfort from the fact that I shall
suffer. The world abhors me. It writhes to know I walk
upon its surfaces…
(*He is suddenly possessed.*)
I JUMP ON IT (*He jumps, stops, laughs.*)
Oh, the pathos of the man who cannot assent, for assent he
must…eventually… (*The CHORUS turns to leave.*)
Stay with me…!

Oh, stay…!

CHORUS: DANCER
    CIRCUMSTANCES ELEVATE UNLIKELY MEN
    THE WAVE THAT LIFTED YOU
    WILL SWALLOW YOU AGAIN
    (*They leave. DANCER turns.*)

DANCER: Thirty years a tutor! And I was handsome, yes, I
    had the looks, I had the acumen, and so many learned
    from me, what could I not teach? For example
    THE AMBIGUITIES OF PARENTAL LOVE
    I saw it all
    THE TORTURES OF DOMESTIC BLISS
    I've seen the instruments
    OH, THE TERRIBLE ORDEAL OF INFANTS
    Especially the rich
    Pity the rich
    I do (*He turns to ROMANOFF.*)
    I am best qualified to govern you, believe me, I have your
    interests at heart. (*He sits, dismissing ROMANOFF with a slight
    gesture.*) Go now, but leave your wife. (*ROMANOFF takes his
    son by the shoulder.*) How appallingly she sleeps. Disaster she
    interprets as a sickness, which can be healed by diet or a
    period of rest…

ROMANOFF: She is depressed.

DANCER: Yes.

ROMANOFF: She deserved nothing but love.

DANCER: Mm.

ROMANOFF: Gratitude.

DANCER: Mm.

ROMANOFF: And loyalty.

DANCER: Indeed.

ROMANOFF: A perfect mother. A perfect wife.

DANCER: Why are you rehearsing this?

ROMANOFF: BECAUSE OUR MISERY IS INCOMPREHENSIBLE
    TO ME. (*Pause. He shrugs.*) Not entirely. I am the guilty one.
    And I have brought these innocents to the brink of murder.
    (*He turns to go.*) Don't kill my son.

DANCER: Why not?

(*A slow, pitiful shrug arises from ROMANOFF's shoulders. He leads the CHILD away.*)

Innocents? (*DANCER gets up.*)

Innocents?

Thank God I am not young, oh, the words of the young, the ponderous vocabulary of youth, their phrases dip like over-laden freighters, morality and rectitude strapped to the decks

INNOCENT OF WHAT?

(*A wind whispers round the room. DANCER looks at the sleeping WOMAN.*)

I am innocent if anybody is…

(*Two young WOMEN appear, pensive, anxious, they wait for his attention. He detects them, looks up.*)

HELEN: Are you in charge now, Citizen?

DANCER: Me, yes.

HELEN: Ridiculous!

DANCER. Isn't it!

HELEN: Only a week ago we were studying the Gallic Wars. The tribes. The topography.

DANCER: So we were…

HELEN: It's all so incomprehensible to us…

DANCER: Is it? So your father says. And yet it is so lucid to me.

GRISELDA: And I hate calling people Citizen!

DANCER: Do you? Say it more often, and it will cease to offend you.

HELEN: What we find particularly hard to understand is why –

DANCER: Please, do not inflict me with the poverty of your understanding. I am no longer a teacher. Your ignorance is no longer a concern of mine. (*GRISELDA weeps. Her SISTER clasps her.*) Oh, how I long to make you weep…how gratifying the spectacle of a young girl's tears!

HELEN: You are vile and –

DANCER: ALL THINGS COWARDLY AND REPREHENSIBLE I KNOW.

(*Pause. He smiles.*)

And once you trusted me.

HELEN: No. Not entirely.

DANCER: Yes.

HELEN: Not entirely, I said –

DANCER: YOU TRUSTED ME. Why pretend to insights you could not possibly possess? None of you has the slightest subtlety of mind –

HELEN: That isn't true!

DANCER: Helen, I know your mediocrity… (*She turns away, bitterly.*) You trusted me, and now you are ashamed. You are ashamed of your own disingenuousness… (*He shrugs.*) What does it matter? We are all dead now…

HELEN: I hate you Citizen…

DANCER: Very well, I am hated…and yet the sun still shines…

HELEN: (*Turning on him.*) IT IS DEAD MATTER, THAT IS WHY. VOLATILE, BUT LIFELESS… (*He stares at her.*) Shall we be killed?

DANCER: I think so, yes.

HELEN: Save my little sister –

DANCER: She is not little, she has merely failed to mature –

HELEN: Oh, stop this fatuous and futile-

DANCER: (*Rising to his feet.*) I CAN'T HELP IT, I CAN'T HELP IT…! (*He pushes them.*) Get outside, now, get outside, find a corner and wait to be killed…! (*They stare. He shudders.*) I am fifty. My chance has come. Fifty and absolute.

GRISELDA: You are not really bad, Citizen…

DANCER: I am –

GRISELDA: No, not really, really bad –

DANCER: I am

    I am that bad

    Believe me.

    You merely cannot bear to contemplate it.

    (*He touches GRISELDA weakly on the shoulder.*)

    Go away now. I am capable of such artificial sentiments, things that make my own flesh crawl…

    (*Suddenly GRISELDA seizes his hand and kisses it. He withdraws it.*)

You see…! You see how colonized we are by other people's gestures! On the rim of the grave even you are insincere! Too many novels, Miss! Too many plays!

(*GRISELDA bursts into tears and hurries out. HELEN boldly keeps her ground.*)

HELEN: I pity you, Citizen.

DANCER: Oh, don't bother…!

HELEN: Pity, I said –

DANCER: I MOCK YOUR PITY. I REPUDIATE YOUR PITY. TAKE YOUR PITY TO DEATH'S DITCH WITH YOU.

(*HELEN stares in disbelief, then goes out. He watches her departure. A MAN has entered, with a sheaf of papers. He looks at DANCER, bemused.*)

FITCH: You'll hurt yourself.

DANCER: Hurt myself? How?

FITCH: All this effort to be vile.

DANCER: No effort, I assure you.

FITCH: ⟨illegible⟩ (⟨illegible⟩)

No one suspects you of disloyalty.

DANCER: Don't they? I suspect myself of it.

FITCH: Well, that is consistent with the earnestness with which you have adopted the revolutionary cause, Citizen, and wholly laudable, but –

DANCER: I do hate that

Forgive me

I do hate that – confectionery – of words I tell you a truth and you offer me these impeccably

I am talking for example of

These immaculately

My sexuality

Its lethal nature

Coiffured words

We must be careful, mustn't we, not to smother things in words?

THIS WOMAN HAS NOT WOKEN YET

No, that helps nobody. (*Pause. FITCH stares at him.*)

FITCH: I have to go…

DANCER: What are these papers? I receive so many papers and quite frankly they are not always read...
Their appearance is detrimental...
And what are they? The usual exhortations to solidarity... quotations from the works of dead economists and completely biased news, no one places the slightest credence in them, you would need to be the most diseased fanatic to even (*He stops.*)

FITCH: Please, put your criticisms on paper and I will forward them to the appropriate committee.

DANCER: Yes, I will.
(*FITCH turns to go. DANCER hurries to him and stabs him. FITCH cries out in disbelief.*)
Oh...!
Oh...!
(*The CHORUS appears, with JANE. A frantic, anxious cascade of music.*)
You see, if they don't listen to me, what occurs!

CHORUS: DANCER
We can forgive the revolutionary death but this

DANCER: I've killed!

CHORUS: THIS

DANCER: It's easy! I'm amazed!

CHORUS: THIS

JANE: He isn't dead...

DANCER: I've killed, I said!

CHORUS: THE TUTOR IS A MURDERER

DANCER: (*Turning on them.*) THE EDUCATOR ALWAYS IS.
(*Pause. FITCH stirs on the ground.*)

JANE: Not dead I said.
(*Pause. Silence but for a thin wind blowing.*)

DANCER: I'll try again.

JANE: You'll have to.
(*FITCH moans. DANCER offers JANE the knife.*)

DANCER: You do it. (*The CHORUS laughs.*)
WHY SHOULDN'T SHE? (*Pause. JANE has not taken the knife.*)
All right... I will... (*He goes to FITCH, who sees him.*)

FITCH: I'm hurt...

DANCER: Yes, you are…so badly hurt you can't come back…
it's…a matter of –
(*He hacks the throat brutally, his eyes shut.*)
CHORUS: DANCER
DANCER
YOU ARE INSANE
DANCER: (*Swiftly rising to his feet.*) You would say that! How
necessary you should think I am insane! Think so if it
relieves you!
(*With a gesture of contempt he tosses the knife away.*)
JANE: He's still not dead…
DANCER: (*Turning on her now.*) IF YOU KNOW SO MUCH
ABOUT IT, DO IT.
(*She is adamantly still.*)
He is in pain there, and really, I am an amateur… (*She
stares.*) Haven't you killed cattle, sheep and things? (*Pause.*)
So what if he's in pain. He was an idiot. (*To CHORUS.*)
THAT IS AN AUTHENTIC IDIOT,
Not me…
CHORUS: DANCER
YOU HAVE STABBED THE AGENT OF THE REVOLUTION
HE WAS ON YOUR SIDE!
DANCER: *My* side?
Do I have a side? (*They are aghast.*)
Oh, how horrified you are to find me pure…
Yes…
Rinsed of all belief…
YOU'D PREFER ANY OLD CATECHISM TO THE ECHO OF
THE UNBELIEVER
Lies
Filth
Encrusted ideology
(*DANCER walks coolly to the dying MAN and slits his throat,
this time effectively and in a routine manner. As he moves
away he senses he is watched and turns to see CHRISTOPHE,
in a corner of the stage. The CHILD tilts his toy watering-can.
A dark fluid trickles out… DANCER turns back to the
CHORUS.*)

DANCER: Humans really are enslaved by books
  I'll give you a book
  Oh, I intend to write one
  I am as narcissistic as the next man
  (*He wipes the blade of the knife and pockets it.*)
  I say a book
  I must warn you, I mean a shelf (*He laughs.*)
  Yes!
  And you will memorize it, oh, whole paragraphs
  word-perfectly…
  (*He looks at the CHORUS. They drift away. JANE looks at DANCER.*)
  Swab away the blood.

JANE: Swab it yourself.

DANCER: Jane, you are a servant

JANE: I am a servant, and so are you.

DANCER: Must we go through this every hour? I tell you for the first and last time, I am a law unto myself.

JANE: You're Billy the tutor with the balding bonce as far as I'm concerned.

DANCER: Oh, your rustic charm…! Swab it, I said.

JANE: No.

  (*Pause. DANCER takes the bucket and broom away from her and begins to wash the floor.*)

DANCER: 'Make my criticisms on paper and forward them to the Committee…'! What does he think I am, a suicide?

JANE: He asked for it.

DANCER: I'm nobody's fool.

JANE: That's true, Citizen. But perhaps it's no bad thing to be a fool…?

DANCER: (*Stopping, appearing to think.*) The ramifications of such an opinion stretch even my imagination to breaking point… (*He lays down the broom, goes to move the body.*) I so detest the wisdom of the people…you take this arm.

JANE: Nope.

DANCER: Oh, come on…

JANE: No I said.

(Pause. DANCER tries to drag the body by its arms. It scarcely moves.)

DANCER: The bulk of humanity suspends its entire existence from three or four bucolic and inane proverbs. This enables it to – *(He heaves.)* tolerate its own annihilation, even… *(He drops the arms and goes to the legs, and pulls.)* Jane… *(She ignores him. He pulls again.)* The lyrics of some whimpering ballad can compensate them for the most appalling blows of fate I CAN'T MOVE THIS BY MYSELF. *(She watches, still.)*

You will remember this moment. My apparent helplessness. My apparent foolishness. You will recollect it. The nadir, possibly, of my existence. I hope you will not rue the day…

(JANE goes out. DANCER is still for a long time. A light, pastoral music. He stares at the sleeping WOMAN. He goes to her, and leaning close to her ear, whispers. He looks to assure ⋯⋯⋯⋯⋯⋯⋯⋯⋯⋯⋯⋯⋯⋯⋯⋯⋯⋯ He tears himself away in a paroxysm of ecstasy.)

I wonder

I wonder if

This

Passion

Is

Sincere?

The distinction between an honest and dishonest passion being what precisely?

Well

I essay

I tentatively

And

Humbly

Propose *(He laughs, shaking his head.)*

Typical tutor

Typical *philosophe*

Nothing is experienced but needs to be explained!

(He reflects. He makes an effort to achieve perfect expression.)

Princesses sleep a thousand years and Queens perish on
the block
We so adore
We so adore to
(*He whispers torrentially into the WOMAN's ear, and turns
away abruptly.*)
And I am after all a modern man
Yes
Nothing quaint or archaic clings to me
THEY ALSO REQUIRE ME TO DIE
Humiliation
Is
Their
Apotheosis…
(*He looks at her, half-pityingly. ROMANOFF enters. DANCER
senses him.*)
I am pitying her death…

ROMANOFF: And what of yours?

DANCER: Mine?
I expect it hourly, and from any source but don't come
near me I have a knife which I have just employed in an
almost but not quite arbitrary manner
THERE IS THE MAN OF THE FUTURE THROAT CUT
Typical future
Short-lived and banal
Promises and inexorable laws of
Engineer of human souls etcetera
Dead now
Never mind
So keep your distance
Would you kindly help me move him I was rather too
spontaneous and he fell right in the door
Next time
Plan it better obviously (*ROMANOFF shakes his head.*)
What are you, a saint? (*ROMANOFF looks away.*)
Some say you are but I keep an open mind
DRAG THE CORPSE AWAY OR I WILL DO SOME CRUEL
THING TO THOSE YOU LOVE. (*ROMANOFF thinks briefly.*)

ROMANOFF: Drag him where?

DANCER: Anywhere, you choose. (*ROMANOFF goes to the dead man, looks.*) I fear my own death for one reason only, that it would render me incapable of experiencing the particular act of love I know myself to be supremely capable of...

ROMANOFF: You...?

DANCER: Yes.

(*ROMANOFF studiedly declines to reply. He leans to the corpse. His hand falters.*)

ROMANOFF: I have never touched a dead man...

DANCER: This act of love may not at first be recognisable as such. I think it will be misrepresented. The subtlest minds may be required to identify and elaborate it. (*Pause.*)

ROMANOFF: AND THAT IS WHY WE FAILED...!

DANCER: Please, you are forever analyzing this thing you call your failure, who cares about your failure, already it is of negligible importance, the preposterous fantasy of academics, and nostalgic picture books

ROMANOFF: THE PRINCE MUST TOUCH... (*Pause.*)

DANCER: Yes... (*He shrugs.*)
But the princess, what of her...?

(*ROMANOFF stands away.*)

ROMANOFF: I decline to do your dirty work for you! Punish as you will. But spare my children –

DANCER: Shhh –

ROMANOFF: Inflict your malice where you will but –

DANCER: Please, you are so – extreme, indulgent –

ROMANOFF: ME?

DANCER: You, yes – indulgent with your fear –

ROMANOFF: YOU THREATENED ME.

DANCER: Did I? I forget... (*He shrugs.*) I threaten everybody... (*He gets up.*)
Come on, help me conceal him or I shall be discovered and consequently you will find yourself in the hands of someone for whom no ties of sentiment restrain his violence... (*He smiles.*)
Oh, believe me, I entertain obscure feelings of devotion for you all! Yes! Now, take his legs!

187

(ROMANOFF hesitates, returns to the body, stoops. DANCER does not move, but watches, and then laughs.)
Yes… *(ROMANOFF looks up.)*
It is so – *(He selects the word.)*
Necessary –
The Prince should be porter to a lout.
(ROMANOFF is patient.)
I am the lout.
(He goes to the arms. Together they hoist the corpse. DANCER does not move.)
I am not presumptuous, am I? I do not call myself History. The Agent of Destiny. Justice. The People's Will. I don't drape myself.
(DANCER nods his head. ROMANOFF staggers. They go out with the body. An effect of sound and light. A cry. The CHILD passes dragging its pillow. The cry again. The sleeping WOMAN is aroused, shocked from her state. She speaks as if resuming a diatribe suspended by a spell.)

CAROLINE: Logic…! The contemptible and threadbare thing how dare you bring it near me its smell offends me!
(Pause. She perceives her situation, looking side to side, almost surreptitiously. A wind rattles.)
That's what I'll say.
Because a princess cannot possibly negotiate the nature of her privilege. Conceding even, that it could be argued would be a profound mistake. I AM NOT IN THE SAME DOMAIN OF LAW LET ALONE LANGUAGE
No
Royalty has no defence
Shoot me
Silence is most eloquent and I shan't utter one syllable of expiation
I am not culpable
GOD IS THE SOLE JUDGE OF ALL MONARCHY
They know that
They want to drag us through their courts
They want to smear us with their language
I WANT A PRIEST, PLEASE! *(Silence. She is still. She smiles.)*

I thought I was modern. I read modern books, but one must be careful of these things, keeping abreast of course but not permitting oneself to be

PENETRATED

SPIKED

SOME SPECIMEN OF ETYMOLOGY PINNED TO THE BOARD

Darling, come here!

(*The CHILD is discovered standing forlornly. She opens her arms.*)

I was asleep! I do sleep such sleeps, don't I, deeper than cats certainly, more like a toad! They sleep whole winters! Come here! (*The CHILD approaches her, slowly. She kneels.*) Who knows why I sleep so? Or what wakes me?

(*She bites her lip. She caresses him.*)

Things are so very out of order...! But what is certain is that order reasserts itself.

It must

That is a law

Do you know what a law is?

A law is what cannot be disputed

So

All this

Inconvenience

Will last for such and such a time

A week perhaps!

But not longer

Promise you

Promise

Promise (*She suddenly crushes him.*)

Little Monarch

How they hate you...!

But don't hate them because it would demean you

Their hatred is the proof we are elect!

(*She suddenly repulses him.*)

Quick now, find your sisters! Find Helen! (*He starts to go.*)

Listen...! (*He stops.*)

When you are the monarch, remember this! To suffer also is the privilege of princes!

(*The CHILD goes out, as ROMANOFF returns. She sees his state.*)

You are covered in mud!

ROMANOFF: Yes...

CAROLINE: Why?

ROMANOFF: Dancer asked me to assist him with a –

CAROLINE: Dancer asked –

ROMANOFF: Not asked exactly –

CAROLINE: Dancer –

ROMANOFF: ORDERED ME –

CAROLINE: DANCER IS A TUTOR –

ROMANOFF: ORDERED ME I SAID. (*Pause.*)

CAROLINE: You see, I am awake. (*She shrugs.*)

I wake, and it is arbitrary, just as it is arbitrary when I go to sleep. Something is preparing me for death.

(*She shrugs again.*)

I say death... (*She looks at him.*)

The death of something...obviously...

ROMANOFF: Everything is my fault.

CAROLINE: Yes.

ROMANOFF: (*Horrified.*) Do you believe that, Caroline?

CAROLINE: Yes.

ROMANOFF: And in what may be our final hours you are prepared to burden me with the entire responsibility for what's –

CAROLINE: Absolutely, yes.

(*ROMANOFF looks at her, distraught. She experiences a surge of pity.*)

Oh, come here, little mouse...

ROMANOFF: (*Fixed to the spot.*) My son – my innocent and inoffensive son –

CAROLINE: Come here, I said... (*ROMANOFF silently chokes tears.*) Always we called one another little mouse...

(*ROMANOFF does not take her hand. It falters.*)

ROMANOFF: I am without sin. Blameless and without sin.

CAROLINE: Yes.

But I require another life.

(*ROMANOFF looks at her, bewildered.*)

The one about to close I…do not feel, on reflection, fulfilled my needs…

(*His mouth hangs open with incredulity. The DAUGHTERS enter.*)

HELEN: Mother!

CAROLINE: Shh!

(*She gestures them impatiently with a hand. They stop, also puzzled. CAROLINE walks.*)

I do not want to die. (*She looks, one to the other.*)

HELEN: We neither! And we are frightened, Mother!

CAROLINE: Yes.

But whereas I think I possess the means of my deliverance, I am not certain either of you do…

(*Pause. They follow her movements.*)

In my sleeps, I hear voices. These voices urge me to –

(*She laughs.*)

Oh, all sorts of things, both poetry and the most obscene –

ROMANOFF: Caroline

CAROLINE: Preposterous and –

ROMANOFF: Caroline –

CAROLINE: (*Turning to him.*) Degenerate things…

ROMANOFF: These sleeps are sickness, Caroline…

CAROLINE: Yes, and like all sickness, they originate in God…

(*She turns to the GIRLS.*)

I tell you this because – in the most unkind way – oh, such a very unkind way – I never felt a greater distance existed between myself and you…

(*They look to their FATHER.*)

When you would think, under such circumstances –

ROMANOFF: Christophe, Helen, Griselda –

CAROLINE: A mother would manifest the opposite tendency, if anything, an excess of intimacy –

ROMANOFF: Christophe, Helen, Griselda –

CAROLINE: A tidal wave of all those maternal instincts which impending murder –

ROMANOFF: CHRISTOPHE

HELEN

GRISELDA (*He shudders. CAROLINE is by contrast, icy.*)

CAROLINE: Licenses… (*Pause.*)

> There is no priest, is there? They killed him in the hospital. (*She laughs.*)
> All the buildings are misused…! The hospital became a slaughterhouse, and as for the schoolroom…
> (*She gestures to the room they are in.*)
> Who knows what we shall learn in here?

HELEN: Frankly Mother, I preferred it when you slept all the time –

ROMANOFF: Helen –

HELEN: I did! When she slept, it was possible to invent her, whereas awake she is –

> NOT NICE, IS SHE? (*She looks boldly at CAROLINE.*)
> Not that it matters, if you are being killed, what –
> (*She falters.*)
> Memory is…!
> (*ROMANOFF goes to console her. She pulls away from him.*)
> No! (*CAROLINE laughs.*)
> We are forever – grasping one another – I don't wish to be grasped…!

ROMANOFF: It is not *grasping*…

HELEN: It feels like it…

ROMANOFF: Always we were intimate…what has happened here? Always we embraced…and you call it grasping…

HELEN: It's suffocating…!

GRISELDA: (*Suddenly.*) Where is Christophe?

ROMANOFF: We kissed, always, and on the mouth, we were not reserved, God knows –

HELEN: That was happiness, kissing from happiness somehow is different from this –

GRISELDA: Christophe isn't here…!

HELEN: PERPETUAL COMFORTING! I do it myself! (*She turns to GRISELDA.*) Don't I? I am the first!

GRISELDA: Christophe isn't here!

(*She turns to go and look for the* CHILD. *As she does so,*
DANCER *enters, the* CHILD *on his shoulders. Instinctively,*
they crowd together.)

DANCER: HE IS NOT CRITICAL

HE IS NOT ETHICAL

HE CAN'T DISCRIMINATE

WHERE IS HIS GUILT, THEREFORE?

(*He turns about, amusing the* CHILD.)

HE DOES NOT ARBITRATE

HE CANNOT CALCULATE

NO ONE COULD LIKE HIM MORE

THAN

ME... (*Pause.*)

Paradox... (*Pause.*)

The executioner's affection for his victim...

Paradoxical! (*To the* CHILD.) Do you know that word?

No?

I paid too little attention to vocabulary, that's obvious, and
far too much to grammar!

(*He lifts the* CHILD *off his shoulders.*)

I found him staring at me! There I was, spade in
hand, ankle-deep in grave-making, and I sensed these
melancholy eyes upon me. At once I ceased my labours,
which were in any case, too strenuous for me. I was
obliged to find another solution to the trivial problem I
had set myself. I am in his debt, I might have put my back
out...

GRISELDA: (*Extending a hand to the* CHILD, *who has been staring*
at DANCER.) Christophe...! (*The* CHILD *does not react.*)

CAROLINE: He hardly speaks now...it is as if he knew the
dynasty concludes with him...

(*A single resonant sound announces the presence of the*
CHORUS, *who have entered unobserved.* DANCER *advances on*
them.)

DANCER: Patience...!

Patience...! (*He claps his hands at them, they inch back.*)

CHORUS: DANCER

DANCER

DANCER: I promise you nothing will occur without your
    acquiescence!
CHORUS: YOU ARE A CALCULATING AND UNFATHOMABLE
    MAN
DANCER: And would you have me otherwise? Are our
    enemies not calculating? Do you want me fathomed by the
    likes of them? This family is steeped in treachery!
    (*He shrugs.*)
    Sophisticated treachery. Educated treachery.
    I am a transient phenomenon, but these…!
    Four hundred years of…!
    (*He shakes his head. The* CHORUS *withdraws, warily.*)
    They have the curiosity of cattle… the comic and yet
    faintly menacing curiosity of cattle…
    (*The piercing sound of a telephone. It transfixes everyone.*
    DANCER *is swaying with anticipation, yet quite unable to*
    move. Apprehension has seized the entire FAMILY. *At last,*
    JANE *appears.*)
JANE: Are you answering that?
    (DANCER *cannot find a voice. It rings on, with increasing*
    violence.)
    Are you or not? (DANCER *doesn't speak. It stops.*)
DANCER: Oh… (*Pause. His body relaxes.*)
    They'll ring back, no doubt. (*It rings again.*)
    They have rung back. (*He goes out, slowly. It stops.*)
JANE: I'm in favour.
HELEN: In favour of what?
JANE: Goodness.
HELEN: Are you? Then tell the world what is happening to us!
JANE: I will do.
ROMANOFF: No, go now!
JANE: I can't go now, I've got so much to do –
HELEN: Please, now!
JANE: I promise, when everything is over, I will tell, I won't
    miss out a single bit of it –
ROMANOFF: No, that's too late, you must go now and –
CAROLINE: YOU ARE MAKING IDIOTS OF YOURSELVES.
    (*Pause.*)

JANE: If you've jewellery…watches or anything…
(*They are silent. She shrugs.*)
I'm not unkind.
I believe in God.
Also, I believe in monarchy.
I believe in all things that are natural.
Like God.
Like monarchy.
And Mr Dancer, I'm sorry to say, is also natural.
Everything that happens, I will tell.
Honestly. (*She goes out. Pause.*)

HELEN: Is that evil?
Is that the absolute in evil?

ROMANOFF: If I had a gun, I would kill. I, who have never killed, would kill and kill…!

CAROLINE: Shut up…

ROMANOFF: A man with such a placid disposition must always look absurd who ii ih i i a i i Axalung th   in, l i ▪

CAROLINE: If you had a gun you would not use it –

ROMANOFF: I WOULD, I WOULD, I WOULD…!

GRISELDA: Please, don't quarrel –

ROMANOFF: During the last offensive of the war it was I who gave the order to advance, I alone accept responsibility, no, I CLAIM IT, I CLAIM THE THIRTY THOUSAND DEAD!

CAROLINE: You are hardly placid at all…

ROMANOFF: I am not placid, no –

GRISELDA: This is ridiculous!

ROMANOFF: I wish I had another life! I wish! I wish!
(*DANCER enters. A fall of silence. He is simultaneously apprehensive and vulgar, arrogant, tender. He walks, feeling their eyes upon him. He gestures, in a Roman manner, to himself…*)

DANCER: The Doorman of our Century… (*A stillness. The wind in the boards.*) Me… (*He shakes his head. He laughs. He stops.*)
Great moments of human endeavour stimulate a sort of poetry…the mundane minds of lawyers are shaken from the attic to the basements…
Earthquakes of phraseology…the sudden discovery of

THE
STYLE
OF
ROME (*He laughs, bending, shaking his head.*)
He was – you could feel it through the crackling of the
telephone, through snow and hail and regiments of
rocket launchers, saboteurs, air raids, you name it, it was
conspiring to spoil the moment but he was not thrown,
he knew this message called for poise and the ponderous
delivery of never-to-be-forgotten syllables, a compromise
between electrification and the oratorical manner of the
late Republic, Cato, Mirabeau, oh, the competition, but
he persevered, and it was excellent in many ways, I don't
criticise
YES
HE
SAYS (*The wind again. He stares.*)
And I, the transient phenomenon, will open the door to a
new – (*He shakes his head, wearily, then recovers.*)
I like the new
The new what
The new anything
The New itself
IT CONCEALS MY TRANSIENCE FROM ME! (*He looks at
them.*)
And your extermination is the threshold… (*He grins.*)
I say extermination because death apparently is
inadequate, there has to be OBLITERATION or someone,
some superstitious, crippled-with-religion, infantile,
irrational – you know the sort of idiot – will excavate and
find a bone, a glove or something and there will be
A CULT OF MONARCHY
Yes
The Citizen at the far end of the telephone has studied
History he reads he spent five years in an English library
eyes down too, no looking up for passing skirt or knicker
he was pellucid on the subject affirmative and absolute that
not a shred of any one of you should persist… (*Pause.*)

A PROBLEM IN ITSELF (*Pause.*)
He left that to me, of course
Mere detail
Couldn't expect him to
What with his responsibilities
I had this staggering compliment
What more could I
Might have made him angry
THE DOORMAN OF THE CENTURY surely knows a thing
or two about (*Pause.*)
Acid, presumably…
(*Pause. ROMANOFF looks at him, shaking his head in disbelief.*)

ROMANOFF: You do not want to do this thing… I do not
believe you honestly wish to do this thing, Mr Dancer…

DANCER: Honestly… I wonder if I hear you right…did you
say honestly…?

HELEN: YOU KNOW VERY WELL HE SAID HONESTLY

DANCER: (*Turning on her.*) It's such a quaint word! Such an
exotic notion, picturesque, obscure!

ROMANOFF: EXAMINE YOURSELF AND –

DANCER: Oh, please –

ROMANOFF: CONFRONT YOUR CONSCIENCE –

DANCER: EXAMINE THE LABYRINTH…! Hands and knees…!
Magnifying glass…!
(*CAROLINE laughs, ROMANOFF, losing control, slaps her.*)
STOP THAT
DETESTABLE
BRUTALITY
STOP THAT

GRISELDA: Daddy…!

CAROLINE: Yes, restrain your father if you can, everything he
says is calculated to aggravate the situation –

DANCER: The resort to violence is the very hallmark of
domesticity… (*He turns away.*)
How I shuddered…
Something in this family made me recoil, as if I'd touched
a loathsome thing which lay hidden under foliage…

HELEN: It is you who is the loathsome thing, and it is you who lay hidden under foliage…! (*He looks at her.*)

DANCER: The toad was once a prince…and the prince…he bears the character of the toad… (*He smiles.*)

Go now, and walk together in the grounds, hand in hand, with that slow pace which always seemed to me not so much a demonstration of assurance, power, continuity, but the restraint of madness…a measured defiance of decline… (*They look to ROMANOFF. He leads them out.*) Take coats…! (*They stop.*) You might catch cold… (*Pause. ROMANOFF looks at the floor.*)

ROMANOFF: This is a pleasure to you…

(*He shakes his head, uncomprehending. They go out. DANCER watches, then claps his hands swiftly. The CHORUS enter, bearing a large table, covered in immaculate white linen and dressed with vases, candelabra, crockery. They stagger it to the middle of the room, go out, and return with chairs. DANCER, in a sort of ecstasy, fusses.*)

DANCER: And all I want is love…!

(*The CHORUS laughs, staccato, in unison.*)

It's true!

I think of nothing else, it is the single and obsessive object of my life! (*And again.*)

You laugh! (*And again.*)

You laugh because the poverty of your imagination blinds you to the possibility! The circumstances seem to abolish it! I assure you, the most comely children are the product of the most squalid copulations, it's the comedy of nature! (*They laugh.*)

Laugh, it's obligatory!

(*They stop. They are suddenly dark.*)

CHORUS: DANCER

THE CIRCUMSTANCES WHICH CREATED YOU ARE

DANCER: Shhh!

CHORUS: THE FLOOD WHICH CARRIED YOU THIS FAR WILL CERTAINLY

DANCER: I am not naïve…

CHORUS: RECEDE

DANCER: I know it all...

CHORUS: LEAVING YOUR BODY HANGING IN THE TREES...

(*DANCER shrugs, eloquently.*)

DANCER: What you describe as a rebuke to me, is no more or less than my desire...

(*He nods as if in gratitude. The CHORUS goes out. A FIGURE is discovered observing DANCER. He wears an overcoat, glasses. There is a quality of authority in him. DANCER catches him in the corner of his eye.*)

Citizen Fitch...! Have you seen him? He is regular as clockwork, and I must confess, his pile of documents becomes almost an addiction to me – we rely on such people to deliver, don't we, in all weathers...?

Perhaps the terrorists got him. I do hope not.

(*The FIGURE just looks.*)

Or are you his substitute? (*And looks.*)

People come and go...

ARRANT: (*Going to a seat, and sitting.*) They say you are learned, Citizen...

DANCER: Do they? Well, they are correct for once.

ARRANT: Are they not always so?

DANCER: Sometimes their innate correctness is distorted by the falsifications of perspective induced by crisis. I compare the wisdom of the people to a figure wandering in a hall of mirrors. Always the individual recognises himself, but in grotesque forms. This nightmare of perceptions does not preclude the existence of a proper mirror, which, the more outrageous the reflections, the more certain he becomes in his faith that it does exist, must exist, and above all, will exist, so long as he does not give up hope. Hope is the problem, given that for most of us, it is not a bottomless well. (*Pause.*)

I am mixing my metaphors...!

Mirrors...wells...(*Pause.*)

Yes, of course I'm learned, what about you? (*Pause.*)

ARRANT: Faith... (*Pause.*)

DANCER: Yes.

ARRANT: In the future...

DANCER: Yes.

ARRANT: Our children's children...

DANCER: Them especially... (*Suddenly.*) I don't have any children...! (*Pause. He laughs.*) So what? Other people do... (*ARRANT stares at DANCER.*) You stare a great deal. I've noticed, since the Revolution, a vast increase in staring. Fitch used to do it! (*Pause.*) Still does do it, I expect...are you staying, or... I've things to do... (*Pause.*) This staring is supposed to wreck the nerves, a sort of permanent interrogation... I don't mind it myself... (*He laughs.*) Of course I mind it, for one thing I think it's rude...

ARRANT: Rudeness?

DANCER: Yes, staring and conversations in which one party confines himself to single words must be construed as rudeness... (*Pause.*) Under the old regime...! (*He laughs.*) I KNOW ALL THE PROPER ANSWERS, CITIZEN! (*He walks boldly to the table, adjusts a glass or two.*)

ARRANT: Let's talk about faith...

DANCER: Faith? Any time! But you begin. After all, you initiated this discussion and I haven't the least idea who you are nor whether you possess the authority to be here, whether you are a charlatan, a counter-revolutionary or simply a man who has stolen a decent overcoat and wandered off the street...! Things are like that now, it is a paradise for imposters, but I don't criticise, I take you at face value, and if you are an imposter, so what, the people have the right to engage their masters in discussion at a moment's notice!

I agree with it! (*He grins.*)

I said masters! You flinched! (*He laughs.*)

Do take off your coat. (*ARRANT looks.*)

There you go! Staring again! At least undo the neck. (*Pause.*)

Citizen. (*Long pause. A wind blows.*)

ARRANT: What distinguishes the rebel from the revolutionary is faith.

DANCER: Yes...

ARRANT: The rebel has none.

DANCER: He has no point of reference but himself.

ARRANT: Consequently he cannot be relied upon.

DANCER: Not relied upon, no. But used, perhaps?
How can you sit buttoned up like that? This room is
sweltering. Are you about to leave?

ARRANT: I discomfort you, Citizen.

DANCER: (*Shrugging.*) I am discomforted by the spectacle of a
man with too much clothing on.

ARRANT: Or too little?

DANCER: That also would offend me! I think it must be the
remnants of some decadent belief in hospitality. The
taking of coats, and so on, a servile instinct I have not
entirely erased from my reconstructed soul, but then, THE
DOORMAN OF THE CENTURY is after all, a menial post...
(*ARRANT looks at him. DANCER smiles.*) I got the order. (*He
jerks his head to indicate a room.*) Down the telephone...
(*Pause. ARRANT unbuttons his neck, opens his coat.*)

ARRANT. What matter is to you, Citizen?
(*Pause. DANCER's eyes are fixed on ARRANT's throat.*)
I said –

DANCER: Love! (*Pause.*) So much murder...torture...
the squalor of blighted lives...requires some perfect
apotheosis... to be justified...

ARRANT: Justified?

DANCER: Yes, oh yes, you see,
THE DOORMAN IS A MORALIST (*He laughs, stops.*)
No, some impeccable, some – immaculate moment of love
– brief as the metamorphosis which brings to birth the
butterfly, perfect, trembling on damp wings and frail as the
dew which vibrates on the stem –
(*He has contrived to place himself behind ARRANT.*)
New in form, and possibly, unobserved –
ONLY ONE SUCH NEEDS OCCUR
(*He grabs ARRANT by the head, forcing it back.*)
FOR
US
TO
SAY (*ARRANT struggles, DANCER slashes his throat.*)

THE SACRIFICE WAS PERFECT (*They struggle. ARRANT chokes.*)
THE SACRIFICE WAS MORE THAN NECESSARY
WE
CRAVED
IT!
FAITH!
FAITH! (*ARRANT lies back in the chair.*)
Jane!
Where are you!
Jane! (*He runs around in a fit of uncontrollable excitement.*)
I'm changing! I'm altering! I'm undergoing something
THAT WAS FAR FROM SPONTANEOUS
(*JANE appears with a bucket.*)
JANE: What!
DANCER: I PLOTTED EVERY MOVE (*ARRANT is dying, but noisily.*)
Shut up!
JANE: You're mad!
DANCER: (*Kicking ARRANT.*) Shut up, shut up!
JANE: MAD
UTTERLY
MAD
DANCER: Faith he said (*He jeers at the dying man.*)
FAITH IN ME!
Finish him off, I can't
JANE: No –
DANCER: DO IT I SAID –
JANE: Absolutely not –
DANCER: (*Going to her, taking her roughly.*) You know your trouble –
JANE: Nope –
DANCER: I'll tell you what your trouble is –
JANE: Don't wanna know –
DANCER: YOU HAVE NO LOYALTY!
JANE: Nope –
DANCER: Neither to the past nor to the future, I find that CONTEMPTIBLE

Do it or I'll have you shot

JANE: Rubbish

THAT HORRIBLE NOISE

DANCER: Well, cover him up! (*They stare at each other like a quarrelling husband and wife. Pause.*) All right, I will! (*He goes to throw ARRANT's coat over him, but senses the presence of CHRISTOPHE. CHRISTOPHE pours fluid from his little can. DANCER pauses, throws the coat over ARRANT. The sound is muffled.*)

I knew him at once

The way they

Swaggering about as if

And staring

I don't stare, do I? Tell me if I do I hate it

AND JUST ARRIVE!

No introductions

Good morning would be nice

I'm too subtle

For my own good, possibly…

(*The grunting stops. He looks, shakes his head.*)

And he called ME the doorman…

How little they know of our rareness, and our beauty…

JANE: Beauty? You?

DANCER: Yes… Me… (*She turns to go out.*)

Jane…

I don't know what to do with these…!

(*JANE shrugs, goes out, leaving DANCER alone. The wind makes the boards creak. He hurries to the body and picks up an arm, but the body is, if anything, heavier than the last. As he pulls and falters, he becomes aware of CAROLINE, who has returned alone, watching him. He allows the arm to fall with a feigned indifference. Music, percussive, brief.*)

Part Two

CAROLINE, alone. ROMANOFF is revealed, staring at her…

ROMANOFF: Your shoes are covered in mud… (*Pause.*)
 Not just your shoes… (*Pause.*)
 Your legs… (*Pause.*)
 Your legs are covered in –
 (*The CHILDREN enter.*)
GRISELDA: (*Seeing the laid table.*) What's this…!
HELEN: This is the old service from the summer house!
ROMANOFF: (*To CAROLINE.*) I hate to see you spoiled in any
 way –
CAROLINE: I'm not spoiled –
ROMANOFF: (*Hurrying to her, kneeling with a handkerchief.*)
 Horrible –
CAROLINE: Not spoiled, I said –
HELEN: Laid for six…
GRISELDA: And the high chair, though Christophe doesn't use
 it any more…!
ROMANOFF: All right, I won't attempt to clean your legs, what
 does it matter if we are clean or dirty?
HELEN: (*To CHRISTOPHE who has wandered near the table.*)
 DON'T TOUCH THE FOOD…
ROMANOFF: (*Applying spittle to his handkerchief.*) No, I think
 it does matter, actually… (*He wipes CAROLINE's legs
 desperately.*) I think it is supremely important…
GRISELDA: (*Staring at the banquet.*) What is this for? If they are
 going to murder us, what is this for?
HELEN: I think they want to make us foolish. I think it is
 grotesque and horrible and –
GRISELDA: The food *is* poisoned, I suppose…?
HELEN: ALTOGETHER TYPICAL OF MR DANCER.
 (*ROMANOFF is working with a passion.*)
 I can see exactly what they want. They want us to sit here
 in a parody of plenty and then possibly on film, certainly
 with photographs, to suffer an agonising death, falling
 across the table, choking on the silverware – (*GRISELDA*

bursts out laughing.) No, it isn't funny, it is the way they think, it is the very essence of their mentality and –

CAROLINE: (*Who has not moved.*) IT'S A WEDDING.

(*Pause. They look at the table.*)

GRISELDA: Yes…! There's a cake…!

(*They look at CAROLINE. Music. DANCER enters. He stops. It is as if he suffers an embarrassment, and chooses not to speak the thing he had intended. He goes to the chair at the bottom of the table and sits in it, thoughtfully. No one else moves. The wind and creaking woodwork. At last he looks up.*)

DANCER: A transient phenomenon…

Celebrates… (*He jumps up, clumsily.*)

Well, that's what we're supposed to do, isn't it? Celebrate! (*He stares at them.*) Revolution has become associated with austerity, we can't have that. The fall of dynasties has forfeited its glamour and become a sordid and obscure transaction occurring in a cellar

THE COMMITTEE LACKS IMAGINATION

I have always said so

I would go so far as to say it defines the thing…!

One would think we were ashamed…

So…

(*He gestures for them to sit. They do not respond.*)

CHORUS: DANCER

THEY WILL HUMILIATE YOU

DANCER: Obviously, they'll try…

CHORUS: FOUR HUNDRED YEARS OF POWER

DO YOU THINK THEY'LL PLAY WITH YOU

THEY'D RATHER DIE

DANCER: They're decadent. Even the boy.

CHORUS: DRAG THEM OUTSIDE

ONE VOLLEY AND FORGET

DANCER: That is precisely what I wish to avoid! That is precisely the mundane practice of all revolutions and I think it fails to grasp

THE

SYMBOLISM

OF

THE

SACRIFICE (*He looks at ROMANOFF.*)

Please…

ROMANOFF: You are asking me to sit at my own table.

DANCER: Yes.

ROMANOFF: To eat off my own plates.

DANCER: Yes.

ROMANOFF: With cutlery that bears my own initials.

DANCER: Yes.

ROMANOFF: You are a man of such mean sensibilities I do
    not think you even comprehend the gravity of your own
    offence…

HELEN: He does…

ROMANOFF: Does he…! Then he also understands why I
    will not concede to him the right to extend me such an
    invitation!

HELEN: (*Turning away.*) I'm sure he does…

ROMANOFF: THE SERVANT OFFERS DINNER TO HIS
    MASTER…!

CAROLINE: Yes!

ROMANOFF: THE MUTINOUS TUTOR INVITES THE PRINCE
    TO EAT OFF HIS OWN CROCKERY!

    (*Suddenly on an inspiration he sits.*)

    I am as subtle as you, Mr Dancer!

    Wretch!

    Animal!

    Simian deformity!

    What's the hors d'oeuvre?

    It had better be good you cur

    Not that you'd know cuisine from the stable floor

    Insect

    Parasite

    I can play this game

    Any game

    Better than you

    Lout

    Rodent

    Did you think me trapped in regal postures?

Stiff and fragile?

Morally obtuse?

A Fabergé of manners and conventions?

Inflexible?

Absurd?

NO

NO

NO

The laugh's on you (*He gestures to his family.*)

Do sit

Do sit (*He spontaneously flings a plate to the floor.*)

Oh, dear, the family crest…!

(*He leans across the table violently.*)

MONARCHY IS NOT MATERIAL, CITIZEN!

(*Pause. DANCER is taken off-guard by this tirade. He stares at ROMANOFF, as do the entire family. The CHILD goes silently to his father and takes his hand. Tears come into ROMANOFF's eyes. Following further instruction, the CHILDREN and CAROLINE take their places at the table. JANE appears at the door in an apron.*)

JANE: Do you want it, now? (*DANCER does not reply.*) Look, Dancer, I am not sweating to pieces in the kitchen while you –

DANCER: Shh!

JANE: Make up your mind what time you might or might not –

DANCER: SHH I SAID…

JANE: I've got a home to go to! (*She goes out.*)

ROMANOFF: Servant problem? (*The briefest pause. He does not look up from the table.*) Listen, if you get us out of here I will pay you one hundred and fifty thousand American dollars…

DANCER: (*As if abstracted.*) Mmm?

ROMANOFF: I said if you –

DANCER: That's nothing to you –

ROMANOFF: No, but a great deal to you –

DANCER: The merest trickle from the great lake of your estate –

ROMANOFF: Very well, five hundred thousand American dollars –

DANCER: Really, this is embarrassing –

ROMANOFF: It doesn't embarrass me –

DANCER: It should do –

ROMANOFF: I have children and a wife to –

DANCER: Precisely, and to save them you are prepared to dispense –

ROMANOFF: Double that figure –

DANCER: To dispense the merest fraction of one part of your annual income –

ROMANOFF: Triple it –

DANCER: The microscopic portion of your wealth you deem appropriate to ransom your so-called loved ones SOME LOVE THIS –

ROMANOFF: I DEEMED IT ADEQUATE TO CORRUPT A WORM LIKE YOU.

DANCER: (*Shouting off.*) WE'LL HAVE IT NOW!
(*JANE appears.*)

JANE: Are you trying to be funny, Citizen?

DANCER: I do not have to try. Apparently I bring it out in others
DO YOU SERIOUSLY BELIEVE MY PASSION HAS A PRICE...? (*Pause.*)

ROMANOFF: Passion?
(*The wind. A single note, discordant. JANE goes out.*)

GRISELDA: Father... I can't eat...

HELEN: Me neither...

ROMANOFF: Stay in your places.

HELEN: I want to go to a priest...!

ROMANOFF: There is no priest, stay in your places...

HELEN: And all this is trickery!

ROMANOFF: Of course it is trickery, but we are not humiliated by the antics of others, History will record how – (*JANE appears with a large tureen. She stands in the doorway.*) In our ordeal we –

GRISELDA: I am not interested in History –

ROMANOFF: We ignore it at our peril

GRISELDA: I want a child… (*Pause.*)
　So what if I'm fifteen? (*She stands.*)
　Mr Dancer
　I think the sins of royalty cannot be extended to the
　children of the children of
　Etcetera
　My body has no politics and
　YOU CAN BE THE FATHER IF YOU WISH
　(*A great silence, in which the sound of the snoring of
　CAROLINE is audible. They look at her, for the first time
　aware she has fallen asleep. DANCER is deeply moved, not by
　GRISELDA, but by CAROLINE…*)
DANCER: She snores…! (*He looks to ROMANOFF, in amazement.*)
　Oh, God…! She snores…! (*He half-laughs, half-snorts.*)
　Impossible…!
JANE: Do you want it or not?
DANCER: Jane! She snores…!
JANE: So do I –
DANCER: Yes, but –
JANE: Shall I serve it up or –
DANCER: SHH SHH PHILISTINE SHH…! (*Pause. The sound of
　sleep.*)
　She dreams…
GRISELDA: You're not listening to me…
　NOBODY IS…!
ROMANOFF: Sit still, please…
GRISELDA: I can't, I want a child…!
ROMANOFF: You will have a child, I promise you –
GRISELDA: How!
ROMANOFF: I don't know yet, sit still…
GRISELDA: MR DANCER I AM PREPARED TO MAKE
　CHILDREN FOR THE REVOLUTION
　KINDLY
　MAKE
　ME
　PREGNANT
　OR
　ANYBODY

PLEASE… (*Pause. She sits, humiliated.*)
I cannot understand how your ideas can interfere with the
functions of my body
I am so healthy
I am so fertile
My womb is not guilty, is it?
HELEN: He is not listening, Griselda…
GRISELDA: No? What is he doing then?
I AM A PRINCESS HOW CAN HE RESIST ME?
(*She laughs derisively.*)
What's in the tureen? Some ghastly thing, no doubt, no, it's
peculiar, this desire to live, do you have it?
HELEN: Yes… (*She looks at her sister.*)
GRISELDA: WHAT'S IN THE TUREEN, SOMETHING TO MAKE
US SICK?
ROMANOFF: Shh…
GRISELDA: Daddy…
ROMANOFF: Shh…
GRISELDA: Daddy…
(*The tureen is placed on the table at a signal from DANCER.
JANE departs. DANCER stands.*)
DANCER: I'd like to serve you…
(*He goes to the tureen and picks up a silver ladle. JANE
reappears.*)
JANE: Psst! (*DANCER is irritated by the interruption to a rite.*) Psst!
DANCER: What?
JANE: There's another one of those Citizens…
DANCER: What!
JANE: Outside.
DANCER: Can't be…!
JANE: Came by car…   .
DANCER: CAR…!
(*The brutal interruption of the telephone. DANCER closes his
eyes. It rings again and again.*)
JANE: Shall I get it?
DANCER: (*Shaking his head.*) It's funny, isn't it, you would
think, in the chaos of a revolution and a civil war, the
complete disintegration of the transport system, the

telegraphic networks and the rest of it, such a resolute
supervision of the minor executives of the People's Will
would be impossible, but no, the contrary is the case, a
profusion of messengers, a plethora of orders emanating
from every corner, and the paperwork…!

I'll see to this. (*JANE goes out. He goes to follow, stops.*)
You'd think I couldn't be trusted.

(*He leaves. The FAMILY remains at the table. The phone
ceases. CAROLINE snores. DANCER returns, stops in the
doorway.*)

They're dead I said. (*Pause.*)

He thanked me. (*Pause. He shrugs.*)

A few minutes either side…what difference does it make?

JANE: (*Coming in again.*) I'm wrong, there's two of them.

DANCER: (*Shaken.*) Two?

JANE: Two Citizens. High ups.

DANCER: TWO.

JANE: That's what I said   (*HOLLOWLY laughs.*)

HELEN: Be quiet!

DANCER: TWO…

CHORUS: DANCER…!

DANCER: Yes, I'm here…

CHORUS: DANCER

WHAT ARE YOU

ARE YOU A LIAR?

DANCER: A liar, yes…! And infinitely resourceful…!

CHORUS: DANCER

YOUR LIES WILL BRING YOU TO THE DITCH

DANCER: I'm too good a rider, sorry…

CHORUS: HISTORY WILL

DANCER: I KNOW ALL ABOUT HISTORY, THANK YOU…!

(*Pause.*)

And as for lies, mine are so thoroughbred they leap the
brooks and hedges of your mediocrity. Give me a great lie,
and I will be its jockey…

(*Two MEN Enter. DANCER turns to face them.*)

Where *is* Citizen Fitch? And not only Citizen Fitch, but
Arrant, where is he? I try to cope but all I have is a flock of
bleating peasants. (*They look.*)
No disrespect, but we know their limitations, don't we?
(*Pause.*)
All right, not bleating. Unenlightened. (*He smiles.*)
Are you my assistants, or am I yours? (*They laugh.*)
Yes! That is how it is here, one does not know! One greets
in pure ignorance God knows what rank of official! It's as
well we have abolished all the old formality!
DENADIR: (*Looking at the table.*) Has one abolished it, Citizen?
DANCER: Oh yes, one has most certainly.
DENADIR: Table cloths, napkins, silverware…one seems to
    have a soft spot for those, notwithstanding…
DANCER: (*Through his teeth.*) One has however, an entirely
    different attitude to objects which once bore particular
    significance, commanded particular responses, and so on.
    It is crucial, Citizens, that we address ourselves not simply
    to the material, albeit we call ourselves materialists, but to
    the meanings with which the material is endowed.
    (*He smiles.*)
DISBANNER: Yer love nice stuff…
DANCER: DON'T TILT WITH ME I AM AN IDEOLOGIST (*They
    stare, puzzled.*)
    The Doorman, me… (*Pause.*)
    The title has no meaning for you? I promise you it will.
    (*He goes to the table.*)
    Are you on your way somewhere or –
DISBANNER: Who are these?
    (*Pause. DANCER hesitates, marshals his resources, smiles, in
    the space of a second.*)
DANCER: Chaos.
    I like it. (*They look at him.*) Chaos.
    How it suits me. (*Pause.*)
    It's my medium. (*Pause.*)
    But you…!
    (*He walks to the chair where CHRISTOPHE is seated.*)

Gentlemen, I can see from your expressions you are
gardeners at heart…
(*He suddenly seizes CHRISTOPHE in his arms and holds his
head in a fixed grip as if he were demonstrating the qualities
of a calf.*)
WHO'S THIS…!
(*He laughs. ROMANOFF jumps to his feet, shuddering, tense.*)
Who's this, he says…!
Look…! (*The MEN stare.*)
Look, then!
(*DISBANNER looks at DENADIR, who nods, to authorise him.
DISBANNER stares at the CHILD.*)
No…
I don't call that looking… (*He drags the CHILD nearer.*)
STARE INTO HIS EYES… (*DISBANNER, hands on knees, stoops.*)
Do you not know the eyes?
The shape of them?
The colour?
Oh, Citizen, are you such an ethereal scholar you never
stooped to pick up the magazines?
(*DISBANNER's eyes meet DANCER's.*)
Not once?
In the dentist's waiting room?
MANY A PASSION HAS BEEN KINDLED THERE…!
(*Pause. Something dawns on DISBANNER.*)
Yes…
This peculiar and distinctive physiognomy is all we
loathe… (*He shakes his head.*)
Whose humiliation and disfigurement can never satisfy our
rage…
(*He propels the CHILD bodily into DISBANNER's arms.*)
Kiss him.
(*DISBANNER smiles grotesquely, and kisses the CHILD, who
squirms. DANCER turns to DENADIR.*)
Here are my papers, where are yours?
(*He thrusts his documents into DENADIR's face.*)
DENADIR: In the car.
DANCER: Get them.

213

(*DENADIR pointedly declines to examine DANCER's authority.*)
When I said kiss him – (*He looks to DISBANNER.*)
I meant once…

DISBANNER: (*To the family, in a spasm of savage delight.*)
I'M TREADING IN YOUR BRAINS YOU!
I'M WIPING MY BOOTS ON YOUR WOMBS!
AND KICKING YOUR EYEBALLS HIGH INTO THE BRANCHES!
(*He stops, turns to DANCER.*)
It is them…?
Is it? (*He returns to his theme.*)
And when I walk away I'll drag your entrails through the gardens…wiping bits on twigs as if I'd trod in shit… kidneys…! Lung clinging to my ankle!

HELEN: Shut up…
(*DISBANNER grins.*)

DISBANNER: It is them, isn't it…?
(*DENADIR goes to DISBANNER and mutters in his ear. He leaves smartly, stops in his tracks.*)

DENADIR: Did I hear a telephone, Citizen?

DANCER: In the hallway, Citizen. You dial seven, for the Central Committee…
(*DENADIR goes out. DANCER knifes DISBANNER, thrusting a hand over his mouth. Instant music. The FAMILY variously rise to their feet, cover their mouths, gasp. CHRISTOPHE holds out his can… The music ceases as abruptly. A peculiar silence. DANCER holds DISBANNER in a fatal embrace. In this silence, CAROLINE can be heard snoring. DANCER listens to this. Then he lowers DISBANNER to the ground. The wind, the creaking of boards. The FAMILY do nothing but watch. One by one, they sit again. JANE enters.*)

JANE: (*Pointing.*) He's on the telephone!

DANCER: Help me move –

JANE: (*Horrified.*) No –

DANCER: Please –

JANE: I can't –

DANCER: Jane –

214

JANE: DON'T WANT ANYTHING TO DO WITH HISTORY!

DANCER: This is not History. This is the opposite of History.

JANE: WON'T HELP A MURDERER.

(*She stares at DANCER. He appears disconcerted.*)

DANCER: Murderer...?

JANE: You!

(*DANCER releases a slow. tentative shrug of the shoulders. He looks to ROMANOFF.*)

DANCER: Get his legs.

ROMANOFF: No, and nor will anybody else.

(*DANCER looks at ROMANOFF.*)

DANCER: You think the transient phenomenon has run out of luck...how little you understand me...and how correct it is I am obliged to do everything myself...to be suspected by every one...and trusted by nobody...how splendid I have slipped from human knowledge like a playing card lying beneath a desk...

JANE. He's coming...!

(*She hurries out. DANCER goes to a chair and sits, extending and crossing his ankles, and joining his fingers as if contemplatively. DENADIR enters, see the body.*)

DANCER: He died. (*Pause.*)

His contribution to the future was significant, but brief...

(*DENADIR looks, coolly.*)

I knew when I saw you, that man was a priest...

I knew it, I could smell the clinging odour of the seminary which no rebellion of the will or cleansing of the intellect can ever shift.

Throw open the windows of the soul! Let the winds of civil disorder and the rhetoric of lawyers whirl the pages of the antique books, sheets in the gutter, splintering crucifixes underneath your boots but still – (*Pause.*)

No, it's painted on your eyes, some profound antipathy to logic... (*Pause.*)

Help me kill this lot... (*DENADIR stares.*)

The Doorman cannot lift the latch...

(*The tension is too great for ROMANOFF, who stands suddenly.*)

ROMANOFF: We love…!
　We love each other…! (*DENADIR stares at him.*)
　Pity us…
CHORUS: (*Quietly, intimately.*)
　DANCER
　CAN YOU CORRUPT THE SO-CORRUPTED
　DANCER
　IS IT POSSIBLE
　YOU'VE MET YOUR MATCH? (*Pause.*)
DENADIR: Pity…? (*Pause. He walks, stops.*) We are replacing
　that by organisation.
CHORUS: DANCER
　HE IS NOT SUSCEPTIBLE
DANCER: We don't know yet…!
CHORUS: DANCER
　HE FATHOMS YOU
DANCER: We know nothing yet!
GRISELDA: (*To DENADIR.*) I think you have such a nice face.
　Such a nice face and you ought to look after it, it's the face
　of an angel. (*DENADIR studies her.*)
　I think if you were capable of murder it would show in
　your face. (*Pause.*)
　Perhaps you don't like to have the face of an angel,
　perhaps it's a burden to you and you think by doing ugly
　deeds your face will change. (*Pause.*)
　No doubt angels have a lot to put up with and would
　happily conceal it. (*Pause.*)
　But it's fate. The weak will always come to you. The weak
　and the destitute. Obviously, you'll hate them for it. You
　will squirm at their dependence and their whimpering, you
　will be enraged to know that your own liberty is trampled
　on by their persistence but… (*Pause.*)
　The perfect are unlucky…have you not heard the angels
　complain…? They do! They groan…!
　(*She looks down at her plate.*)
　They grasp at anything which will suffocate the pity that
　consumes them…
　(*Pause. The wind and the boards.*)

DENADIR: It's true I have wings under my overcoat I hide
   them obviously I fold them occasionally a single feather
   drifts to the ground what's that they say what's that white
   thing? (*He bursts out laughing.*)
   YOU PARADE YOUR SENSIBILITY
   THE BLOOD OF THOUSANDS OOZES FROM BENEATH
   YOUR FINGERNAILS
   (*Suddenly he throws down a set of motor car keys. They lie on
   the floor, the subject of everyone's gaze. A long pause.*)
   There is a car
   It's parked by the lodge
   A full tank of benzine
   Maps and
   (*Suddenly he suffers a paroxysm of mental pain that doubles
   him. They watch. He sobs.*)
DANCER: None of them drives, unfortunately…
   (*He goes to DENADIR, and with a gentleness, runs his
   hands along the man's arms. DENADIR weeps on DANCER's
   shoulder. DANCER kills him with the knife in this embrace.
   A cry.*)
   It's better…! (*A cry again.*)
   No, this is better…! (*And again.*)
   The torments of a pure soul!
   I couldn't bear to witness it! (*He staggers, lowers him.*)
   Martyr!
   Martyr to an instinct which all life abhors!
   (*He looks at the dying man, then turns to GRISELDA.*)
   Console him… (*She is staring in fixed horror.*)
   Console him, then…! (*She goes unsteadily, kneels, weeps.*)
ROMANOFF: He would have saved us…
DANCER: Yes…
ROMANOFF: HE WOULD HAVE GOT US OUT OF HERE!
DANCER: Of course he would! I saw it in his eyes!
ROMANOFF: THEN WHAT –
DANCER: Do you think we have had a revolution in order that
   idealistic priests masquerading as policemen could indulge
   an appetite for gestures by liberating oppressors such as
   you? What do you think the revolution is, a stage?

ROMANOFF: Yes, what else is it? (*Pause. DANCER shrugs.*)

DANCER: Yes, and this performance, however predictable, threatened to overshadow me… (*He calls for JANE.*)

HELEN: You kill people. You just keep killing them

DANCER: Yes, it's so much easier than I thought –

GRISELDA: (*Holding up a tiny crucifix.*) Look! He wore this round his neck…!

JANE: (*Entering.*) WHAT?

DANCER: (*To GRISELDA.*): Wear it yourself…your eloquence entitles you to some reward…

JANE: CHRIST YOU'VE GONE AND –

DANCER: Both of them, yes –

GRISELDA: (*Through a sob.*) I CAUSED HIS DEATH…!

ROMANOFF: Nonsense! All you said was true and beautiful and nothing caused his death but this monster and his delinquency!

DANCER: Excellent. Unfortunately, she is too sophisticated for your platitudes. (*To JANE.*)
Help me move these to the –

ROMANOFF: I DETEST YOU, Dancer. I CURSE YOU.

JANE: You keep asking me to shift these bodies

DANCER: I know, and you keep refusing, but –

JANE: I'M INNOCENT AND THAT'S HOW I'M STAYING.

DANCER: Do you think I want to kill these people? They keep turning up, one after another, it's like hacking the limbs off a centipede…! (*He shudders.*)
Horrible…
And their banality…their philistine instincts, glamorised by philosophical quotation, their cruelty, legitimised by slogans, they don't know what cruelty is…! It's pure savagery to them…! Indulgence…! (*He shakes his head.*)
It is such a difficult time to love…to surpass oneself… to triumph over the servile characteristics of a rebellious character like mine…and love…difficult…oh, difficult…

CHORUS: DANCER
DANCER
SOME LAPSE SOME COMPLICATION
MAKES US DISTRUST YOU

WE CRAVE THEIR EXECUTION AND YOU GIVE THEM
DINNER

DANCER: It's no more than a ritual, I assure you...

CHORUS: WE DEMAND THEIR DEATHS

DANCER: Yes...

Yes...and the people must be gratified, of course. I feel
your breath, hot on my neck...not very sweet breath, but
sweet breath is almost certainly evidence of degeneracy...
(*He leans over the sleeping CAROLINE, so her breath falls on
his face. Silence. A note played. He is ecstatic. Suddenly, he
turns and sweeps the car keys off the floor.*)

How fortunate I am I do not need a chauffeur!

ROMANOFF: (*Standing.*) Take us. Drive us to the frontier.
Redeem your stunted life by a single act of perfect charity.
(*DANCER laughs quietly, shaking his head.*)

DANCER: Do you think I have not thought of that? From the
very first day of the uprising, do you not think I anticipated
that? Whilst you were seriously troubled by a point of tactics
whilst the disintegration of the army cost you hardly any
sleep, I was rehearsing the very moment of your passion,
and the role I'd play in it...

ROMANOFF: Yes, I believe you.

DANCER: Most men would, of course. The gratification, the
celebration, the reputation the everything heroic and
magnanimous, who could refuse? (*Pause.*)

Only me. (*Pause.*)

Unfortunately, I am cursed with subtlety.

(*He makes a tremendous throw, sending the keys far into the
night. A wind.*)

I have to guard against myself. We all long to evade our
destiny...

ROMANOFF: (*To HELEN.*) Come here...! Come here...!
(*She goes to her father, weeps in his arms.*)

Griselda...!

GRISELDA: (*Not unkindly.*) No...

ROMANOFF: Christophe...!

(*The CHILD goes to him. The group rock, tearfully, in each other's arms. DANCER watches. Then, to rupture the tension, bursts out.*)

DANCER: Firstly, I mastered the vocabulary. Less than one hundred words, I promise you, is adequate, two hundred makes you an expert, entitling you, to a limited extent, to innovate! Yes, I am a most convincing exponent of the theory of revolution whilst at the same time disciplining myself against the temptation – always present in a man of real intelligence – to intervene in the higher levels of debate – a fatal error because is renders you – (*Pause.*) Please stop that – (*HELEN wails.*) It renders you an object of suspicion to the – (*GRISELDA cannot help herself, and wails also.*) Please...! (*Pause.*) The very individuals you most hoped to – (*JANE now shakes with grief. DANCER watches with a peculiar disbelief.*) satisfy...

(*The sound fills the stage, ROMANOFF himself grieving loudly. In this orchestration, DANCER moves, like a fascinated child in a museum of anguish. His delicate steps take him round the table to where CAROLINE still sleeps. He takes her head between his hands and kisses her, deeply, lengthily. Through their grief, the others are slowly made aware of this. They cease, their horrified gaze falling on the spectacle. ROMANOFF, repressing an urge to attack DANCER, moves away, thoughtful and observing from a distance.*)

CAROLINE: (*As DANCER withdraws his lips.*) I sleep – I can't describe the clinical reasons – I sleep to isolate myself – as if like some insect I might undergo a change of such proportions I would not, on waking, recognise myself... I do recognise myself... And the sleep's hell. Perhaps it is for butterflies. Perhaps there is a price to be paid for such brief apotheosis. (*Suddenly.*)
I keep dreaming I'm on trial...!

ROMANOFF: I think, this time, there will be no trial...

CAROLINE: Pity. I would have conducted myself very well, if the dream is anything to go by. I would not be acquitted, but they would suffer the humiliation of committing a judicial murder. The public would know this, and...

(*She shrugs.*)

How romantic…! As if the public cared…!

HELEN: Mother…

CAROLINE: Yes… (*She looks to DANCER.*)

JANE: LET 'EM GO…! LET 'EM GO, DANCER…!

DANCER: Jane…

JANE: I CAN'T BEAR THIS…!

DANCER: It's difficult…

JANE: BODIES, MORE BODIES…!

DANCER: I know…

JANE: I try to be historical, I try to be – to be – what's it –

DANCER: Objective –

JANE: That's it, I do and –

DANCER: You've done splendidly –

JANE: CHILDREN…!

(*Pause. DANCER looks at her.*)

DANCER: Yes. (*Pause.*)

AS ALWAYS, CANCER DANCER has a personal interest in this.

(*He goes to JANE, touches her lightly on the shoulder.*)

Which, even were the ground not thoroughly patrolled… would render your pleas meaningless… (*JANE wipes her eyes with her sleeve.*) Help me move these dead men out…who… for all their cruelty…were simple…raging but possibly also…kind…

(*Pause, then JANE assists him to drag away the two dead men. CAROLINE goes to DANCER, boldly.*)

CAROLINE: You won't escape the consequences of this, Mr Dancer –

DANCER: No –

CAROLINE: On the contrary, you will be the next to be eliminated –

DANCER: Yes –

CAROLINE: The shame of this will oblige them to destroy every piece of evidence, including the witnesses –

DANCER: Yes –

CAROLINE: You and the man who murders you and him who murders him, they all –

DANCER: I UNDERSTAND THAT VERY WELL –

CAROLINE: MY LIFE IS PERFECT, LOOK AT ME. (*Pause.*)

HELEN: Mother…

CAROLINE: Shhh –

HELEN: Mother, we are all –

CAROLINE: I AM FIGHTING FOR MY LIFE AND YOU SHOULD
FIGHT FOR YOURS
(*A cold wind, she shrugs.*)
Or if you prefer not to, don't…
(*ROMANOFF watches her, having returned from moving the
bodies.*)
If you would rather acquiesce…with dignity and so
on…do… I don't criticise… (*Pause.*)
I am not a good mother, am I? I plead for myself, and my
humiliation, if it is humiliation, embarrasses you.

HELEN: You shouldn't stoop to such a –

GRISELDA: Oh, let her, let her stoop…!

HELEN: SUCH A HORRIBLE AND –

GRISELDA: I stooped! Stoop yourself!

HELEN: NEVER

GRISELDA: It would do you good to stoop for once –

HELEN: Shut up!

GRISELDA: No, it would do…!

HELEN: You'd take your clothes off for this monster, you just
said so, what kind of family lets a child – (*CAROLINE laughs
bitterly.*)
WHAT KIND OF FAMILY. (*Slowly, JANE goes out.*)
We have offended her…

CAROLINE: Yes. The poor cannot bear their masters to be
human. *They* can be human, but not us…
(*GRISELDA grasps HELEN in her arms.*)

DANCER: The beautiful exists…but only because the hideous
exists… I am the hideous, and the agent of the hideous… I
have never concealed it from myself.

CAROLINE: I don't find you hideous, Mr Dancer…

DANCER: Please…

CAROLINE: I am perfectly serious, I don't find you –

DANCER: TIME'S VERY SHORT
TOO SHORT

FOR TRANSPARENT COMPLIMENTS
AND THE *ARRIÈRE PENSÉE*, MADAME!
(*He laughs, shakes his head.*)
I find...
How infuriating...
I find...
So few who are in any sense worthy of great sacrifice,
so few, and possibly – one must grasp the nettle – such
individuals do not exist, but this does not diminish in the
least, the will to sacrifice, misery of miseries, it possibly
enhances it... (*Pause. He looks at CAROLINE.*)
I adore you...
And you are – spiritually – poor... (*Pause.*)

CAROLINE: I resent that, Citizen.

DANCER: Of course you do...

CAROLINE: I am beautiful, a princess of royal blood, and
you –

DANCER: I am an ugly and murderous fellow, yes (*Pause.*)
There is a cake there, but where is my bride? (*Pause.*)

CAROLINE: I'm here –
(*Pause. She looks to her HUSBAND. He makes a slight move
of his head, encouraging her. DANCER puts his hands to his
cheeks.*)

DANCER: The innocence of me...!
Even these – (*He indicates the CHILDREN.*)
Are more –
Sophisticated! (*ROMANOFF steps forward.*)

ROMANOFF: I'll give the bride away...
(*DANCER is puzzled. The telephone rings. He is still. It rings
and rings.*)
Shall I?
Wouldn't you like that?
(*Ignoring him, DANCER walks out of the room. They speak at
once.*)
It's all right, I know what I'm doing

HELEN: (*To CAROLINE.*) Don't quarrel with him –

ROMANOFF: I know his type –

HELEN: Whatever he says, do it –

ROMANOFF: Humour him –

HELEN: Things that horrify or possibly disgust you, still –

ROMANOFF: Grit your teeth and –

HELEN: Crawl, Mother –

ROMANOFF: I never thought I'd say this but –

HELEN: Creep, Mother –

ROMANOFF: The lives of our children depend on the denial of our feelings –

HELEN: Submit –

ROMANOFF: Caroline –

HELEN: Submit –

ROMANOFF: Caroline…! (*He stretches out an imploring hand.*) I shall suffer every second of your degradation…!
Every second…!
(*His hand, extended over the table, is ignored by her. It remains.*)

HELEN: We so admire you…!
(*DANCER enters, slowly. He walks as if in deep thought, ignoring them. He stops. He turns at last.*)

DANCER: I have been ordered to place myself under arrest.
(*Pause.*)
I've done so, obviously. (*Pause.*)
The higher wisdom of the Committee, the exigencies of the Terror, who could quarrel with it? Not me.
(*He looks at them.*)
A Transient Phenomenon expects nothing less than to be crushed beneath the wheels of Progress. I don't hesitate. I fling myself headlong.
Privacy.
Idiosyncrasy.
Call it what you like.
Must be extinguished like a cigarette.
His words, not mine.
The personality is no longer the exotic garden of indulgence but the park of the people.
His words, not mine.
Gates down. Walls down. The squeals of dirty infants in the summer house… (*Pause.*)

My words, not his...
Really, he has a fine mind, the Citizen at the terminus of all
the telephones. And not bereft of sensibility, no...!
(*Pause. It is darker, the evening closes in. The wind blows
in the silence. Suddenly, as if in horrible anticipation,
CHRISTOPHE runs from his FATHER's arms to his MOTHER.
She clasps him...*)

CAROLINE: Shh... (*She strokes his hair.*)

DANCER: (*Looking into the night.*)

    Hated nightfall
    As long as there was day
    I sensed the power to distinguish
    Will from appetite
    What thrilled me in the sun
    Is threatening by night
    Hated nightfall
    I'll lie awake all hours
    Plotting injury to those I love
    And you will pass an unclean hand
    Over the eyes of malcontents
    The senile dissidents
    And those
    Who find a recompense in cruelty...
    (*CAROLINE, steering her SON into the direction of his
    SISTERS, goes towards DANCER, who gazes into the evening.*)

CAROLINE: Save yourself... (*DANCER turns to her.*)
    Yourself and me...
    (*He examines her, not without suspicion.*)
    You because you believe in nothing.
    And me, because I represent everything.
    The cynic.
    The symbol.
    Lucidity.
    And illusion.
    Take me to a foreign city and we can live as poor as
    beggars in a room...
    I will be a mystery to you.
    Naked.

On a mattress.
Poverty
Exile
And
Desire… (*DANCER looks at her…*)
My body is not perfect –
DANCER: I've seen it –
CAROLINE: Three children leave their mark –
DANCER: Seen it I said –
CAROLINE: But an empress is an empress and – (*Pause.*)
Seen it, how? (*DANCER shrugs…*)
DANCER: All night on a balcony…nothing to me…soaked to the skin and clinging to a creeper…nothing to me…
(*GRISELDA laughs, stops.*)
ROMANOFF: Wretch…! Monkey and wretch…!
(*GRISELDA forces her hand into her mouth.*)
DANCER: Underneath the curtain an inch of light…adequate for me!
ROMANOFF: Pitiful and melancholy dwarf!
DANCER: (*Staring at CAROLINE.*) And the underwear…!
(*GRISELDA bursts out again.*)
Yes!
Absurd! (*He looks to GRISELDA.*)
She knows! The tutor scrambling in the laundry, there's religion for you…!
CAROLINE: (*Measured.*) If ever a man needed to sleep with an empress, that man is you…
DANCER: Sleep with…? Sleep with, she says…as if that mundane act could compass the terrible extent of my devotion…how little you know of love, Caroline.
CAROLINE: Instruct me, then…
DANCER: How shallow you are…as I always knew…so shallow it wounds me where I am most pervious to pain…
CAROLINE: Teach me…
DANCER: I preferred you sleeping…then at least I was deceived –
CAROLINE: TEACH ME I SAID. (*DANCER falters.*)

Night after night. Noon upon noon. Teach me. I have had a life of poverty. Drag me to a room and we will pulp our misery in the pursuit of some smothering ecstasy DRAG ME.

(*DANCER stares, moved by her vehemence. She tears her dress from the shoulder.*)

This is my flesh and it is dead. Unlit as Arctic winter. Breathe on me.

DANCER: (*Struggling against her.*) Fifteen nights in Paris…belly to belly underneath the roof –

CAROLINE: Yes –

DANCER: Venice… Deauville… Longchamps… Nice…

CAROLINE: Yes –

DANCER: The thrashing of limbs and dreams in mouldering resorts –

CAROLINE: Yes! Yes! Why not! Or on some lonely look-out tower clinging to the cliff where we will caress each other under changing skies with the intense devotion of the archivist… (*She stares at DANCER.*) I've not been entered… believe me… I'm unrevealed…

(*DANCER is in acute pain…he sways.*)

DANCER: It'll only – it'll simply –

GRISELDA: Do go, Citizen… (*DANCER turns, shocked at her encouragement.*) I thought I was unhappy but how small my unhappiness is compared to yours…leave us, do… Oh, my poor mother! What she says is true!

(*ROMANOFF covers his face in grief.*)

DANCER: Yes…and the way she says it…is the proof…

(*CAROLINE flings herself on DANCER, sliding down to his knees. DANCER, profoundly moved, looks at ROMANOFF.*)

ROMANOFF: It isn't too late, Dancer…you can go…

DANCER: (*As if lost.*) Go…?

ROMANOFF: LOVE HER AND GO.

(*DANCER yearns towards CAROLINE, but a movement catches his eye. CHRISTOPHE, with his watering can, climbs onto the table and proceeds to pour the contents over the cake, dark as blood. DANCER watches with fascination. The spell is broken. A low laugh comes from him…*)

DANCER: That was not the love I had in mind... I would lie with the silence of a spent lover and grieve under the seagulls for the apotheosis I had shirked... (*He looks to CAROLINE.*) Madame, you –
(*With a percussive shock, an arm, holding a rifle extended, is thrust through the floor. The rifle is flung down with a clatter. The arm remains fixed in the air. CAROLINE falls forward onto her hands, sobbing. ROMANOFF goes to dash to her.*)

ROMANOFF: Oh, Caroline –
(*He is stopped by the appearance of a second rifle thrust through and flung down as before. He takes account of it, then goes to CAROLINE and places his hands on her shoulders.*)
I'm sorry
I'm so sorry
I'm so sorry
So sorry
So sorry

CHORUS: DANCER
FORGIVE US
WE SUSPECTED YOU OF
AMBIGUITY
LUKEWARM IN YOUR DEVOTION
TO THE FUTURE
AND INCLINED TO
CLEMENCY

DANCER: Clemency...? But History doesn't know the word...
(*DANCER seizes the tiered wedding cake in his arms... He staggers under the weight... A pipe plays a dance off-key. CAROLINE goes to a chair, sits, sleeps. DANCER revolves with the cake as the CHORUS laugh. His dance takes him past the figure of CAROLINE.*)

CHORUS: MOCK HER
MOCK HER
THE BITCH'S GARMENTS ARE WOVEN FROM OUR
POVERTY
HUMILIATE HER
SHE FUCKED WITH PRIESTS

DANCER: (*Revolving.*) She did, did she...?

(*Some laugh in staccato contempt. Others excite themselves in chanting.*)

CHORUS: MONARCHY

MONARCHY

ANOTHER WORD FOR DEPRAVITY

DANCER: You know everything…!

CHORUS: AND THE HUSBAND WAS ANYWAY

COMPLETELY

IMPOTENT! (*They laugh derisively.*)

DANCER: I never knew…!

(*DANCER falls at CAROLINE's feet, clutching the cake. A silence. A wind blows. GRISELDA sings a psalm. JANE enters, clutching a saucepan. GRISELDA stops.*)

JANE: There's a woman outside says –

DANCER: A woman…?

JANE: A woman yes and –

(*DANCER takes the knife from his pocket again. JANE is horrified.*)

Dancer… (*She swallows with apprehension.*)

Dancer, you can't –

(*DANCER plunges the knife into the cake. He looks at JANE, then at the others.*)

DANCER: My bride's arrived… (*JANE stares.*)

Do share my cake… (*He extends a slice. JANE is motionless.*)

You are afraid…

The consequences of partaking of my wedding cake… appal you…

(*He tosses the slice. It strikes JANE on her apron, falls…*)

JANE: Dancer…you are a stupid, stupid man…

DANCER: (*Hacking another slice.*) LET THEM EAT CAKE! (*He tosses it wildly over his shoulder.*) She was not cruel…she was struggling with incomprehension, Marie Antoinette…

(*He flings another. Into the silence, a WOMAN OFFICIAL of the Revolution. It is as if they all knew her and expected her. JANE, desperate, turns to her.*)

JANE: Can I go now?

I did nothing except when I was forced and even then my soul revolted

Can I?

At all times my inclination was to say no thank you

Thank you I would rather not

Another time

Etcetera

God knows my innocence

GOD I LOVE HIM GOD (*She closes her eyes. She goes to move.*)

I'm wiping up, I –

ALBEIT: Stay where you are.

(*A musical effect. ALBEIT goes among the family, touching them lightly on the shoulder one by one and indicating they should move to the back of the room. She touches CAROLINE last. She does not move.*)

DANCER: She sleeps...the Empress...

(*ALBEIT indicates to the CHORUS with a movement of her head. They come and lift CAROLINE in the chair. CHRISTOPHE goes to his mother.*)

She sleeps because she cannot tolerate a world whose poverty of spirit includes even her...

JANE: I WANT TO WIPE UP, PLEASE!

DANCER: Oh, let her wipe up. She is a servant, and they deteriorate without their servitude I've noticed –

ALBEIT: (*To the CHORUS.*) Arrest this man. (*JANE drops the saucepan with a clatter.*) And her.

DANCER: Oh, Jane, and you did nothing!

JANE: DONE NOTHING, NO!

CHORUS: (*As they jerk DANCER and JANE into chairs.*)

DANCER

SOME MISUNDERSTANDING OBVIOUSLY

SOME TEMPORARY

SOME

SOME

IDEOLOGICAL

COMPLEXITY

ALBEIT: Where are the Citizens named Fitch and Arrant, Disbanner and Denadir?

ROMANOFF: Dead! They're dead!

ALBEIT: (*To DANCER.*) Where are the Citizens, I said –

ROMANOFF: He killed them
   He tortured them
   He slit their throats before our eyes
   Abominable monstrosity
   NO LOYALTY TO ANYTHING EXISTS IN THAT DEFORMED
   AND POISONED SOUL
HELEN: Father!
ROMANOFF: The world revolves and dynasties can come and
   go but that diabolical and cynical parcel of depravity –
GRISELDA: SHUT UP
ROMANOFF: SHUT UP?
   NEVER WILL I
   CEASE IN MY INDICTMENT OF – (*He is inspired.*)
   Citizen, look in the soup tureen. They were feeding us
   human remains.
HELEN: (*Incredulous.*) What…?
ROMANOFF: Yes, oh, yes, he was up to all sorts of –
JANE: HUMAN REMAINS?
ROMANOFF: The heads, yes, hacked them off and boiled
   them, arms and legs –
HELEN: What…!
ROMANOFF: In the soup…!
HELEN: Father!
ROMANOFF: (*To ALBEIT.*) The ones you mentioned, I don't
   know their names –
HELEN: Father, please…!
ROMANOFF: (*To ALBEIT.*) CLEANSE THE WORLD, MADAME!
   (*ALBEIT hesitates…*)
JANE: What heads…? I spent hours finding mushrooms for
   that soup – (*ALBEIT strikes JANE across the face.*)
ROMANOFF: Good…! Good…!
CHORUS: DANCER
   DANCER
   THE VEGETABLES WILL TESTIFY AGAINST YOU
   THE BANQUET WILL RISE UP AND POINT
   AN
   INCRIMINATING
   FINGER…

(*Pause, then* ALBEIT *goes to the soup tureen.*)

HELEN: It's impossible…!

ROMANOFF: Shut up.

HELEN: Impossible –

ROMANOFF: Shut up you idiotic child nobody requires your interventions!

HELEN: (*Aghast.*) Idiotic child…?

ROMANOFF: (*Whose gaze is fixed on the table.*) That's what I said…!

HELEN: I forgive you…how hard it is but I forgive you…

ROMANOFF: (*Staring madly at* ALBEIT.) Good!
(ALBEIT *removes the lid of the tureen. She looks in. She calculates. She replaces the lid.*)

JANE: There you are, now you can see what's what I'd like permission to – (ALBEIT *silences* JANE, *taking her face between the fingers of one hand menacingly and twisting her.* JANE *is still. Her head hangs.* ALBEIT *walks up and down.*)

ALBEIT: Chaos… (*Pause.*)
How it licenses depravity… (*Pause.*)
And we, constructing on the ruins of the past a new society, encounter in the strangest places exotic delinquencies…
(*She looks at* DANCER.)
Cannibals
Perverts
Amoralists

ROMANOFF: ABANDONED BY GOD AND REVILED BY MAN…!

JANE: Cannibals?

ALBEIT: Old and rotting systems whose debauched relations bring to birth in their senility transient phenomena such as this…

ROMANOFF: CLEANSE, MADAME…!

JANE: What cannibals…?

ROMANOFF: CLEANSE…!

DANCER: Oh, how they hate me, Jane…in this, these arch-opponents are of one accord…for I am the antithesis of History, which has manacled their souls…

(*ALBEIT seizes him by his hair and forces back his head. She lifts an item of cutlery from the table. At once, the* CHORUS *flock to observe his ordeal.*)

CHORUS: DANCER

DANCER

WE FEARED YOU WOULD DISPLAY THIS (*He lets out a cry.*)

ARROGANT

AND

PETULANT

(*He cries again.*)

DISHARMONY...!

JANE: (*Horrified.*) Leave him...leave him...!

(*He cries again. The* GIRLS *cover their mouths.*)

ROMANOFF: (*In a rambling, disconnected tone.*) We were tired, obviously we were tired, but it was not just tiredness –

HELEN: Don't die...! Don't die, Dancer!

ROMANOFF: No, I think one must acknowledge tiredness such as ours owed something to the greater lassitude of God, I think God Himself was tired –

(*DANCER, concealed behind the gathered* CHORUS, *lets out a profound groan...*)

I think His silence was the withdrawal of His love which possibly we had ceased to value...and in consequence He turned – not far – the slightest averting of His face is after all, sufficient for the eclipsing of all happiness –

GRISELDA: Shh!

ROMANOFF: (*Mildly now.*) Shh...why?

(*The* CHORUS, ALBEIT, *stand back from* DANCER. CHRISTOPHE, *irresistibly drawn to* DANCER, *slips off his* MOTHER's *lap and silently peers at him.* JANE *extends her hand to hold* DANCER's...)

JANE: Dancer... Oh, Dancer...that woman's blinded you...

GRISELDA: We love you... We love you...!

HELEN: Yes, oh, yes...!

DANCER: (*Croaking.*) Yes... I know you do...

ROMANOFF: Oh, Dancer, what are you... WHAT ARE YOU...!

DANCER: Afraid...

ROMANOFF: Afraid...?

DANCER: Afraid death even...will be poorer than my
imagination predicted...

ROMANOFF: OUR SOULS WILL MEET IN PARADISE!

GRISELDA: Yes! Yes! And Mr Dancer will be – oh, will be –

HELEN: Content!

GRISELDA: Content at last!

JANE: It's all right, Dancer...it is...even if it seems...not
right...at all...

ROMANOFF: I TAKE HIM IN MY ARMS!

GRISELDA: We all do! We all do!

*(DANCER is aware of CHRISTOPHE's proximity. His head
turns to him...)*

DANCER: Listen...

Listen...

*(The wind blows. The sound of CAROLINE's snore.
CHRISTOPHE lifts his watering can and pours the contents
over DANCER's uptilted face...)*

WOUNDS TO THE FACE

Characters

A WOMAN AT A MIRROR

A MAN

A SURGEON

A SOLDIER

A MOTHER

A LOVER

A BRIDE

A PRISONER

YOUTHS

MONSIEUR

A VISITOR

A WIFE

A TERRORIST

A SECOND TERRORIST

A DICTATOR

A DOUBLE

A SECOND DOUBLE

AN EMPEROR

AN EMPRESS

A PAINTER

A GUARD

A ROUÉ

A PROSTITUTE

A SECOND PROSTITUTE

NARCISSUS

A GREEK

A SECOND GREEK

A PATRIOT

A WOMAN WITH A PARASOL

A MAN

FIRST, TO LOVE YOURSELF

A WOMAN at a table and mirror. The litter of make-up. She works.
She suffers. She flings down some tool with vehemence.

WOMAN: An hour I've been here! (*Pause.*)
An hour...! (*Pause.*)
Firstly, there is no point, none whatsoever, in disputing
what cannot be dissented from, the face is the face, what I
was given, what I came into the world behind and which it
is impossible to disown or disassociate myself from, we are
implacably united dreams notwithstanding, tastes, opinion
notwithstanding, no, it's this and no other, start from the
facts, live with the facts and stop this futile and nauseating,
OH, GOD, AN HOUR, dissidence!
(*Pause. She looks. Suddenly she grabs up a pencil.*)
An hour so what! I am not content to endure without
protest the severe injustice of being trapped behind, no,
gnoled in, yow, [illegible] in a face I have profound
objections to, I refuse to yield to circumstances I was not
party to, I register my disobedience! (*Pause.*)
More than an hour now...
(*She peers into the glass.*)
I do not like it. Never did I like it. Not from my first look
did I and having said so perhaps I now might lay aside my
just criticism of God, His idleness, His wit, His sarcasm and
so on and proceed to – (*Pause.*)
I cannot move from this stool... (*Pause.*)
It is quite possible I shall never move again from off this
stool because I cannot reach agreement with my face, I
cannot make a compromise or an accommodation with
my face to live and let live, no, we hate each other and it
clings there like an uninvited insect I will not walk into the
world behind this thing I actually detest, how did I get like
this, an hour ago I was nothing like this I'VE MISSED THE
TRAIN THE BUS AND THE CONNECTION. (*Pause.*)
Really, this mirror gives me more trouble than a dozen
children, violent husbands, anything, perhaps it lies,
mirrors do lie, it's possible a different mirror would

convey a different picture, wholly possible, this mirror is against me and reflecting falsely I ACCUSE MIRRORS YES BECAUSE THEY ARE DISHONEST everybody knows, one says one thing, one says another, I am tired of being made a fool of INTO THE GARDEN AND THROW A BRICK AT IT or if it's not the mirror it's the lights, my position vis-à-vis the window, a dozen things might influence what I am seeing and consequently what I am seeing is by no means truth but some distortion, I have allowed myself to suffer a distortion! Idiot! (*She laughs.*)

Really, an hour and a half for nothing...!

(*She picks up a tool. She cranes. A MAN is discovered observing her.*)

MAN: An hour and a half today...not bad...some days she spends an entire morning there, and never once lifts her eyes higher than the mirror's rim. I observe, and am not observed. (*Pause.*)

At first, this pleased me. I was gratified by my own cunning, privileged to see and be unseen, but now...

(*Pause. The WOMAN gazes at herself, with a studied objectivity.*)

The opposite because what are her efforts for if not for me? I cannot tolerate such an expenditure of effort on the creation of a face that exists apparently for itself alone, I am offended, I considered breaking her window with a stone, or more subtly, in a faked accent telephoning, and with an affectation of concern, announce she is not so solitary as she believes herself to be, a catapult would do it, look, I am exposed to my full-height in the window and still...! (*Pause.*)

Blind...!

(*Spontaneously, the WOMAN weeps with rage and disgust. Three placards simultaneously descend, identical images of the face of the DICTATOR. A gang of YOUTHS rush in and attack the placards, defacing them. A sound of an explosion, as of a grenade. A SOLDIER enters, whose face is swathed in bandages except for the mouth. The YOUTHS hurry away, shouting.*)

SOMETHING CAN BE DONE IN ALMOST EVERY CASE

A SURGEON, white-coated, enters. He looks for a long time at the still figure of the maimed SOLDIER.

SURGEON: I am not insensitive. How hard it is to hold, however. How hard. Always ready to take flight, an anxious bird which trembles in the hands. Some don't. Some can't. I however, try. (*Pause.*)
Your jaw has gone, and one half of your face, the eye included. The nose, entirely, and the mouth, the palette, a cavern now. You feel this damage, and the scale of it. I have never seen a worse case but there have been worse. A worse case always. Raise your hand if you follow me.
(*The SOLDIER raises a hand, lets it fall.*)
And we have such skills now, such infinite resources, our aim is to restore you to the level of a tolerable life, a complex notion, I agree, one might dispute its meaning, raise a hand if you can follow me.
(*The SOLDIER does so, lets it fall again.*)
The face is after all, a structure, it is a particular organisation of muscularity and bone, fibre, membrane and if never replaceable, it can be reproduced, and if not made identical, similarity can be achieved, say if you follow.
(*The SOLDIER's hand rises and falls.*)
Some wars ago, before photography, the remade face was pure speculation, therefore a work of art, whilst technical, also a field for dream, but now we have so many images to hang our efforts on, one might say we improve on the authentic YOU WILL BE FOREVER HIDEOUS AND SIT ALONE IN ROOMS...
(*Pause. The SOLDIER raises his hand.*)
They hover in the corridors of Europe, behind avenues of trees, and do not talk. Ghosts have little need of conversation, you will find...
(*The hand falls. The SURGEON goes to the SOLDIER.*)
And did she whisper how she loved your face, and with the tender touch of adoration trace your brows, brushing your

241

lips with hers and swimming hour after hour in your gaze, and in the darkness find assurance in the contours of your face? (*The SOLDIER is silent.*)

That's all for today. I expect we shall see much of one another from now on.

(*He starts to go out, but senses the SOLDIER has raised a hand. He stops, without turning.*)

Yes, kill yourself if you wish. I would.

(*He goes out, passing an aged WOMAN, who looks grievingly at the SOLDIER.*)

MOTHER: What does he say...? (*Pause.*)

My son, what does he say?

SOLDIER: I am not the only one.

MOTHER: No, but –

SOLDIER: High walls and trees, he says. (*Pause.*)

MOTHER: And what about –

SOLDIER: Benches. Gravel in the gardens. And fountains, possibly...

MOTHER: Yes, but –

SOLDIER: But conversation not to be anticipated, apparently –

MOTHER: THE FACE, WHAT OF THE FACE, MY SON?

SOLDIER: No face, Mother. There's none.

(*A long pause. The MOTHER suffers, braces, determines.*)

MOTHER: Then you will need me. For a man without a face will earn no love from women. On the contrary, they will shudder and love will come from me alone, me, the solitary source again...!

My breasts tingle!

My breasts...dear one... (A *MAN enters, looks at her.*)

YOU WILL ENDURE ME, LONG AFTER I HAVE GONE

LOVER: I was looking at your photograph! (*He smiles.*)

The peculiar fashions of your youth...! And even, it seems, a way of smiling, which is almost certainly the smile of a period, the smile of twenty years ago, I am not sorry you have aged, you have shed a certain shallowness and gaiety with the years and now your beauty is quite painful to behold, dead vanity, and the ruins of an arrogance lend you such dignity, it is as if you were disappointed, not once, but over and over again, which I find attractive, perhaps peculiarly, and you are lucky, I suppose, to have acquired me as a lover at your age...

MOTHER: Lucky, and I never cease to think it.

LOVER: When I could find any number of mistresses whose eyes were sky blue with undamaged life...

(*He unbuttons her.*)

MOTHER: I sometimes gasp at my good fortune...

LOVER: What do people think, I wonder, seeing me visit you?

MOTHER: They do see, do they? I thought, by visiting me at night, you spared them the embarassment of speculating on the subject...

LOVER: It is clandestine, but of necessity...

MOTHER: I understand that, I was not criticising you – (*The LOVER kisses her passionately.*) Not criticising you at all...! (*She unbuttons him. The kisks with her.*) Sleep now...

LOVER: How much I want to...!

MOTHER: Sleep, and I will wake you. Have I ever let you down? Always, I arouse you in time.

LOVER: Yes, you do...and yet sometimes I feel I cannot read your face...suppose you love me but...

MOTHER: Love you...! Do I *love* you...

LOVER: Too much? (*Pause.*)

MOTHER: Possibly. (*She smiles.*) I often think, possibly this love is too great for the normal world...

LOVER: (*Scoffing.*) The normal world! God forbid the normal world!

MOTHER: God forbid it, yes!

(*She lowers his head.*)

Sleep now...

(*The LOVER sleeps, blissfully. She kisses his face, taking from her skirts a thin, cruel blade which she suspends over him. Again, she kisses him, and then plunges it fiercely. He emits a terrible cry.*)

You carry me, the consequences of me now, I cannot be denied...!

(*He rushes from the room.*)

If I bear age, then you bear temper! We wear each other's pain…!

(*Sobs from offstage. The LOVER returns, a towel over his face.*)

Sorry.

Perhaps you can boast one day of the madness you induced.

Ridiculous face.

Goodbye. (*The LOVER is still.*)

LOVER: Help me.

Help me, I have a wife!

MOTHER: Go to the wife, then. (*The LOVER peers over the towel.*)

LOVER: I'll say I was attacked.

MOTHER: Yes, say that. Shall I call a cab?

LOVER: By men. Attacked by men for no reason.

MOTHER: It happens all the time.

LOVER: My handsomeness offended them, I'll say…they marked me for no reason…

(*The LOVER goes out, slowly. A mirror descends in front of the chair on which the SOLDIER is sitting. He stares.*)

THE PERIMETERS OF AN OATH

The MOTHER stands behind the SOLDIER, and then, with an effort of will, begins to unravel his bandages. At last he is exposed. They both stare into the mirror. Their horror, their will, suspends them. A knock on the door.

MOTHER: Don't come in. (*Pause.*)

Or come in. (*Pause.*)

Don't…! (*Pause.*)

Or do, if you want…

(*A young WOMAN enters. She goes to the mirror and stands behind the SOLDIER. A long pause.*)

THE BRIDE: I can't marry you now… (*Pause.*)

SOLDIER: Someone threw a grenade, but badly…

THE BRIDE: Now now…

SOLDIER: Instead of landing in the enemy, it bounced back…

THE BRIDE: Not now...

SOLDIER: It hit a post, and bounced.

THE BRIDE: I cannot...now... I cannot...

SOLDIER: If the post had not been there. Or if the weather had been different. If I had been more agile. Or if his nerves had not spoiled his aim. (*Pause.*)
Another would be faceless and I. (*Pause.*)
Of course I think this all the time. (*Pause.*)
What if the post had rotted in the rain...?

THE BRIDE: Always philosophical...

SOLDIER: The same man. The same.

THE BRIDE: I

CANNOT

MARRY

YOU

SOLDIER: The same but in different proportions...

THE BRIDE: ONE LOVES THE OUTSIDE, FORGIVE ME, THE OUTSIDE ALSO (*Pause.*)

SOLDIER: I do think this piece of wood has much to answer for. Its effects on your character, for example, I wonder where –

THE BRIDE: Forgive me, I said...!

SOLDIER: Where this post is now... As they carried me away I tried to mark the place, this post was in my mind, it possibly exists still, holding up a barn door and not significantly decayed, it rains on this post and in summer it grows warm in sunshine...

THE BRIDE: I cannot lie beside you now...

SOLDIER: And then I think, this post was once a tree, and had a crop of leaves on, oak or beech, how I should like to lie beneath its arching bough, in your arms, obviously...

THE BRIDE: PLEASE SAY YOU UNDERSTAND... (*Pause.*)
I WOULD SO LIKE TO TAKE THAT UNDERSTANDING
AWAY WITH ME... (*The SOLDIER is still, silent.*) By withholding that, you are not philosophical at all... (*Pause.*)

SOLDIER: Now I am particularly exercised if it was pine or beech the post which like a cricket bat so deftly drove the bomb into my face...! Not oak, I think, we exhausted oak

in the war's first year UNDERSTAND YOU SAY oh, always
understand, the world is thick with the slippery paste
of mutual understanding, understand yes, which is not
forgiving is it, I understand the post, but forgive it, no, we
cannot marry it is an outrage to decency, obviously...

THE BRIDE: I LOVED YOUR FACE AND IT HAS GONE. (*She
turns to go. She encounters the MOTHER's gaze.*) How you hate
me, and will never speak of me again, I know. But there
are women like me everywhere, uttering this same pitiful
revulsion in a dozen different tongues... (*The old WOMAN
smiles grimly.*) How you make me hate you for that look...
(*She goes out. A WOMAN in prison garb enters, stands with a
mirror in her hand, but resolutely avoids seeing herself in it.*)

MOTHER: They all want forgiveness! But we are unforgiving!
We walk along the middle of the road! Horror! Horror!
Ring a bell to make the children hide! That woman and
her awful son! She had one life, and now she has another!
He had one face, and now he has another!

ARBITRARY IMPRISONMENTS

*The PRISONER holds the mirror at arm's length, turning it cruelly
towards herself and then averting her face to avoid the image. She
repeats this action from another angle, yearning towards it, recoiling,
laughing with fear and relief. She drags a worn photograph from her
pocket, examines it, stuffs it away.*

PRISONER: Twenty years in a hole. (*Pause.*)
Twenty in a hole IT CAN BE DONE and I was not resilient.
(*Pause.*)
In a pit open to the sky never mind the reason and then
the tide came in, it always does, eventually the tide comes
in bringing the dead on its crests but also the living
LEAVE YOUR HOLE a voice said and put a hand down
which I took, the greatest handshake in the world I defy
you to propose another, twenty years in a hole, it can be
done, and for no reason, probably my face, my face was
hated by someone OR LOVED POSSIBLY LOVED that

also was a reason for denunciation LOVED BY SOMEONE
AND THEREFORE DOOMED TO A HOLE I understand
that – better I was in a hole than gave myself to others
oh, I understand that passionate possession, twenty years,
twenty without a mirror. (*She holds up the photograph.*) Of
course I've changed. Not necessarily, but very likely I
have changed, the climate in that hole, it varied from
freezing to suffocation, so hardly do I entertain the idea
I am recognisable, no, this is quite – (*She suddenly tears up
the photograph and scatters it.*) The face of a dead woman to
all intents and – (*She drags the mirror past her face, shrieks,
closing her eyes at the crucial moment to avoid seeing her image.*)
I am such a coward! Such a flagrant! And I rubbed shit
into my flesh! This was for warmth initially, I wore it, I
weaved it into rugs, was there ever a parallel desire to
exist, I was an insect but not quite an insect for I obviously
harboured VANITY! (*She thrusts the mirror beneath her and sits
firmly on it.*) DON'T LOOK! But presumably, were I to look, and
obviously I will look, the moment will certainly announce
itself, I'd be less horrified than I anticipate because the
peculiar conditions in which I've lived, the characteristic
properties of holes and bogs might have – I speculate –
PRESERVED ME – don't mock it happened to some Celts
their bodies were as perfect as the day they or Romans
possibly no Celts it was and underneath the crust of my
endurance the youthful face of unused beauty still –
(*Bawling off. Three placards of the dictator descend. The
YOUTHS burst in, tearing and ripping the images.*)
He's dead, then?

YOUTH: Yes, and all the holes filled in!

PRISONER: Dead, and I thought he was immortal…

YOUTH: Every morning, his mug in the classroom!

SECOND YOUTH: Every morning, in the workshop!

THIRD YOUTH: And on the bus, his mug bore down on you!

PRISONER: So there was one thing good about the holes, for
twenty years I never saw it…!
(*She cackles. The YOUTHS start to run away.*)
Don't go…!

YOUTH: We're off to rip his mug off other walls!

PRISONER: Wait! I've also got a face… (*They stop.*) Describe it,
would you?

SECOND YOUTH: Find a mirror –

PRISONER: I have a mirror, but I'm afraid to use it!
DON'T GO I SUFFERED. (*Pause.*)

YOUTH: A nose. In the middle. (*They snigger.*)
And underneath, a mouth…

PRISONER: (*With a bitter smile.*) Very good…

SECOND YOUTH: Either side of the nose, an eye –
(*They giggle again.*)

PRISONER: That's perfectly good to start with –

YOUTH: Ears. Teeth, I imagine – (*She bares her lips.*)
Teeth, yes –

SECOND YOUTH: (*Mockingly.*) Teeth…!

PRISONER: And old?

YOUTH: Teeth rather –

PRISONER: OLD OR NOT?

YOUTH: Dirty, certainly –

PRISONER: Ignore the dirt –

YOUTH: Dirty and –

PRISONER: THE DIRT'S A CRUST…!
(*She drags a cloth from her clothes, spits on it and begins to
scrub her face.*)
Don't go…!

YOUTH: All people from the holes look identical to me! (*The
YOUTHS hurry off.*)

PRISONER: ONLY A CRUST!

NOT ABSENT, HIDDEN MERELY

*An ARISTOCRAT of the seventeenth century enters, wearing a velvet
mask. He bows to an elegant woman VISITOR who observes him.*

MONSIEUR: The Bastille is a world. (*He sits.*)
Huge, this world. (*Pause.*)
It is a grave mistake to think the plains of Africa are wider
than this room. (*Pause.*)

Of course this knowledge comes only to him who most
requires it. (*Pause.*) Is that not the case with all knowledge?
It grows on grief. A mould. A bacillus. And very floral,
sometimes. (*Pause.*)

Also, I sleep a lot. (*He laughs.*)

LAUGHTER IN THE BASTILLE

Yes

Plenty of it

Don't believe everything you read… (*Pause.*)

THE VISITOR: You have such a beautiful voice.

MONSIEUR: That too, I cultivated here. Prior to my sentence I
slurred my speech.

THE VISITOR: Such a perfect voice a woman might adore you
for it…

MONSIEUR: Or a man. The gaolers ask me to recite. In
exchange they bring me innocent requests. Soap. Scissors.
Pencil stubs. And the mask is not uncomfortable. The
Venetian who made it measured every feature with infinite
care. Alas for them, because they had seen me they were
put to death. No one living has observed me since. (*Pause.*)

THE VISITOR: Remove the mask. (*MONSIEUR laughs.*)
Remove it, I have a longing to kiss you.

MONSIEUR: Only in solitude am I allowed my face.

THE VISITOR: This is solitude – (*He laughs.*)
Don't laugh at me…!

MONSIEUR: No, it is I who is foolish, for believing solitude
exists. I am constantly observed. Sleeping, defecating,
in sickness and in health, my unseen mother watches
over me.

THE VISITOR: How can they punish you, or I, for that matter.
It would not take so very long, this kiss. Men and women
die for less.

MONSIEUR: The penalty is not extracted from me, but
from others whom I love. (*He stands, with a swift, nervous
movement.*) Beyond this sanction, nothing much offends me
here, no one is ill-disposed to me. After all, it is not me
they hate, but the identity. Not what I am, but who I was,
and that is beyond all repair and alteration. I SHOULD

LIKE TO KISS YOU ALSO never mind never mind I always say that never mind the words are written on my ribs and I once put them to music –

THE VISITOR: Make love to me!

MONSIEUR: I said it is impossible to slip my mask –

THE VISITOR: In the mask then, and let the watcher watch.
(*Pause.*)

MONSIEUR: No. (*The VISITOR glares at him.*)

THE VISITOR: No? And are you so supplied with lovers you disdain to –

MONSIEUR: I have no face, and cannot make love, therefore.
(*She shrugs.*)

THE VISITOR: I will imagine your face. And what I imagine will be commensurate with all I have conceived this passion for.

MONSIEUR: I CANNOT BE IMAGINED WHEN I AM.
(*Pause. He smiles. He shrugs.*)
I mean… I AM…
(*THE VISITOR drags her skirt over her head with an impulsive gesture, and is still, fixed to the spot. MONSIEUR watches her, agonised. At last, with a movement towards her, he goes to tear the mask from his face. A VOICE booms from a hidden place.*)

VOICE: Keep the mask on please, Monsieur…!
(*MONSIEUR stops in his tracks.*)

MONSIEUR: Yes…

VOICE: All right, Monsieur, thank you…
(*Three placards of a dictator descend. The YOUTHS rush in to deface them. The SURGEON is passing in the street.*)

WE PUNISH THE PICTURE

The SURGEON stops to watch.

SURGEON: The real face. That also must exist. But where?

YOUTH: Cut his moustache off, so the radio said, and hiding.

SURGEON: A single plane left here this morning.

YOUTH: So what? We'll send assassins.

SURGEON: And plastic surgery? I somehow think he won't
remain like that...

YOUTH: Exterminate the surgeons! (*The YOUTHS laugh.*)

SURGEON: Yes, well, that's one solution...

(*He joins the SOLDIER and his MOTHER. He takes off his
hat.*)

Nice day! The birds indifferent to the revolution, evidently,
since they sing the same old tunes... (*He undoes his bag.*)

SOLDIER: I lost my face for one regime, perhaps another will
give me another... (*He laughs brutally.*)

SURGEON: Sardonic humour is a most benign resource to
those who cannot come to terms with meaningless pain.
I frequently encounter it.

SOLDIER: MY LOVER QUIT.

SURGEON: Did she? And am I supposed to be indignant?
Isn't it enough that I have to probe the ruins of your
physiognomy, but I have to listen to your grievances
as well?

SOLDIER: I only mention it...

SURGEON: And when your mother dies, you'll tell me that, I
suppose? (*He opens a book.*) Now, here you see some faces
I have saved. (*He flicks through.*) I say saved. Saved from
what? They are not saved, they are inventions. Not one
gives me the slightest satisfaction, though many call them
miracles. (*He selects one.*)

Regard this miracle. Him I distinctly improved, but
you were handsome, you started from altogether higher
principles, which is why I recommended suicide...

MOTHER: We are so grateful! We thank God!

SURGEON: Do you? Why? It's me you should thank.

MOTHER: (*Peering at the book.*) This gives us hope...

(*The SURGEON looks at her.*)

SURGEON: You are weeping...

MOTHER: Yes...because so much is bad...and yet...there is
still good...

SURGEON: (*Looking at the book.*) Him I did badly. Him I felt
antipathy towards... (*He tears out the picture, screws it up.*)

When one rebuilds the face, one rebuilds the character. It's inescapable.

SOLDIER: I'm staying as I am.

SURGEON: And this reconstruction of the soul is yet another maiming, we must be frank…

SOLDIER: AS I AM WITH ALL RESPECT

SURGEON: The forcing of a character into the mould of altered features, what a journey, what an epic… I watch… I gasp… (*He thrusts the book back in his bag.*)

Stay as you are, yes. Flaunt your bitterness. Make them squirm who, if they did not cause your pain, are guilty certainly, of painlessness… (*He thrusts his hat on his head.*) Good day! (*More placards descend and are attacked. To YOUTH.*) Found him yet? They say he's in the city, after all.

YOUTH: They're hunting for him in the sewers!

SURGEON: (*Moving on.*) The sewers! That's where he belongs!

(*The YOUTHS laugh. The SURGEON passes through. The damaged HUSBAND appears in a door. He holds the cloth pressed to his face.*)

SHE KNEW AT A GLANCE

LOVER: Darling…!

Help, darling, help…!

(*A WOMAN appears, is filled with horror.*)

WIFE: What…!

LOVER: It's all right…it's all right…it's –

(*The WIFE lets out a cry.*)

Not much…just a – just a – (*She walks slowly to him.*)

Slash over the face…

(*She removes the towel. Her hand goes to her mouth to stifle shock. He presses the towel back.*)

THE WIFE: Why… ?

LOVER: (*Shaking his head.*) No reason.

Louts.

Did not like it.

Louts…

WIFE: Louts?

LOVER: Did not like my face, presumably.
   Drunkenness and.
WIFE: Did not like your face…
LOVER: IT HAS TO BE PUNISHED THIS DRUNKENNESS
   What are we
   Walking down a street and
   What are we
   I said no
   No I said
   I was so inoffensive
   We must live abroad we must
   A country with no louts
   Or fewer louts
WIFE: Did not like your face, why ever not?
LOVER: WHY ME I SAID
   I'M INOFFENSIVE
   WE DO NOT LIKE YOUR FACE THEY SAID
   Not face I don't think another word
WIFE: Not like your face?
LOVER: That's what I said
   Can you get another towel or bandage
WIFE: NOT LIKE YOUR FACE IT'S INCOMPREHENSIBLE
LOVER: Of course it is it's drunkenness it's what louts do it's
   everywhere it's
WIFE: Your face is beautiful
   (*The LOVER stops.*)
   Your face is perfect. (*Pause.*)
LOVER: To you. But not to others, evidently, wash me I am
   caked in blood…
   (*The WIFE stares.*)
WIFE: It is not possible that anyone would spoil your face.
   It is perfect and would command the silence even of a
   drunkard whose dislocated soul oozed hatred for the
   world… (*Pause. The LOVER stares at her.*) I know that face. It
   is inviolable. And never could be marked by malice.
   (*He shrugs.*)
LOVER: So you say but –
WIFE: Not by malice. Only love.

(The LOVER stares. A FIGURE enters in a hood and goes to sit at a dressing-table.)

THE HOLY ORDERS OF A TERRORIST

TERRORIST: Killing today. *(He plucks his hood, adjusts it.)*
Killing today and my hood took her eight hours. Eight hours' labour! What a tailor! What a perfectionist that woman is the stitching is what she calls Flemish Flemish stitch she says, running the tape measure around my face, do you want the top to peak or topple fold or stand up proud, perhaps to hug the contours of your face, these things are fashions, too, some years ago they were all wool, but now, a vast selection of materials and linings, too, what once was simple and expedient is now the subject for individual taste, style, even eccentricity, so she did this and I approved it, I approved it at the drawing stage.
(He stands up, pulling his jacket close.)
Killing today and I already famous the subject of some ballads though ballads are no distinction in these parts the film script is a far greater compliment but I place little faith in admiration, what was it Alexander said, Alexander the Great, sycophancy is the mongrel at the heels of power, I don't call myself another Alexander but
(He stops. He leans on the table to look closer into the mirror.)
Killing today and that little feeling which I have learned to call a flower growing in my lung the very last of nerves and most important after all to keep a little fear, the traces of an inhibition, cultivated, to be so very cold would mock the passion that inspires bravery. *(Pause.)*
Killing today and I'm not alone.
(He laughs. A second hooded FIGURE is seen by him in the mirror.)
Are you for me or against me? *(Pause.)*
Oh. *(He sits.)*
You're ill-disposed and what a lovely morning. Are you the enemy or envy? *(Pause.)*

It is so pretentious not to speak, it is so louche, or is your voice a poor thing, peep peep, does it go, a broken reed? All right, stay silent, I'm sure I've met you something in you tells me we're acquainted, come on, take the hat off, son. (*Pause. The FIGURE is still.*)

Oh, what a lovely day and my own children on their way to school, my three daughters, I never liked those lunch boxes with pictures of the Royal Family on, if you think I will plead for my life you are mistaken, I am the subject of a dozen ballads and a film in preparation in America, three lovely girls my wife she plaits their hair and spotless you should see the washing line on Monday mornings a dozen little dresses blowing in the wind HAVE YOU GOT A FACE OR NOT (*He rips away his own hood.*)

And first thing this morning I thought someone else was doomed THREE LOVELY GIRLS ORPHANED BY A FACELESS MAN I do love your ambition I had ambition once hope will be hope but a more famous who his executioner is WHAT IS IT SHAME OR SOMETHING? (*He laughs. Pause.*)

I'm at the end of my life, then. (*Pause.*)

I have a girl friend in the Monastery Flats you know her probably give her the full account the way I did not flinch or cringe do me that favour will you WHAT DOES IT MATTER IF I RECOGNISE YOU NOW so what too late too bad too everything YOU ARE ONE MAN AREN'T YOU ONE MAN AND NOT ANOTHER be a human being have a face... (*He turns in his chair to face the intruder.*)

Don't obliterate it...don't...

(*He turns his temple towards him.*)

Just here...one round is adequate...

Oh, don't obliterate it, don't...!

(*Three placards of the dictator descend. The YOUTHS rush in, proceed to deface it. They hesitate, sensing the presence of a stranger. This STRANGER has the dictator's face.*)

THE DICTATOR'S DOUBLE

The YOUTHS turn, incredulous.

DICTATOR: He no longer looks like that.
(*The YOUTHS slowly gather about him.*)
And never did. (*They peer.*)
The face was a creation. (*He smiles.*)
You know the way they work. Experts. Photographers.
Psychiatrists. Utter fiction. You wouldn't know the real man
if he stood in front of you. And that's power, the sheer and
staggering effrontery of power, you'd think he would have
said 'so what, my mug's my mug, love it or else!' But no.
He went and had it manufactured, that's the only word,
the Department of Social Propaganda manufactured it
OH, THE EXPERTS IN THAT BUILDING you know the big
one by the river, the brains and skills assembled in that
place, philosophy, astrology, sociology, it's not his face
at all it's the OFFICIAL IMAGE. (*He smiles at them.*) And a
face like that does not arrive without controversy, I assure
you. The committee came up with a dozen options, none
of them truthful, none of them the least bit representative,
but what's that got to do with it, no, it was a scene of
bitter wrangling, and he was relatively innocent, he
was – imagine it – the victim of their arguments, he had a
headache after twenty minutes but it took six weeks, after
all the face was doomed to reproduction, stamps, marriage
licences, even in the Gonorrhoea clinic, and not one was
really him, it was A FARRAGO OF APPROXIMATIONS –
(*They suddenly menace him.*)
Pol – ice! (*He laughs, shaking his head.*)
This is ridiculous, if I was him, do you think I'd go about in
this moustache, first thing to go, and the hairstyle, I'd have
shaved my head, if you want to know I am the newsagent
from Casca and a well-known idiot –
(*They lurch to seize him. He tears off the MOUSTACHE.*
They stop in their tracks.)
William.
The idiot

And newsagent. (*Pause.*)

YOUTH: Asking for trouble, William…

DICTATOR: It must be trouble that I want. And I've met others!

(*They shake their heads and go off, passing the SURGEON. The DICTATOR replaces his moustache.*)

SURGEON: Good.

It won't work twice of course…

DICTATOR: (*Shrugging.*) Got newspapers to deliver…

(*He starts to leave.*)

SURGEON: A little surgery…makes all the difference…

(*THE DICTATOR stops.*)

DICTATOR: Surgery? I like my face. It haunts them. It is a masterpiece of wit and coercion. How they need it! How they justify their misery by it, their failures, their stunted lives, let them employ it, it is an icon and an alibi. What do you want me to do? Sit in a Swiss hotel with benign features? I would not deprive them it in our mutual creation, we made it together, I the inflicter, they the endurers, now, give me away why don't you, join the crowd, how gratifying to hate the already hated, long live the common opinion, let's all dance…

(*He turns to go. The PRISONER enters with her mirror.*)

PRISONER: I'M GOING TO LOOK…!

DICTATOR: (*Indifferent.*) Are you…

PRISONER: I'm going to look!

DICTATOR: Look, then, who cares?

(*He goes out. The SURGEON remains, watching.*)

PRISONER: I count to three and –

(*She holds out the mirror, shutting her eyes.*)

I count to three –

It's got to be done at some point, obviously –

SURGEON: Has it, why?

PRISONER: Shop windows, puddles, sooner or later I will catch a glimpse, so it's better I'm prepared ONE! Most important that I have at least a modicum of self-control, my destiny and so on TWO a little bit a little under my control THREE!

257

(*She opens her eyes. She sees the mirror. She drops it. She sways. Pause.*)

I've gone. (*She looks at the SURGEON.*)

I've gone.

SURGEON: What's the matter? Don't you like the face?

PRISONER: Not my face.

SURGEON: Not yours?

PRISONER: My mother's. And I've gone…

(*Sound of traffic. Two MEN enter from either side of the stage. They stop, catching sight of each other.*)

THE NECESSITY OF FULL POSSESSION

They stare into each other's faces. They laugh with bewilderment. The laugh dies away. The FIRST DOUBLE launches himself violently against the SECOND. They struggle, moving first one way, then the other. They cease, exhausted.

FIRST DOUBLE: Even the eyes are the same…!

SECOND DOUBLE: It occurs all over the globe and why it should enrage you I can't think, surely a cause for celebration if anything given the number of human types a miracle, I find it amusing personally, and that hurt my neck…

FIRST DOUBLE: You've got to die.

SECOND DOUBLE: Don't be ridiculous, it happens all over the globe…

FIRST DOUBLE: I couldn't care less about the globe, the globe leaves me indifferent, I am not influenced one way or another by the behaviour of others here or elsewhere on the globe, do not appeal to me on grounds of what is tolerable elsewhere, I detest you and you must die –

SECOND DOUBLE: How can you detest me, you don't know me –

FIRST DOUBLE: YOU HAVE MY FACE.

SECOND DOUBLE: Or you have mine –

FIRST DOUBLE: No, you have my face, I said –

SECOND DOUBLE: Anyone would think I'd stolen it –

FIRST DOUBLE: That may well be the case –

SECOND DOUBLE: RIDICULOUS…!

FIRST DOUBLE: (*Menacing him.*) You are not continuing to exist with a face that does not belong to you, you are not posturing and preening and presuming to walk the streets with a face that is not your own, impostor…!

SECOND DOUBLE: (*Unnerved.*) Wait…! Please…let's just…

FIRST DOUBLE: I CLAIM THE FACE! AND YOURS IS FRAUDULENTLY OBTAINED!

SECOND DOUBLE: (*Moving back.*) The same could just as well be said of –

FIRST DOUBLE: I CLAIM IT!

(*He flings himself cruelly on the other.*)

SECOND DOUBLE: Oh, God…! (*They struggle, vilely, to and fro. At last, exhausted, they come apart again.*) This is madness… madness!

FIRST DOUBLE: GIVE UP YOUR FACE…

SECOND DOUBLE: Utter… madness…

(*He tries to escape. The other holds him.*)

FIRST DOUBLE: I am stronger than you, or if not stronger, more determined. You are conciliatory and I am not, and that alone ensures I will eventually overcome you and kill you, so –

SECOND DOUBLE: (*Wailing.*) What have I done…!

FIRST DOUBLE: You've done nothing, but the injustice of it alters nothing. Wail as much as you like but you cannot keep the face –

SECOND DOUBLE: Mother…! Oh, Mother…!

FIRST DOUBLE: Yes, they are to blame! So much to blame for everything…!

(*With a cry the SECOND DOUBLE attempts to bolt. Roaring, the FIRST pursues him offstage. An EMPEROR enters. He looks at an easel, which is covered by a cloth.*)

HE SAW HIMSELF, OFFICIALLY

As he gazes, the EMPRESS enters. She stops. She gazes. She laughs.

EMPEROR: Moment of truth.

(*The EMPRESS goes swiftly to tear aside the cloth.*)

Don't yet, thank you!

(*Her hand is suspended in mid air. It falls.*)

Moment of truth…

What does that mean? I love the phrase, but the meaning? IT HAD BETTER BE GOOD OH GOD IT HAD. (*Pause.*) Perhaps we won't see it today. Perhaps today the conditions are not perfect for truth to announce itself. I personally believe truth comes better on some days than others, climate, digestion, all sorts of things might influence its – (*A PAINTER enters, stands patiently.*) I chose you. Knowing fully. Utterly apprised. Laid myself prostrate before your merciless and scrutinizing brush AM I NOT A HERO how many kings would yield themselves to someone with a reputation as sour and uncomplimentary as yours? Have you flayed me? Have you whipped me, humiliated, ridiculed? Let me say before you tear away the cloth I shall not destroy it nor consign it to a cellar, I fear contempt, no man more, but what I chose I also submit to, the most powerful man in the world must acknowledge there is no immunity from judgement however unsound that judgement may be, please show me what you've done. (*The PAINTER pulls away the covering. The EMPEROR goes to look. A very long pause.*)

EMPRESS: May I? May I also?

(*The EMPEROR goes, looks out of a window. She walks to the canvas. THE EMPRESS walks away, slaps the PAINTER's cheek. He winces, nurses the place. The EMPRESS goes out.*)

EMPEROR: I'm sorry. My wife is impetuous.

PAINTER: Now I'll be murdered, I suppose…some hired lout will carve me in an alley…

EMPEROR: Shh…

PAINTER: Not the first time some enraged female has –

EMPEROR: Shh…shh…

PAINTER: You say shh, but I've been beaten in the past and –

EMPEROR: Beaten?

PAINTER: Beaten yes and my fingers trodden over for less offence than –

EMPEROR: You are an ill-used man, a martyr –

PAINTER: People who cannot stomach truth should not commission pictures! (*Pause.*) My hands were in bandages for weeks… (*He shrugs.*) So what, it's a dangerous profession.

EMPEROR: I'll have it hung at once, and the public granted access. Let them troop by and arrive at their own conclusions.

(*The PAINTER bows, and goes to leave.*)

IT IS SUCH AN UGLY THING. (*He stops.*)

You know it is.

And hurts me like a lash.

PAINTER: We entertain such high opinion of ourselves.

(*He goes to leave again.*)

EMPEROR: Kiss me. (*Pause.*)

PAINTER. Kiss you…

EMPEROR: Yes. I am the Emperor and I want to be kissed.

(*The PAINTER goes to kiss his cheek.*) Not there.

PAINTER: Where?

EMPEROR: My arse, of course.

Is it not also a face?

PAINTER: I prefer not to.

EMPEROR: What's preference? (*The PAINTER cogitates.*)

PAINTER: I won't do that. (*Pause. The EMPEROR walks a little.*)

EMPEROR: I think you want to overthrow the State.

PAINTER: No, I am merely a –

EMPEROR: MY FACE IS THE STATE. YOU HAVE ATTACKED MY FACE. That's treason.

PAINTER: No, I regarded this commission in the same light as –

EMPEROR: Please, no false innocence –

PAINTER: As – as –

EMPEROR: This disingenuousness is not becoming –

PAINTER: Any face which has – certain characteristics and

EMPEROR: There are faces and faces –

PAINTER: Faces and faces, yes, two eyes, a nose –

EMPEROR: Imperial nose –

PAINTER: A mouth and –

EMPEROR: IMPERIAL MOUTH –

PAINTER: In a particular configuration –

EMPEROR: IMPERIAL CONFIGURATION –

PAINTER: You don't allow me to finish my –

EMPEROR: YOU CANNOT PAINT AN EMPEROR AS YOU WOULD A BARTENDER, THAT IS A BARTENDER. (*Pause.*)

PAINTER: The way I saw – the way my eyes read the subject was –

EMPEROR: Treason. The eyes committed treason, even if the will was loyal…

PAINTER: What do you want to do, then, blind me?

EMPEROR: Yes. (*Pause.*)

PAINTER: I'll do it again. (*He goes to cover the painting.*)

EMPEROR: No, that's silly –

PAINTER: Yes, I'll do it now. Come here and stand by the window

EMPEROR: That really is –

PAINTER: (*Manoeuvring him.*) I see you differently, already differently, the light here is so much more – PENCILS! And half-profile, that full-face was –

EMPEROR: (*Shaking him off.*) Absurd!

(*Pause. The PAINTER smiles thinly.*)

PAINTER: Quite. (*The EMPEROR smiles also.*)

EMPEROR: Obviously you did your duty to yourself. There is no quarrelling with your integrity, and I would never stoop to wreck a work of art, FOR THAT IS WHAT IT IS. (*Pause.*)

On the other hand, I am the subject, I have an investment. I am not meat on a slab, am I, nor trees on a hill, I am not inert matter, and you have injured me.

PAINTER: Perhaps, after all, I should simply kiss your arse…? I am not a good man. I merely have a gift. This gift's a sickness, and it's cost me dear.

EMPEROR: I am so injured, you must suffer for it, anything else would smack of compromise.

PAINTER: Destroy the painting, then…!

EMPEROR: Never. It is a work of art.

(*He claps his hands. A GUARD appears.*)

Blind this man.

PAINTER: WHAT

WHAT

OH WHAT

EMPEROR: One of us must be blinded. Either I must be in order not to see what you have shown me of myself, or you, in order to be blamed for a truth that never should have been permitted.

PAINTER: Lock me in a room but let me keep my sight!

EMPEROR: But it's a burden to you, you said so yourself –

PAINTER: In some ways, but –

EMPEROR: Without eyes you will not be led into such dangerous representations, and yet, being an artist by instinct you will perhaps produce things with your fingers and these may be, unlike your paintings, a celebration of mankind, loving, charitable things, the bitterness having been discarded during your long passage through pain… it happens…

PAINTER: Yes, it does happen, but –

EMPEROR: (*He nods to the GUARD.*) I think it's best…

(*The PAINTER screams, crawls.*)

PAINTER: Oh, let me, let me lick your arse…!

EMPEROR: (*Covering his eyes.*) Shh! I cannot bear it! Shh! (*The GUARD drags the PAINTER away.*) And you'll be a legend! Which is more than I shall be… (*The EMPRESS enters. The EMPEROR looks at the portrait again.*) I think when one is portrayed as a beast, one must be a beast, or the world's a – (*A terrible cry, off.*) Nonsense, surely?

EMPRESS: If only he had told the truth…which is that you are kind…

EMPEROR: Yes! And had he done so, I should, in character, have been kind to him!

THE ECSTASY OF THE UNREPENTANT

The WOMAN at the dressing table. She works with a lipstick. The MAN observes.

WOMAN: I crept. I hugged the shadows of the shops. But still they persecuted me. I wanted one thing only – not to be observed. But this desire merely seemed to draw attention to me. They knocked into me.

MAN: Impossible.

WOMAN: They collided with me out of malice.

MAN: Imagination.

WOMAN: NOT SO, THEN! ONE COMMANDED ME TO SMILE! (*She glares. She returns to her mirror.*) My misery offended him. I said my father had just died. This appealed to him. This seemed plausible. (*She tosses down the lipstick.*) ROSE IT SAYS, I DON'T CALL THAT ROSE!
(*She covers her face.*)

MAN: Oh, listen…listen, I find you beautiful…

WOMAN: It's not enough…

MAN: You must be reconciled to your appearance.

WOMAN: I will be reconciled. When you are reconciled to your poverty, I will be reconciled to my ugliness.
(*The SOLDIER enters, bandaged. He stands observing her. She observes him in the mirror. She begins, irresistibly, to laugh.*)
Oh, it is the war wounded. Oh, it is the man who has no face at all. Oh, and I am in for some moral education. Oh, and oh, again! (*She turns to face him.*) You have found a new career. You are going to be an itinerant exemplar. Surely an asset to the entire community, for who would groan at their condition, having once set eyes on you? You leave repentance in your wake, and the poor are reconciled to poverty and the unhappy obliged to confess they do somewhat exaggerate NOT ME HOWEVER. (*The SOLDIER just looks.*) All these lipsticks…but it can't be the colour, only the shape… (*He extends a hand to her. She sees it, does not respond.*) No…it's false…it's false!
(*The MAN, embarrassed, humiliated, goes to assist the SOLDIER, who dismisses him with a savage movement of the*

hand. The struggling DOUBLES pass over the stage, desperate,
with appalling cries. The soldier's MOTHER enters.)

MOTHER: My son! My little one! You do wander! You do
stray! Teatime now and buns the ones with icing on, or the
custard-filling, you say!

SOLDIER: How I wish that you had died instead of me.

MOTHER: Yes. I too, wish that.

SOLDIER: I would not hesitate to put you in my place.

MOTHER: Nor I to stand in it.

SOLDIER: You pulped. Not me.

MOTHER: Yes.

SOLDIER: You raw. Not me.

MOTHER: Indeed.

Indeed.

(*The MOTHER extends a hand to lead the SOLDIER. He obeys.*
As they depart, a ROUÉ of the eighteenth century enters. His
coat is smothered in identical photographs of himself as a
child.)

I WAS NOT ALWAYS THUS, BUT ADORABLE

The pleasure gardens of the Palais Royal.

ROUÉ: Here again. Tonight I planned to read. But I've
read everything. So I redesigned the garden. But this I
accomplished in no time at all. Here again, therefore.
And looking for the face that might postpone my death.
Certainly I should have stayed in the library. Or wrote a
little thesis on Etruscan urns. Certainly I have made the
same mistake again. And I was warned! The authors of
the ancient world were unanimous and vehement as to
the futility of my, the pathos and absurdity of my, but still
I, always I, HERE AGAIN, LADIES! (*A PROSTITUTE laughs.*)
Yes! Ridiculous your game, and ridiculous mine!

PROSTITUTE: Gloomy tonight.

ROUÉ: In a cheerful way.

PROSTITUTE: Gloomy in a cheerful way.

ROUÉ: That's the benefit of culture, madame, but move along, I'm not absorbed by you and standing there you might obstruct another meaningful encounter.

PROSTITUTE: You don't like women, excellency…

ROUÉ: No. But what man does? I adore them, isn't that sufficient? (*The PROSTITUTE turns to go.*) I HAD A LOVER ONCE. (*She stops.*)

PROSTITUTE: So you say, on each and every –

ROUÉ: Loved and loved in return, are you interested?

PROSTITUTE: Heard it before, sir –

ROUÉ: Of course you have –

PROSTITUTE: Same old story –

ROUÉ: Same old coin, and how beautiful she was…!

PROSTITUTE: More beautiful than me –

ROUÉ: Undoubtedly, a face which was –

PROSTITUTE: The rarest combination of ancient cultures! (*Pause.*)

ROUÉ: Yes, exactly, how well you put it, how succinct…! And she married a man of such pleasant manners –

PROSTITUTE: More pleasant than yours –

ROUÉ: Much more pleasant, yes, a man who cherished her and brushed her hair…

PROSTITUTE: Dark hair…

ROUÉ: Which I might have…plucking the grey, and letting those fall to the floor…

PROSTITUTE: Thirty years –

ROUÉ: Thirty years, yes, sleeping like children, belly to arse… (*Pause. The PROSTITUTE kisses him, pityingly.*)

PROSTITUTE: Ten pounds…

ROUÉ: Not cheap to tell you a story! But I appreciate to keep a straight face calls for uncommon qualities! Anyone new tonight? (*He pays her.*)

PROSTITUTE: The new! The new! Always the new!

ROUÉ: The new contains the fallacy of hope! IT WAS WRONG, I SHOULD HAVE MARRIED HER. Because in truth, she was spoiled also, by his kindness. All lives are wrong. All lives… (*He sees a young WOMAN.*) Is your life wrong, Miss? (*She stops.*) Not seen you before.

SECOND PROSTITUTE: Never been here, sir.

ROUÉ: (*Going to her.*) If my face horrifies you, forgive it, I pay well, ask her.

SECOND PROSTITUTE: It doesn't.

ROUÉ: No? Not horrify you? Fifty years of wrong decisions THAT MUST MAKE THE YOUNG RECOIL!

SECOND PROSTITUTE: No, sir. (*She points to the snapshots.*) Who's he? (*He shrugs modestly.*) Sweet face that boy.

ROUÉ: He had, and blushing…! No girl was ever like it, so much shame and tenderness struggled in his cheeks is thirty pounds agreeable?

PROSTITUTE: He has some funny tastes, His Excellency does –

ROUÉ: Funny tastes, yes, I speak and make love with my eyes open, kiss me.
(*Pause. The SECOND PROSTITUTE goes to kiss his face.*)
No!
Not him.
But me… (*He extends the photographs on his lapels. She obeys.*)
Oh, lucky youth! Oh, delirium! KISS ME AGAIN!
(*She does so. He gives her some of the money.*)
The disbelief! He has no breath, the breath has left his body…! KISS ME AGAIN…!
(*She kisses the photograph a third time.*)
I so love to witness his confusion! You lure him from his studies, what's HORACE TO A WHORE'S ARSE, after all, when you are eleven? Mutter things! Whisper! Make his life IMPOSSIBLE!

SECOND PROSTITUTE: (*Addressing the photograph.*) You are a very charming boy – (*The ROUÉ passes her a note.*) And with such a *serious* expression!

ROUÉ: Go on…

SECOND PROSTITUTE: Those lovely eyes which must have come from your mother…

ROUÉ: From her, who else…

SECOND PROSTITUTE: They bore deep into me and make me feel quite naked…!

ROUÉ: Yes…

SECOND PROSTITUTE: Do you like me very much? And want to feel me underneath my clothing? Put your hand here if you want to, do you want to, and are afraid I'll stop you? I shan't stop you… (*The ROUÉ gives her another note.*) Not too quickly…! How your hand goes burrowing and your eyes are still severe…! Your eyes say one thing and your hand is – oh! Not yet quite familiar enough with –

ROUÉ: WHAT CAN NEVER BE FAMILIAR…

(*The SECOND PROSTITUTE kisses the photograph spontaneously.*)

SECOND PROSTITUTE: Already you want to meet again! Already you are planning the next occasion!

(*She kisses it again and again. The ROUÉ is weeping silently.*) My beautiful…! My never innocent…!

(*She is suddenly self-aware. She gets up. She tucks the money away.*)

ROUÉ: Come again….he's always here…

(*The SECOND PROSTITUTE goes to leave, turns, kisses the ROUÉ's mouth with spontaneous adoration.*)

SECOND PROSTITUTE: Idiot! Oh, idiot…!

(*Three placards descend, already defaced. The YOUTHS rush in, and throw a noose over a beam. Others drag in the SURGEON, bound.*)

THE ABOLITION OF BEAUTY IN THE INTERESTS OF SOCIAL HARMONY

SURGEON: The Revolution is diseased! I declare this publicly, the sickness of the Revolution is upon us! If surgeons are liable to execution, who is safe, surely the limits of insanity have been passed, I am the hero of the hospitals! What am I guilty of?

YOUTH: The mockery of God.

SURGEON: Even the language is archaic! Mock who? How mock?

YOUTH: You have been tried in accordance with –

SURGEON: I have been condemned in accordance with nothing! What civilised –

SECOND YOUTH: We are not civilised, you are –

SURGEON: The healer is murdered for his powers!

YOUTH: You are not a healer. You are a critic of God. And if cosmetic surgery is civilisation, we rejoice in the restoration of barbarity! Noose, Citizen! Beat the drum!

SURGEON: I have given happiness where only misery prevailed! Ask any of my eight hundred patients, what nature so illiberally scattered my craft repairs. The ugly praise my name!

YOUTH: There are no ugly. (*Pause.*)

SURGEON: No ugly? Are there not?

YOUTH: Not from today. Nor beautiful. Only the will of God. (*The WOMAN AT THE MIRROR throws down her cosmetics.*)

WOMAN: Yes! Long live the Revolution!

SECOND YOUTH: What's beauty but a word? And you cut flesh, for a word. Cut the dictionary instead.

SURGEON: Wait…the word exists…because the thing exists…

YOUTH: Not any more! (*He takes the WOMAN by the face, firmly, presenting her to the SURGEON.*) Deny her perfection in the eyes of God.

SURGEON: The eyes of God? God's blind. It's Man who discriminates –

YOUTH: IS SHE NOT PERFECT? Say! (*Pause.*)

SURGEON: I am bound to say…my taste obliges me…to confess some doubts about –

YOUTH: ONE MORE TIME I ASK YOU, IS SHE PERFECT, SURGEON, CRITIC OF GOD? (*Pause.*)

SURGEON: There is a man somewhere would find her so.

YOUTH: Noose!

(*The YOUTHS go to tighten the rope round the SURGEON's neck. The SOLDIER appears, leading his MOTHER, whose face is swathed in bandages. He stops. He points to her.*)

SOLDIER: She – (*He shrugs.*)

She – (*They observe him. His face is undamaged.*) It's love…

(*He shrugs again. A YOUTH of Hellenic beauty enters, playing a reed pipe.*)

THE COLLABORATOR RESERVES PART OF HIMSELF

NARCISSUS: Girls pester me…

ROUÉ: Obviously…

NARCISSUS: Girls fall ill for me…

ROUÉ: I should fall ill myself…

NARCISSUS: And die…!

ROUÉ: That's as it should be. Love's unhealthy.
  (*He picks up his chair and starts to leave.*)

NARCISSUS: Where did you get that awful face?
  (*The ROUÉ stops.*)

ROUÉ: Awful…?

NARCISSUS: Rotted and disintegrating –

ROUÉ: Rotted?

NARCISSUS: Pitted, grooved, and –

ROUÉ: Pitted, me?

NARCISSUS: Wreckage of a face, it chills my bone, it makes
  my mouth go dry PLEASE LOOK AWAY I'M SORRY YOUR
  GLANCE IS LIKE A CURSE…!
  (*The ROUÉ bows, turns, walks slowly out. NARCISSUS taunts
  him.*)
  I know what you are thinking!
  THE
  COMPENSATIONS
  OF
  SENILITY
  How do you get that scaly stuff around the eyes?
  And that crust of yellow skin?
  As for the eruptions…!
  (*He chokes with laughter, He goes to put the pipe between his
  lips. He detects the presence of a STRANGER, who holds an
  unusual box under his arm. Pause.*)
  The Greeks were overcome by the Barbarians, who
  swarmed over their land, burning, looting, cutting off
  hands, and because the Greeks were beautiful, they hated
  them, and made a box. (*A SECOND STRANGER enters, waits.*)
  Some say the Barbarians were too ignorant to make this
  box themselves, but some Greek did it, out of spite, a
  renegade who hated his own race and was perhaps himself

imperfect in the face. However, the box was invented and its efficiency recommended itself to the Barbarians, whose first enthusiasm for disfiguring had been spent. The sad fact is, had this box never been invented, rather few Greeks would have had their faces maimed, because hate and envy always die down in the end, whereas this machine was light and practical, transportable, and in the hands of experts, has left its mark the length and breadth of the land…

(*He looks to the STRANGERS.*)

I've got a dispensation. (*They are not persuaded.*)

All right, you want to see it. (*He puts a hand into his pocket.*) Fuck.

Never mind, they all know me.

Narcissus. (*They stare.*)

Oh, dear, you are feeling menacing today. I'm the royal boy, all right? Your king is my – (*He gestures.*)

All right? (*They take a step towards him.*)

Listen, if you put that fucking thing on my bonce you are in for a – (*He feels again in his pocket.*)

GOT IT! All right?

(*He shows the card. They stare contemptuously.*)

Look, I don't know who you geezers are, but when this gets back to my good friend the Most High and Mighty King of the Barbarians you can start to panic, he won't be greatly pleased and might decide to box your heads for all I know –

GREEK: Shut up. (*Pause.*)

NARCISSUS: Oh, fuck you're Greeks…

Fuck and fuck again…

Look, lads, what's this about?

SECOND GREEK: Be sensible. It won't take long.

(*He walks forward with a wrist strap.*)

NARCISSUS: Hold it! I think you – HOLD IT IT I SAID! Letting you blokes wander round like this, untrained and so on – (*The MAN clasps his wrists.*)

MIS – TAKE! MIS – TAKE!

SECOND GREEK: It only takes a minute.

271

NARCISSUS: Please, I am exempted from the Face
Programme!
(*The GREEKS hold him in a tight grip and place the box over
his head. Cries come from within, One of the men takes a
handle from his pocket and inserts it in a slot. He is about to
turn it when a cry comes from offstage.*)
PATRIOT: Hey!
GREEK: It's Narcissus, the bumboy and collaborator!
(*The PATRIOT goes to the box, slides back a panel, sees the
occupant, shuts it again.*)
PATRIOT: Yes, well done, now take it off.
GREEK / SECOND GREEK: TAKE IT OFF?
PATRIOT: Yes. No matter how much he deserves it.
(*An outraged pause.*)
GREEK: Turn the handle, John!
PATRIOT: REMOVE THE MAIMING BOX.
(*The GREEKS are reluctant.*)
GREEK: This roving, poncing youth of utterly degenerate and
diseased character has betrayed his people by copulating
with the Barbarians whilst our people lost their faces
APPARENTLY HE LAUGHED!
NARCISSUS: I never!
GREEK: LAUGHED while boys and girls screamed in their
villages THE COUNTRYSIDE IS SMOTHERED IN MAIMED
CHILDREN TURN THE HANDLE!
PATRIOT: Wait! And listen!
GREEK: I would rather die than not do this. I have followed
him for fifteen days. I will do it or kill myself and that's an
oath. And now you have a dilemma because if this bastard
is allowed to keep his face I'll hang myself, tell that to the
Greeks. (*Pause.*)
PATRIOT: You do not question my love of the Greeks, I
daresay? I need not provide you with my credentials?
GREEK: Nope.
PATRIOT: So I address you from THE VERY SUMMIT OF OUR
PRINCIPLES. This youth Narcissus is the most beautiful
who lives, and in his features lives the essence of the race

called Greek, there is no finer specimen HIDEOUS AS HIS
CHARACTER THROUGH WEAKNESS AND AMBITION IS.

GREEK: Who denies it? It makes me want to turn the handle
twice as fast.

(*He goes to it, but draws it from the socket, and playfully slaps
his hand.*)

I respect you, and I hope you will respect me also…he has
to suffer, or I will, and I'm innocent.

PATRIOT: This youth is more, and greater than himself.
Precisely for his beauty he is immune even to just revenge.

GREEK: AND HE IS PRIVILEGED, THE WHORE! IS HE NOT
GIFTED BY THE GODS BUT WE GO FURTHER AND HEAP
FORGIVENESS ON THE –

(*He shakes his head, speechless with bitterness. A cynical laugh
comes from inside the box.*)

PATRIOT: Yes, it will always be thus, and we must swallow bile
again…

(*He nods to SECOND GREEK, who removes the box.
NARCISSUS rubs his eyes, looks at the GREEK.*)

NARCISSUS: I thought you said you'd hang yourself…

PATRIOT: The most beautiful Greek is the whore of the
Barbarian…

NARCISSUS: Yup.

PATRIOT: Still a Greek, however… (*NARCISSUS goes to leave.*)

NARCISSUS: (*Stopping.*) When you lot win… I'll be yours…

PATRIOT: Quite so…

NARCISSUS: Don't take too long about it. Narcissus, he also
spoils…

THE SOLDIER'S CRUELTY IS RESERVED FOR HOME

The SOLDIER looks at the MOTHER, who is still with resignation.

SOLDIER: It's what you wanted. (*Pause.*)
And I must not allow my sense of gratitude to spoil my life.
(*Pause.*)
Which it could do. (*Pause.*)
The sacrifice being so – (*He shrugs crossly.*)

THERE IS SOMETHING SO COMPLACENT ABOUT YOU,
MOTHER. (*Pause.*)
The fact is I think I have to flee from you. I think to see
you there, parked by the fireside day and night, I –
(*Pause. Exasperation seizes him.*)
You were not buying love, were you? Is love a bargain,
then? YOU HAUNT ME AND I MUST BE FREE.
(*The BRIDE appears, standing silently in the door.*)
Twice she's given birth to me...and would do, over and
over again... (*The BRIDE extends a hand, a command.*)
Pain and more pain...the evidence of love...
(*He turns to go, hesitates, goes to his MOTHER and kneels by
her.*)
Let me tell you what your pleasure is...to know I walk the
world in a decent obscurity, and no eyes follow me, but
the eyes of women who would have me share their beds.
DOTE! DOTE ON THAT YOUR TRIUMPH, MOTHER!
(*He seizes the BRIDE, and with infinite, particular,
incredulous solicitude, exposes her body.*)
MOTHER: Breathless...! (*The SOLDIER stops, his hand poised.*)
Anticipates!
(*He turns to look at the bandaged face of his mother.*)
Soon!
Soon she!
Murmurs!
Limbs all
Weeping
Hair all
Plunders
Weeping
Pleading
Not yet
Pleading
And
(*Pause. The SOLDIER removes the belt from his trousers and
without haste proceeds to strangle his MOTHER. The WOMAN
enters.*)

WOMAN: The surgeon's dead. (*Pause. She watches indifferently.*)
I had mixed feelings. On the one hand so much talent, so
much skill. Nullified. On the other, did he not fix on hope
like some vile crow? Not that my opinion weighed with
them!
(*The SOLDIER drops the belt. He takes the BRIDE in his arms,
passionately. They run off, hand in hand.*)
No, they were hell-bent! They were deaf to arguments!
(*The YOUTHS pass, noisily.*)
YOUTH: Throw away your lip-sticks!
WOMAN: I will do!
SECOND YOUTH: In the bin the rouge and the mascara!
WOMAN: Funny words! (*They go.*)
Obscure properties!
(*The WOMAN goes to the mirror. She looks. A WOMAN with a
parasol enters a garden.*)

PERHAPS SHE LIED. BEING INVISIBLE

*The WOMAN with the parasol turns, perambulating. A MAN enters,
observes her a long time.*

MAN: If you lie, I shall know…
WOMAN: Yes. And that is why I turn my back to you.
MAN: Your face will undergo involuntary changes. For
example, you will blush…
WOMAN: There are many reasons for blushing.
Sometimes, the very idea of being disbelieved produces
embarassment…
MAN: Yes, but your eyes will falter. Your mouth also will
indicate that what it speaks is false. If it is false… This is
something I revere in you. I applaud the honesty of your
features.
WOMAN: Yes, you applaud it because it gives you access to
feelings which I prefer to guard. I cannot tell you how I
loathe this in myself. I practise lying before mirrors.
MAN: To no avail.
WOMAN: As yet.

MAN: You will destroy the beauty of your character.

WOMAN: I cannot wait.

MAN: Why should you want secrets?

WOMAN: Because I do not want to be entered like a public place! (*She turns to him.*)
I require my secrets. Inviolable avenues and little gardens, gated, fenced, and spiked my private – (*She issues a torrent.*) I have another lover – no I don't – I do – he adores me and I adore him – not really – but he gives me something – nothing much – this is nonsense – I am yours – yours only – beautiful man he – no other man at all – preposterous – am I blushing – and now I feel guilt when I have nothing to be guilty of and if my lip trembles make of it what you want…! (*Pause. She begins to laugh.*) Your face!

MAN: What of it?
(*The WOMAN laughs, covering her mouth.*)
What of my face!

WOMAN: CONFUSION AND EMBARRASSMENT! (*She stares.*) You don't know what to… (*She turns her back quickly.*) I don't like that face, recover quickly, you look foolish, which I cannot bear in a man.

MAN: You dislike an expression which you yourself inspired –

WOMAN: I CANNOT LOVE A MAN WITH A FACE LIKE THAT.
(*The MAN hangs his head.*)
I wish I'd not seen that… (*Pause.*)
Obviously, this other man was necessary to me.
(*The MAN drags a handkerchief from his pocket and drapes his face with it.*)

MAN: Please, stop torturing me… (*The WOMAN turns, looks at him.*) Please… (*Pause. Then with deliberation.*)

WOMAN: He places one hand firmly on my arse… And with the other, draws up my skirt…in public sometimes, this…! In museums, or in restaurants… (*Pause. The MAN is still.*) And this hand is possessive, confident, and not polite… far from polite, it is – inspired and yet discreet…oh, so discreet he never pinches, pumps me, no, it is –

MAN: SHUT UP. (*Pause.*)

WOMAN: And in his room, at the top of these stairs, dark
stairs, he curses in his haste! And I am – flung, oh, toppled
and –
(*The MAN tears away the handkerchief. Instantly she covers her
own face with her parasol.*)

MAN: Why do this to me...! (*Pause.*)

WOMAN: (*Behind the parasol.*) It isn't true. Inspired by some
book, not true at all. I read too much. You always say it
isn't good to read.

MAN: I'll kill you if it's true. (*Pause.*)
Look at me.

WOMAN: No.

MAN: However foolish my expression, believe me I will kill
you if it's –

WOMAN: I DON'T KNOW IF IT'S TRUE OR NOT. (*Pause.*)
It's true that – what I just described – is what I wish.

MAN: Wish anything you like but is it –

WOMAN: I can't see your face and whether your are serious in
your threat to kill me I can't be sure, and therefore whether
what I said is fiction or confession is dependent now on
pure intuition YES I LOVE HIM AND HE HAS MY SOUL!
(*She lowers the parasol. Their eyes meet. Pause.*)
You were serious...! I can see it in your eyes! So serious,
but I was lying.

MAN: You were not lying.

WOMAN: Was I not?

MAN: Not lying, no.

WOMAN: Teasing, rather.

MAN: Teasing, no.

WOMAN: My sense of humour governs me, you know. Why
I have this humour, God knows, it protects me possibly
from some terror I can't face, only with him am I not
humorous...
(*The WOMAN AT THE MIRROR looks up, over the rim.
Her mouth hangs. The light shrinks until her face alone is
illuminated. In the darkness, the passage of THE DOUBLES,
at the terrible end of their struggle.*)

SECOND DOUBLE: No...no...mercy...!

Mercy…!
Forgive…!
Forgive…!
(*A silence. The eyes of the WOMAN AT THE MIRROR close. A dirty rain falls, staining her. She is a gargoyle. The light goes.*)